PHPP Illustrated

A Designer's Companion to the
Passive House Planning Package

2nd Edition

Sarah Lewis

RIBA Publishing

Published by RIBA Publishing,
The Old Post Office, St Nicholas Street,
Newcastle upon Tyne, NE1 1RH

ISBN 978-1-85946-775-6/PDF 978-1-85946-773-2

Commissioning editor: Ginny Mills
Production controller: Richard Blackburn
Designed and typeset by Tom Cabot/Ketchup
Printed and bound by Page Bros, Great Britain

RIBA Publishing is part of RIBA Enterprises Ltd

Acknowledgements

I would like to extend a special thanks to the following experts and
colleagues, without whom this book would not have happened:

Alan Clarke
Andrew Farr
Diana Dina – bere:architects
Eric Parkes
Jan Steiger – Passive House Institute (PHI)
Justin Bere – bere:architects
Karl Parsons – WARM: Low Energy Building Practice
Kym Mead – Mead: Energy & Architectural Design Ltd
Maiia Guermanova
Nick Grant
Nick Newman
Sofie Pelsmakers
Tom Mason – Architype
Dan Towers – Hamson Barron Smith
Tad Everhart – CertiPHlers Cooperative
David Edwards – Passive House Institute (PHI)

A special thanks to John Trinick (WARM) for his input on common
PHPP mistakes, and Michael Lewis for his support throughout.

Contents

Foreword

The Passive House Planning Package (PHPP) is one of the most accurate energy efficiency calculation and design tools, as has been repeatedly shown through various monitoring projects. The development of the latest version focused on ensuring this reliability and applicability of the calculations to climate conditions all over the world. PHPP9 has considerably enhanced features in order to support all sorts of uses within the project design process, as they are to be found in the practical day-to-day work of architects, engineers and energy consultants.

One of these key new features is the variant calculation, allowing the user to easily enter and evaluate several efficiency design options of single components or whole buildings. This considerably enhances the possibility to enable the user to take informed efficiency design decisions and support clients in choosing the best options for their projects. The new EnerPHit Retrofit Plan (ERP) and the parallel calculation of retrofit steps is another new feature that takes into account that within the refurbishment sector, step-by-step retrofits represent the largest investments. The PHPP and the ERP thereby provide reliable consultancy and the design of step-by-step retrofitting processes to the end-users. A new concept of data entry support with error messages and plausibility checks further support the user to work with the PHPP easily and with great results.

Finally, a new efficiency evaluation method has been implemented into the Passive House concept and PHPP, the so called PER system (Primary Energy Renewable). This concept allows testing the efficiency design of the projects in a future renewable energy supply environment, after the transition of our energy supply systems. The concept also includes the evaluation of storage losses of renewable energy, thereby allows the combined assessment of energy efficiency and renewable energy gains. The new Passive House Classes, Plus and Premium, are based on this system and allow the designers and consultants the design and evaluation of future-proof buildings.

This second edition of PHPP Illustrated comprehensively explains the new features and concepts and supports to better understand the possibilities and benefits of these new concepts. It also features PHPP's 3D data entry and efficiency design tool, *design*PH, in detail and gives an outlook to the future developments. Furthermore this book comes as helpful visual guide, the explanations are clear and easy to follow for designers and designers to be, guiding them through the necessary inputs and helping them understand what the outputs mean for their buildings. In providing professional guidance on using the acclaimed Passive House design tools known as the Passive House Planning Package and *design*PH, this book will help further the Passive House Standard and consequently contribute to a better built environment.

Dr Wolfgang Feist
Founder and Scientific Director of the Passive House Institute; Professor at the University of Innsbruck Department of Energy Efficient Construction and Building Physics

How to use this book

This book is for designers, students and experienced practitioners who have an interest in using the Passive House Planning Package (PHPP) as a design tool. This companion helps readers to gain a better understanding of how their designs and decision-making affect the energy balance of their buildings.

The book:
- illustrates the key principles common to all Passive House buildings
- sets out the preparation and information required to successfully use the PHPP
- provides clear and easy to follow steps for entering and understanding a building in the PHPP
- highlights the common mistakes of first-time PHPP users and provides useful tips
- provides guidance on using the new SketchUp plug-in for PHPP.

This designer's guide focuses on the sections of the PHPP relating to design decision-making and is to be used as an accompaniment to the full PHPP technical manual, which is included with every copy of PHPP.

5

Introduction

What is PHPP?

The Passive House Planning Package (PHPP) is a tool and not something to be feared. It is actually very easy to use once you get the hang of it and does not require advanced abilities in computer modelling. Complex dynamic models were used to create the PHPP, but the PHPP itself is a series of interlinked Excel spreadsheets in one workbook.

Therein lies one of the great advantages of the PHPP; the Excel workbook can be used by anyone with access to Excel or Open Office and basic Excel training, so architects can share the workbook with mechanical, electrical and energy consultants. The reliance on standardised software allows avenues for cross collaboration and encourages technical dialogues to develop. Data can also be easily and quickly extracted to provide useful graphs for clients or consultants.

The PHPP is a design tool and should not be confused with compliance tools such as Standard Assessment Procedure (SAP) and Simplified Building Energy Model (SBEM). Many architects and designers contract out SAP and SBEM assessment. However, I believe it does not make sense to contract out PHPP work, as designing with the PHPP is an interactive process and should be carried out in-house as part of the design process.

The PHPP is a vital tool and I would always recommend it be used from an early stage to give you and your design the maximum benefit. Deciding a building is going to be a Passive House (and introducing PHPP) at a late stage in the design process is not efficient, as late changes are always more expensive and difficult to enact. If this is your first Passive House it is invaluable to work with other experienced Passive House consultants as they will be able to provide guidance on whether what appears to work in the PHPP will be successful in reality.

The PHPP has been developed for designing Passive House buildings but is also a useful tool to design other low-energy buildings, providing very accurate results. It can even be used to model existing buildings pre-retrofit, albeit with less accurate results . Obtaining accurate results for low-efficiency buildings is notoriously difficult in any programme due to the increasing influence of unpredictable boundary conditions.

This book complements the technical manual. The manual has been translated from German and can be difficult to navigate as an English-speaking PHPP beginner. This book aims to bridge the gap, setting out clear and easy to follow steps for designing and understanding a building in PHPP, while the technical manual provides the additional detail on the underlying physics of the standard.

The content of this book also differs from full Certified European Passive House (CEPH) courses, which are intensive and cover the fundamental principles of PHPP including the economics, through

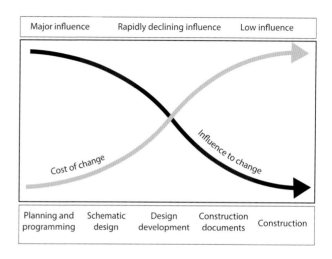

Figure 0.1 *Cost-influence graph*

to the underpinning mathematical calculations upon which the theory is based. Although this is very valuable information, the courses are aimed at architects and energy consultants with experience in designing and delivering low-energy buildings. The full qualification is very technical in nature. This book is focused solely on providing practical guidance for using and understanding your design decisions in PHPP.

0.0 What is a Passive House?

A Passive House is a very well-insulated and draught-free building designed to provide the highest level of comfort. The methodology set out by Dr Wolfgang Feist built upon a collaborative research project to address the problems of unhealthy, unsustainable and unaffordable homes initiated by Bo Adamson during the 1960s to 1980s. Coming from a background in physics, Dr Feist and his team at the Passive House Institute (PHI) developed the methodology into the leading standard for low-energy buildings, offering an optimum standard of thermal comfort and user satisfaction.

> "Passive House is the world's leading standard in energy-efficient construction. The Passive House Standard stands for quality, comfort and energy efficiency. Passive Houses require very little energy to achieve a comfortable temperature year-round, making conventional heating and air conditioning systems obsolete. While delivering superior levels of comfort, the Passive House Standard also protects the building structure."

Source: www.passivehouse-international.org

Over the last few years the number of completed Passive House buildings has grown rapidly. Now there are over 60,000 residential and non-residential structures of all types around the world, with the vast majority in Europe. Of these more than 14,000 are certified according to Passive House Institute (PHI) certification criteria.* Fewer Passive House projects have been completed beyond Europe but there are now examples across extremely diverse climatic regions, from the hot and humid climate of Lafayette, Louisiana, USA to as far north as Finland, where winter temperatures fall to −30°C.

* www.passivehouse-international.org/index.php?page_id=65

Chapter 1

Key Principles of a Passive House Project

1.0 Key Principles of a Passive House Project

An existing certified Passive House has been used throughout this book to help contextualise the guidance. This case study is a home from the Carrowbreck Meadows development in Norwich which, on completion, was the largest certified Passive House development in Greater Norwich. The Carrowbreck home is used here to explain pictorially the key elements universal to all Passive House projects. Designers working with the imperial system can refer to a conversion table at the back of the book, figure 9.2, page 260, to assist in reading this chapter.

Passive House buildings can be constructed from almost any building material. Our case study home is constructed in clay block but could just as easily have been, for example, timber frame, brick, block or straw construction.

Figure 1.1 *(right above) Carrowbreck Meadow in the evening*

Figure 1.2 *(right) Carrowbreck Meadow Avenue*

Figure 1.3 *Carrowbreck Meadow Case Study Plot, Floor Plans NTS*

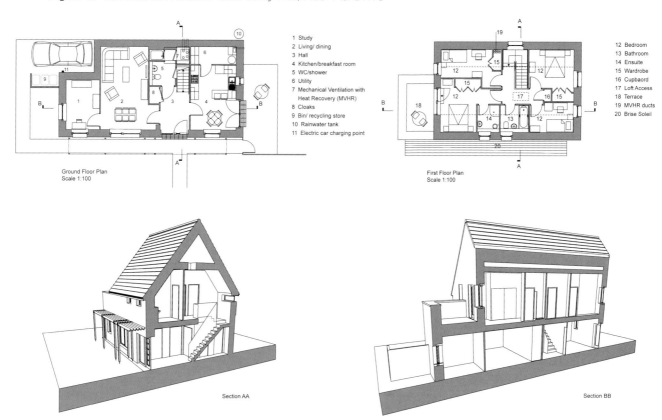

1 Study
2 Living/ dining
3 Hall
4 Kitchen/breakfast room
5 WC/shower
6 Utility
7 Mechanical Ventilation with
   Heat Recovery (MVHR)
8 Cloaks
9 Bin/ recycling store
10 Rainwater tank
11 Electric car charging point

12 Bedroom
13 Bathroom
14 Ensuite
15 Wardrobe
16 Cupbaord
17 Loft Access
18 Terrace
19 MVHR ducts
20 Brise Soleil

Ground Floor Plan
Scale 1:100

First Floor Plan
Scale 1:100

Section AA

Section BB

Figure 1.4 *Carrowbreck Meadow Case Study Plot, Sections NTS*

Key Principle 1: The building envelope

- A continuous thermal envelope all around a building acts like a woolly jumper, minimising heat transfer.

- It is very important that there is no gap in the thermal envelope.

- U-values* of 0.10–0.15 watts per metre squared per degree kelvin ($W/(m^2K)$) are normally required for a new build in the UK.[†] The PHPP may require slightly higher or lower U-values depending on the building and site.

- Passive House U-values normally require thicker components, i.e. walls, floors and roofs, than a standard building, or require the use of high-performance insulation materials.

---

* U-value is a measure of heat transfer through a building element. Units explained: W = watts; m^2 = metre square; K = kelvin.

[†] Refer to Section 2.5 (page 58) for requirements for retrofit projects.

Figure 1.5 *Key Principle 1: the building envelope*

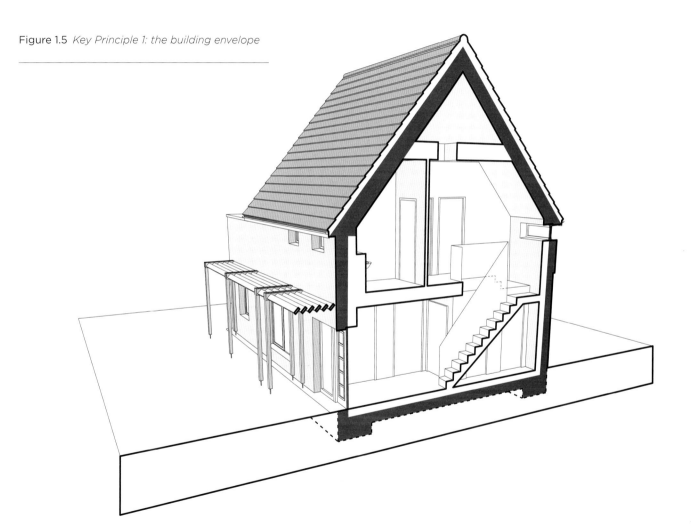

Key Principle 2: Draught free

- The airtight layer plays an important role in reducing the heat losses from draughts, as well as protecting the fabric from interstitial condensation. Passive House certification requires $\leq 0.6h^{-1}$@50Pa in a new build and $\leq 1.0h^{-1}$@50Pa in a retrofit. This measurement is the total air changes per hour (called an n50 test).

- The expression for the results of the n50 test is not the same as that used for SAP and SBEM in the UK (called the q50 test), although the same physical test can be used to measure both values. In the UK the result is given as a rate of air infiltration of the exposed building fabric (m^3/m^2h @50Pa).

- For the n50 test it is important to measure the internal volume (Vn50*) correctly – usual UK assumptions overestimate this and users may wrongly think the building meets the standard.

- The air test is carried out under a pressure of 50 Pascals (Pa) and for Passive House certification the result must be an average of the pressurisation and depressurisation tests. This is not currently a requirement of UK building regulations.

- The air test result can be established only after the building has been finished on site. It is best to complete an air test as soon as the airtight envelope is complete, for easier rectification. This reduces the risk of missing the limiting value in the final test. At design stage, it is best to be conservative and use the limiting value (noted above), unless users have a proven track record in achieving better results on site.

---

* The **Vn50** is the internal volume according to the EN13829 standard, which states the following: '3.2: Internal Volume – deliberately heated, cooled or mechanically ventilated space within a building or part of a building subject to the measurement, generally not including the attic space, basement space and attached structures.'

There are the following additional exceptions: do **not** include the air volumes within partition walls, suspended ceilings and floor cassettes, behind plasterboard, and in inaccessible closed-off areas under stairs (apart from these areas, the stairwell is included). Attics can be included if accessible and fully within the thermal envelope. Generally door and window reveals are also excluded.

It is not easy to make direct comparisons between n50 and q50 readings.

'If a vapour check has as little as a 1mm x 1mm tear within a square metre area, the U-value can reduce by a factor of 4.8!'
Institut für Bauphysik, Stuttgart*

* *pro clima Intelligent Airtightness & Windtightness Building Systems, Product Portfolio*, published by Ecological Building Systems Ltd, 2014.

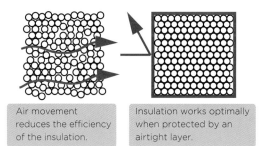

Air movement reduces the efficiency of the insulation.

Insulation works optimally when protected by an airtight layer.

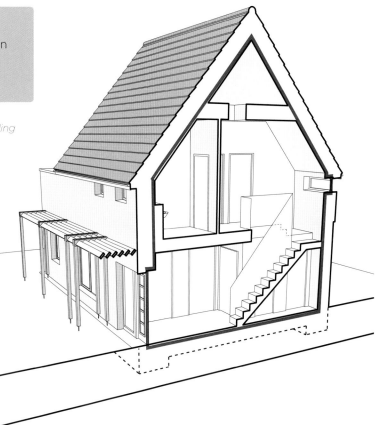

Figure 1.6 *Key Principle 2: draught free*

15

Key Principle 3: Solar gain

- Passive House is not to be confused with Passive solar. While high-performance south glazing can provide a net heat gain over the heating season, unless the windows are needed anyway, they are a very expensive way to heat a building. 'Free' solar heat costs about 10–20 times as much as gas.[*] However, if the window is needed then it is free heat.

- Windows are an essential element in the overall success of the building fabric, with high-quality windows being key to ensuring thermal comfort for occupants. Instead of acting as holes in the fabric that contribute to heat loss, which is the case in most buildings, Passive House windows can result in net heat gains on the south façade.

- The quality of a window depends on two essential characteristics: the U-value of the window (glass and frame combined), U_w, and the g-value, which is a measurement of how much solar heat gain is admitted through the glass.

- Passive House window component certification requires as a minimum a U_w of $\leq 0.80W/(m^2K)$. This is calculated using a 'standard glazing unit' (1.23m x 1.48m) but you should not need to worry about this as all certified window manufacturers use this same standard when calculating their U_w. You do not need to use certified windows, but if you are using non-certified products you have to be sure they are of suitable quality.

- The U_w installed should be $\leq 0.85W/(m^2K)$, which takes into consideration the detail of how the window is installed in the wall. In the UK it is possible to achieve certification if the U_w is not met but this limiting value provides a useful target.

- The window frames do not contribute to solar heat gains but do contribute towards heat losses (with good-quality triple glazing, frames always lose more heat than the glazing), so it makes sense to reduce the frame-to-glass ratio as much as possible.

> When designing a Passive House it is important to remember the windows are key to the balance of maximising heat gains in the winter and minimising overheating in the summer.

[*] Nick Grant, Passive House Trust Technical Director, UK Passive House Conference 2013

Figure 1.7 *Key Principle 3: solar gain*

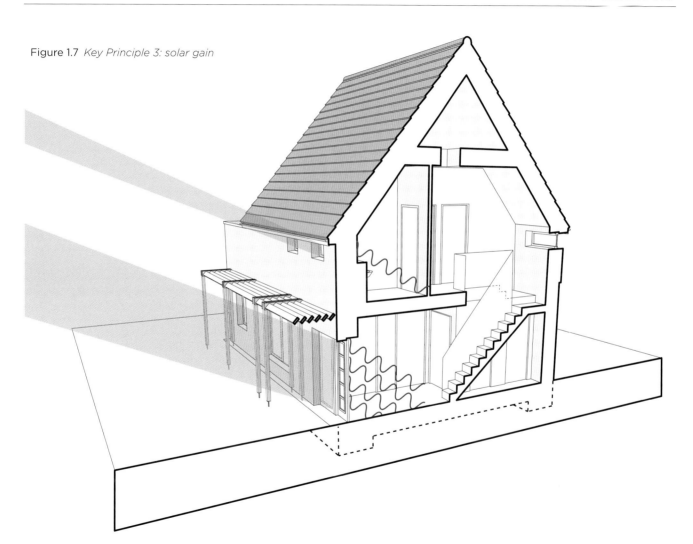

- Just remember that to maximise heat gains the U_w should be as low as possible and the g-value should be as high as possible. Common g-values are around 0.5, meaning 50% of the solar heat hitting the window passes through it into the building. However take care that higher g-values don't lead to summer overheating.

- The PHPP provides summaries of the contribution that the windows are making to solar heat gains and heat lost to the outside, so that the windows can be adjusted to work optimally for the building.

- The most important things to remember about windows are they must:

  - be triple glazed with low-e or equivalent glazing (in the UK at least, in other climates this can vary)
  - have an insulated glass edge bond (referred to in the UK as a warm edge spacer)
  - have a highly insulated frame (this requirement can sometimes be reduced in the UK through agreement with certifiers and excellent detailing)
  - be very well detailed where they meet the building (to reduce thermal bridging)

Key Principle 4: Controlling solar gain

In a Passive House, windows provide a useful part of the energy required to meet winter heat demands (around a third). But what about summer overheating? *

- It is a requirement for Passive House certification that temperatures exceeding 25°C do not occur in a building for more than 10% of the occupied year and ideally not more than 5%.

- When planning for future climate scenarios and variations in internal heat gains (IHG) due to occupancy, habits and kit, I always aim for this figure to be lower than 5% and if possible see how this can be reduced to 1%.

- Just as in a non-Passive House project, shading devices can be brise-soleil, external retractable blinds and shutters, as well as foliage and trees (especially useful when they are deciduous).

---

* The PHPP will help you evaluate this risk and if necessary provide guidance on the quantity of shading required. Full details in Chapter 4.

- The PHPP does not place any restrictions on the shading devices that can be used but helps the designer understand the impact of their choices on winter heat gains.

- For residential projects it is possible and desirable to design out the need for expensive and complicated shading devices.

Overheating is also reduced through cross ventilation and night purge ventilation.

While night ventilation is critical for summer comfort, noise, insects or fear of intruders may mean that overly optimistic ventilation rates are not achieved in practice.

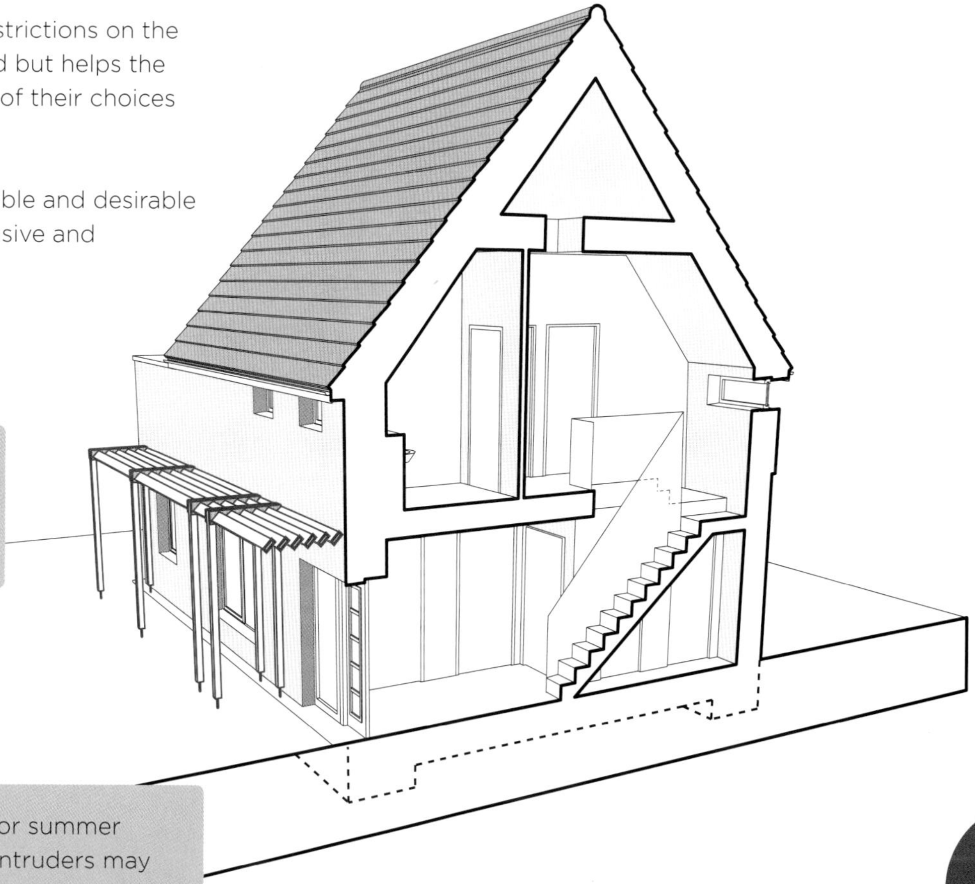

Figure 1.8 *Key Principle 4: controlling solar gain*

19

Key Principle 5: Thermal bridge free detailing

A thermal bridge is a localised weak area in the envelope of a building where heat flow is substantially greater than in adjacent areas. These can be repeating or non-repeating. For example, a repeating thermal bridge could be the regular timber studwork in an insulated wall. A non-repeating linear thermal bridge may occur where a wall and floor meet.

Thermal bridges result in localised reduced interior surface temperatures in winter, which can lead to increased heat losses, surface mould or even condensation. The same thermal bridge can lead to increased interior surface temperatures in summer allowing unwanted heat in the building/raising the cooling load. To help simplify the calculation of thermal bridges for the PHPP, the PHI has created a simplified criterion for thermal bridge free detailing, which is that if the thermal bridge (Ψ) is $\leq$ 0.01 watts per metre of length of the thermal bridge per degree Kelvin (W/(mK)) it does not need to be calculated and can be classed as thermal bridge free.

How to calculate thermal bridges is covered in detail in Chapter 7. However if thermal bridge free detailing is adhered to, you can significantly reduce the number of details you have to analyse.

The surface area of the thermal envelope is calculated based on the external dimensions of the heated building when carrying out PHPP modelling. This differs from the convention used by SAP and SBEM, which require the envelope area to be calculated based on internal dimensions. The result is that PHPP slightly overestimates the heat loss from the building elements (wall, roof, floor) thus it has already taken into account heat loss from most geometrical thermal bridges and in some instances over-accounts for them. Refer to Chapter 3 for a more detailed explanation.

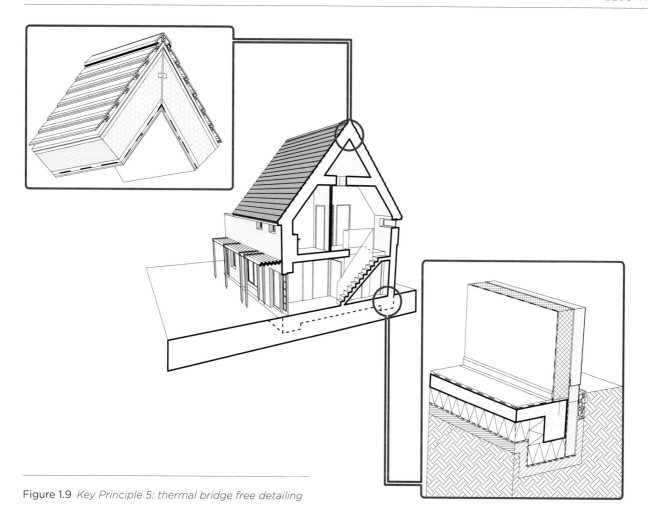

Figure 1.9 *Key Principle 5: thermal bridge free detailing*

Key Principle 6: Fresh air with heat transfer

This principle is all about providing optimal indoor air quality (IAQ) for the health and comfort of occupants. In traditional buildings people often open windows in winter to get some fresh air circulation, but even opening windows twice a day does not allow sufficient air change and in the winter it can be very uncomfortable, not to mention the increased energy use.

The typical solution for building regulation compliance is the trickle vent, which people don't tend to use correctly because they either don't know they are there, or they don't know how to use them. Trickle vents also require dusting/cleaning at intervals, which is rarely carried out in practice. Even when used and maintained optimally the trickle vent still results in significant heat loss, as there is no heat recovery available.

- The Passive House requirement for fresh air is for $30m^3$/hr per person, while the building ventilation rate must be around 0.3 air changes an hour (ACH); this will be covered more in Chapter 3. If no ventilation rate is input into the PHPP it assumes 0.4 ACH, which is a good place to start. If this figure were to be achieved just by opening windows, the windows would need to be open for

The 0.3ACH value is not directly comparable/ should not be confused with the 0.6ACH target for airtightness, which is carried out at high pressure, where as this is at normal atmospheric pressure.

five to ten minutes every three hours all day, even at night, which is not very practical. So we need comfort ventilation based on the requirement for fresh air supplied through Mechanical Ventilation with Heat Recovery (MVHR).

- MVHR continuously removes air from the kitchen, bathroom, toilet and other rooms with high pollution and humidity. At the same time, the MVHR pumps fresh air from outdoors into the living room, bedrooms and functional rooms preheated with the heat from the outgoing air, without mixing airflows.

If a non-certified unit is being used you must take 12 percentage points off the manufacturer's stated efficiency eg 90% becomes 78%

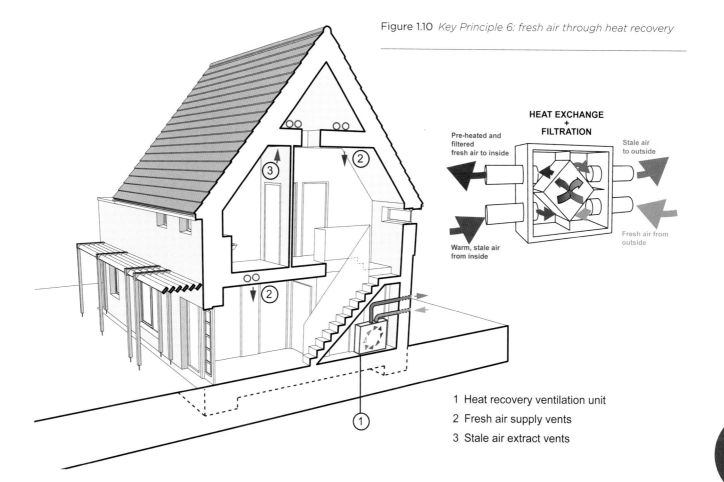

Figure 1.10 *Key Principle 6: fresh air through heat recovery*

HEAT EXCHANGE + FILTRATION

Pre-heated and filtered fresh air to inside

Stale air to outside

Warm, stale air from inside

Fresh air from outside

1 Heat recovery ventilation unit
2 Fresh air supply vents
3 Stale air extract vents

23

- The PHI certifies MVHR units and only units with certified thermal efficiency of ≥75% (with a fan power of ≤0.45Wh/m^3) should be specified.

- Typically a high-quality MVHR unit saves 10 times more energy than it uses. Residential systems typically use 22 watts, costing around 10p per day; this is comparable to having one low-energy light bulb on.*

- In the UK, outside of the heating season the heat recovery function is bypassed in residential buildings with filtered fresh air still being supplied. In non-residential buildings the ventilation system is often designed to switch to extract only with natural ventilation providing the fresh air. The design of the MVHR system is central to the success of a Passive House project and working with experienced service consultants is beneficial.

- Beyond the UK, in climates with hot summer months, the MVHR is just as important on a hot summer day as it is on a cold winter day. It rejects heat in the fresh but hot outdoor air

ACH for UK building regulations requires 0.43ACH (0.3l/s/m^2). The building regulations standard appears to have evolved from a natural ventilation scenario for control of VOCs. In Passive House projects the MVHR has different settings and as long as the boost or highest setting can meet the building regulation requirement this is normally sufficient. The concern with designing for building regulations rather than the lower Passive House requirement is that the building can be over-ventilated, causing dry air conditions, especially in large buildings and specifically those with low occupancy and hence low moisture generation.

by transferring it to the cold, stale exhaust air. Creating a comfortable internal environment without auxiliary cooling (air conditioning).

And remember you can still open your windows whenever you like. If this is during the heating season some heat loss will occur.

* www.greenbuildingstore.co.uk/page--mvhr-frequently-asked-questions.html

1.1 Preparation

Site analysis

Designing a Passive House is no different from designing any other type of low energy building. Careful consideration should be given to the particular site. The Passive House Standard can be achieved with many different building forms and orientations, however it is much easier if the building is positioned optimally on its site. When working with an existing building there might still be opportunities to influence new elements or existing landscaping.

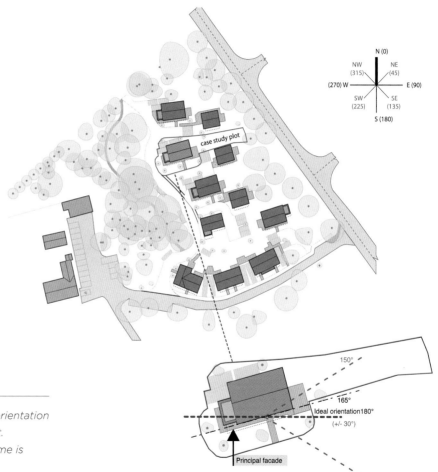

Figure 1.11 *Orientation: Plan showing the orientation of the Carrowbreck Meadow development. The principal facade of our case study home is orientated 15° from due south.*

So what is optimal?

Passive House buildings make use of solar energy during the heating season. It is therefore a good idea, in the UK, to orientate your building along an east/ west principal axis, maximising the use of the south façade. In the winter the heating load will be at its highest and the south façade will have the most opportunity for solar radiation. Consequently if a site allows a building to be positioned within 30 degrees of south it will maximise the use of the solar gains when they are needed most.

What if I can't position my building optimally?

There will be situations where it is not possible to position a building optimally due to existing site constraints, especially on tight urban sites. Equally there may be times when positioning a building optimally does not work because it does not fit with the overall concept, or does not make the most of views or other site attributes. This does not make a Passive House build impossible; it does, however, mean the building will have to work harder elsewhere. For example the fenestration would need to be designed very differently and a compact form may become essential. A poor orientation can increase annual heating demand by at least a third.*

The most important thing to recognise is the optimum position and have a clear, rational argument for any necessary deviation.

*   BRE Passive House Primer

What site information does the PHPP require?

For the PHPP to accurately model a building's energy demands, it has to be given the context. Inputting this data is covered in detail in Chapter 3, but to summarise the following information is vital in order to get started with PHPP:

- location
- shading
- exposure.

Location of the Norwich Passivhaus.

Geographical location is important so that appropriate weather data can be selected. Take into account any specific features of the site that may result in a large variation from the standardised weather data for the area, is the project at a high altitude? The PHPP makes adjustments for altitude (−0.6°C for every 100m increase in altitude) automatically when you input the actual site altitude.

Take into account all external elements that shade the site. This includes hills, buildings, trees and

Greater Norwich, Norfolk

Figure 1.12 *Location of the Carrowbreck Meadow development*

27

any elements of the building that permanently or temporarily shade the windows.

The more the building is shaded the lower the solar gains will be during the heating season and the higher the heating energy demand will be. Conversely during the cooling period shading reduces the risk of overheating.

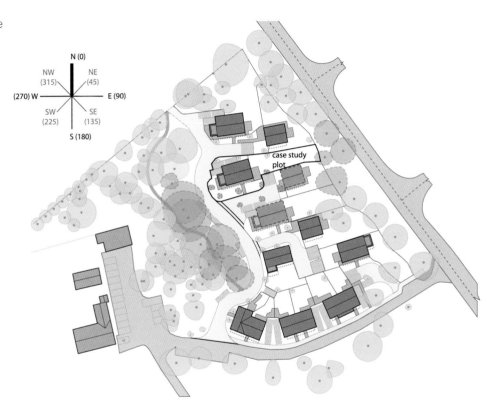

Figure 1.13 *Shading: Plan showing shading elements taken into account for our case study plot at Carrowbreck Meadow*

Assess the sheltering provided by the situation of the building. Do other structures surround the building or is it in an exposed rural setting? Are all sides of the building exposed to weather or is one or more protected by adjacent structures or landscape?

The more exposed the building is to the wind the greater the heat losses will be. In the UK it is helpful for the building to have some form of wind protection.

Figure 1.14 *Exposure: sheltering considerations for the heavily wooded Carrowbreck Meadow development*

29

1.2 Schematic Design

The building's form has a huge influence on its energy demands. It is good to test a number of forms in the PHPP before progressing with one design. This is a great reason to work with PHPP in-house and not rely on contracting this work out. The SketchUp plug-in from PHI, called *design*PH, can be particularly useful and time-saving at these early schematic design stages. This is covered in more detail in chapter 6, new to this second edition.

How does form affect the energy demand?

At the most basic level, the more compact the building the less energy it will require. The ratio of the external building envelope to the internal volume (A/V ratio) is critical to the energy balance. A significant proportion of heat loss in buildings occurs as transmission loss through the envelope, so the higher the proportion of envelope to internal volume, the more area for potential transmission heat loss in the winter (and heat gain in summer).

Passive House projects come in all shapes and sizes so design creativity need not be restricted. However, form becomes particularly important when working on small projects and/or projects with a tight budget.

Evaluating the efficiency of the form

The external building envelope to the internal volume (A/V) ratio is a good way to evaluate the efficiency of form. The smaller a building is, the more important the form becomes. A small building that has the same form as a larger building will actually have a worse A/V ratio. This is worth keeping in mind when developing the schematic design. The larger the building is, the less the energy penalty of a complex form.

Figure 1.15 *(opposite) A/V ratio – effect of size on the A/V*

Our case study house has
an A/V ratio of
467m²/364m³ = **1.28m²/m³**

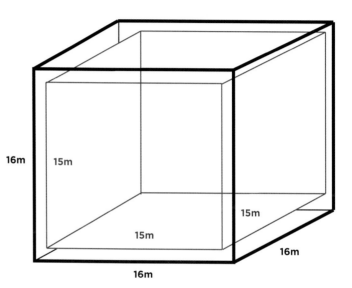

16m

15m

15m

15m

16m

16m

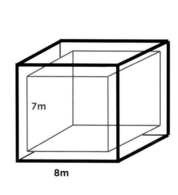

7m

8m

3m

4m

Small cube

External surface area = 96m²
Internal volume = 27m³
A/V ratio = 3.6m²/m³

Medium cube

External surface area = 384m²
Internal volume = 343m³
A/V ratio = 1.1m²/m³

Large cube

External surface area = 1536m²
Internal volume = 3375m³
A/V ratio = 0.46m²/m³

Effect of multiple storeys on the A/V

The A/V ratio is also affected by the number of storeys the building has. This is something to consider at an early stage in the design process. **Figure 1.16** shows that for a building with an internal treated floor area (TFA)* of 100m^2 (equivalent to a small family home in the UK) and a cuboid envelope with a consistent wall thickness of 500mm, the most efficient A/V ratio is achieved in a two-storey design. Every design will have a different optimum layout; this diagram has been included to illustrate different variations and shows why a single-storey building is often not the most efficient form for a Passive House. A single-storey Passive House is certainly possible, but allowances have to be made elsewhere as a result, for example, by increasing the performance of the envelope.

Provided below is some advice to consider at schematic stage:

- Small buildings and bungalow houses are likely to have an external surface area to internal volume (A/V) ratio of ≥1m^2/m^3, making these the most challenging
- Large compact buildings or terrace houses will reach a ratio of 0.6–0.7m^2/m^3.
- Tower blocks will achieve an even better ratio of 0.3–0.4m^2/m^3

It is worth remembering at this point that a complex form will, in addition to having a high A/V ratio, be more challenging when eliminating thermal bridging and maintaining a continuous airtight envelope. If designing and building your first Passive House, the additional challenges of a complex form could be quite significant and collaborating with more experienced team members and/or contractors would be beneficial.

* the TFA is the 'treated floor area' and is explained in detail in Chapter 3.

Figure 1.16 *(opposite) A/V ratio optimisation*

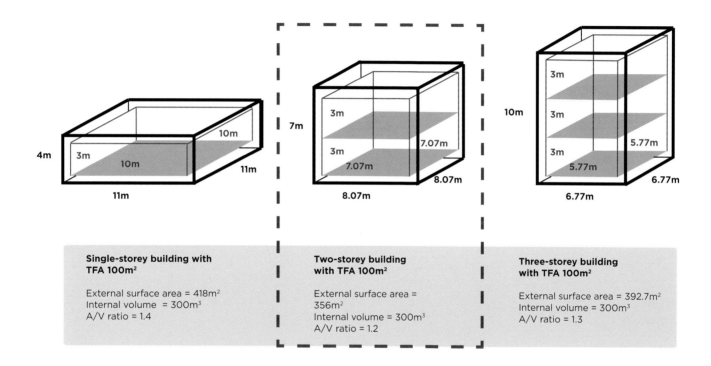

**Single-storey building with
TFA 100m²**

External surface area = 418m²
Internal volume = 300m³
A/V ratio = 1.4

**Two-storey building
with TFA 100m²**

External surface area =
356m²
Internal volume = 300m³
A/V ratio = 1.2

**Three-storey building
with TFA 100m²**

External surface area = 392.7m²
Internal volume = 300m³
A/V ratio = 1.3

External surface area to internal treated floor area (TFA) – the form factor

Another, and often more common, way to evaluate the efficiency of form is to look at the relationship between the external surface area and the TFA. The examples here look at variations on the two-storey 100m^2 house from the previous page, varying the complexity of the envelope.

It is reasonable to achieve an external envelope surface area to TFA of ≤3 (although in very small buildings achieving ≤4 can be challenging). If the design includes large areas of voids/double height spaces the form factor will be higher and it will be more challenging to achieve the Passive House Standard.

When assessing the A/V ratio and form factor it is important to keep in mind that the size of the project will have a big effect on the values it is possible to achieve. Our case study house has high values due to its size, and still would even if it were a perfect cuboid, however it still achieved the Passive House Standard. Generally residential buildings in the UK are smaller than their German counterparts so will have more challenging A/V ratios/form factors.
At the schematic stage of the design process the key question to ask is whether it is worth constructing a complex form. If the answer is yes, then the performance of the fabric, orientation and window positioning will probably need to be adjusted in order to compensate, which could in turn become prohibitively expensive and/or impractical. Taking this into consideration, the designer must carefully consider the benefit of design decisions for their own sake. Taken as a whole, the performance of the building will improve if design decisions are a response to the contextual environment in which the building sits, and the form is influenced by the efficiency of the space created.

Figure 1.17 *(opposite) Surface area to TFA - the form factor*

Our case study house, has an external surface area to TFA ratio of $467m^2 / 121.2m^2 = $ **3.9**

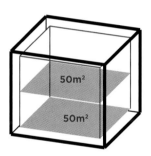

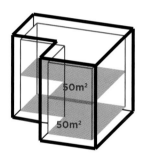

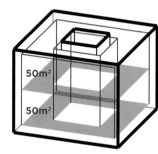

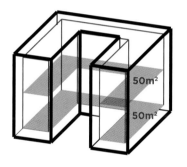

Cuboid

External surface area = $356m^2$
TFA = $100m^2$
Ratio = 3.6
(A/V = 1.2)

L-shaped

External surface area = $394m^2$
TFA = $100m^2$
Ratio = 3.9
(A/V = 1.3)

Courtyard

External surface area = $492m^2$
TFA = $100m^2$
Ratio = 4.9
(A/V = 1.6)

U-shaped

External surface area = $524m^2$
TFA = $100m^2$
Ratio = 5.2
(A/V = 1.8)

Chapter 2

Getting Started with PHPP

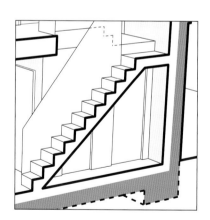

2.1 Introduction

As with all new programs, getting started can be a bit daunting. It's important to allow for time to experiment with the program and for becoming familiar with the new terminology. A glossary is included at the end of this book covering some of the essential technical terminology.

As already mentioned, the PHPP is an Excel workbook, first published in 1998. At the time of writing PHPP9.6a is the most recent edition. PHPP9 is designed to work with the now commonly used Excel format .xlsx for the first time. PHPP9 is not compatible with the previous Excel file format .xls or with Excel 2003. PHPP was designed for metric unit inputs but is now available for imperial unit inputs as well (IP PHPP).

When purchased, the PHPP includes the PHPP technical manual which provides essential information and explains the building physics behind the Passive House Standard. Complementing but not replacing the manual, this guide focuses on the interactions between a designer and the PHPP. Further information and technical details can also be found at www.passipedia.org – a Wikipedia-style directory for Passive House information.

It may seem unusual that an Excel workbook of stationary energy calculations can be used to accurately design and predict the energy demands of a building, but the PHPP does have a tried and tested track record in terms of accuracy, calculating energy balances to an average accuracy of +/- 0.5kWh/m²a (this assumes very accurate inputs).[*]

The PHPP has been developed for low-energy buildings and to obtain these accurate results from the program the building being studied must be a low-energy building. Remember, a Passive House will have a heat demand of ≤15kWh/m²a. It is, however, worth noting that the accuracy of the PHPP will be affected if the actual conditions in the building/environment differ from the various pre-set PHPP assumptions, such as internal gains (it is not uncommon to find these higher in the UK, especially in small buildings), internal temperature of 20°C, and heating season temperatures and sunshine as per the climate data set.

Before getting started, make sure the correct version of PHPP is being used for your project.

[*] http://passiv.de/en/04_phpp/04_phpp.htm

39

It is important that the most recent edition is used, as this is necessary for certification. Upgrades are not expensive once a first copy has been purchased. PHPP9 contains many new and useful tools which are explained throughout this second edition of the book.

This chapter provides an introduction to the certification criteria for Passive House projects as summarised below. This book focuses on criteria relevant to cool temperate regions (eg UK), but will highlight where these vary for other regions.

- **Section 2.2** provides an explanation of the recommended component performance standards, summarised in a useful reference table.
- **Section 2.3** introduces the New Passive Houses Classes
- **Sections 2.4–2.6** set out the mandatory Evaluation Criteria, which are calculated by PHPP, for new build (Section 2.4), refurbishment projects (Section 2.5) and PHI low-energy buildings (Section 2.6)
- **Section 2.7** provides an explanation of how cooling requirements are assessed.
- **Section 2.8** concludes with a flow diagram based on the one included in the PHPP technical manual, as a visual representation of which Excel sheets are to be filled in. Each subsection in the following

chapters references this chart to maintain a clear reference point.

The chapter is structured this way to guide the reader through the process in a method as compatible with the design process as possible.

By starting with the key component performance criteria, the designer can make some assumptions regarding the fabric of the building at an early stage. Understanding the Evaluation Criteria is essential to understanding what the goals are while progressing through the following chapters.

The questions and answers addressed in this chapter are restricted to those necessary to obtain a clear and comprehensive understanding of the Evaluation Criteria.

The PHPP will display a multitude of Excel sheets when first opened. Don't panic, start by reading the first tab called 'Brief Instructions'. This tab explains what the different coloured cells mean, which cells require you to input data, which show important results, etc. It also provides a list of all of the worksheets in the PHPP and explains which are required for certification.

Figure 2.1 *(opposite) Brief instructions sheet*

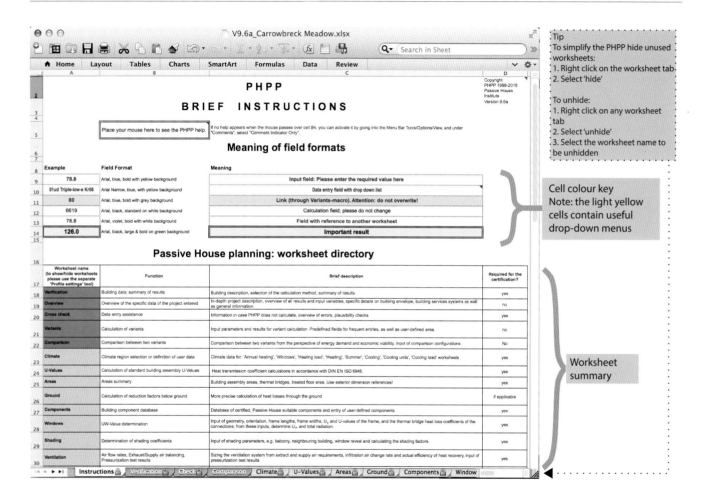

V9.6a_Carrowbreck Meadow.xlsx

PHPP

BRIEF INSTRUCTIONS

Copyright
PHPP 1998-2016
Passive House
Institute
Version 9.6a

Place your mouse here to see the PHPP help. | If no help appears when the mouse passes over cell B4, you can activate it by going into the Menu Bar Tools/Options/View, and under "Comments", select "Comment Indicator Only".

Meaning of field formats

Example	Field Format	Meaning
78.8	Arial, blue, bold with yellow background	Input field: Please enter the required value here
01ud Triple-low-e Kr08	Arial Narrow, blue, with yellow background	Data entry field with drop down list
80	Arial, blue, bold with grey background	Link (through Variants-macro). Attention: do not overwrite!
6619	Arial, black, standard on white background	Calculation field; please do not change
78.8	Arial, violet, bold with white background	Field with reference to another worksheet
126.0	Arial, black, large & bold on green background	Important result

Passive House planning: worksheet directory

Worksheet name (to show/hide worksheets please use the separate 'Profile settings' tool)	Function	Brief description	Required for the certification?
Verification	Building data; summary of results	Building description, selection of the calculation method, summary of results	yes
Overview	Overview of the specific data of the project entered	In-depth project description, overview of all results and input variables, the specific details on building envelope, building services systems as well as general information.	no
Cross check	Data entry assistance	Information in case PHPP does not calculate, overview of errors, plausibility checks	yes
Variants	Calculation of variants	Input parameters and results for variant calculation. Predefined fields for frequent entries, as well as user-defined area.	no
Comparison	Comparison between two variants	Comparison between two variants from the perspective of energy demand and economic viability. Input of comparison configurations.	No
Climate	Climate region selection or definition of user data	Climate data for: 'Annual heating', 'Windows', 'Heating load', 'Heating', 'Summer', 'Cooling', 'Cooling units', 'Cooling load' worksheets	yes
U-Values	Calculation of standard building assembly U-Values	Heat transmission coefficient calculations in accordance with DIN EN ISO 6946.	yes
Areas	Areas summary	Building assembly areas, thermal bridges, treated floor area. Use exterior dimension references!	yes
Ground	Calculation of reduction factors below ground	More precise calculation of heat losses through the ground	if applicable
Components	Building component database	Database of certified, Passive House suitable components and entry of user-defined components	yes
Windows	UW-Value determination	Input of geometry, orientation, frame lengths, frame widths, U_g and U-values of the frame, and the thermal bridge heat loss coefficients of the connections; from these inputs, determine U_w and total radiation.	yes
Shading	Determination of shading coefficients	Input of shading parameters, e.g. balcony, neighbouring building, window reveal and calculating the shading factors	yes
Ventilation	Air flow rates, Exhaust/Supply air balancing, Pressurization test results	Sizing the ventilation system from extract and supply air requirements, infiltration air change rate and actual efficiency of heat recovery, input of pressurization test results	yes

Tabs: Instructions | Verification | Check | Comparison | Climate | U-Values | Areas | Ground | Components | Window

Tip
To simplify the PHPP hide unused worksheets:
1. Right click on the worksheet tab
2. Select 'hide'

To unhide:
1. Right click on any worksheet tab
2. Select 'unhide'
3. Select the worksheet name to be unhidden

Cell colour key
Note: the light yellow cells contain useful drop-down menus

Worksheet summary

2.2 Component Performance Criteria

The key criteria for certifying a Passive House are referred to as the 'Evaluation Criteria' and are set out in **sections, 2.4–2.6**. In order to assist readers in meeting these key criteria, the PHI also provides recommended qualities for each of the components within the building, such as walls and windows. By following these guidelines, in addition to other parameters such as shading and orientation, readers should find that the Evaluation Criteria are easy to achieve. These recommended qualities for components should be thought of as reasonable target values, unless agreed otherwise with the certifier or through discussion with experienced Passive House consultants. A summary of these limits for cool temperate regions (eg UK) is provided in **Figure 2.2**, and full details can be found in the technical manual. The official Passive House Institute climate regions can be seen in **Figure 2.3**.

This table provides a summary of all of the recommended component qualities in cool temperate regions for easy reference. Throughout this section of the book, as project details are being inserted into the PHPP, this table can be used to confirm that all the elements of the building meet the recommended target values. These criteria can be considered the

For EnerPHit projects there are some special exceptions. Refer to the technical manual for full details.

core of the Passive House Standard but it must be understood that simply meeting these criteria does not guarantee Passive House certification. Certification requires in addition that all of the 'Evaluation Criteria' are met and to establish this completion of the PHPP is required.

Figure 2.2 *(opposite) Component limits*

Mandatory Envelope Performance – Passive House – All regions

Draft-free $\leq 0.6h^{-1}@50Pa$
External building envelope should be thermal bridge free $\Psi \geq 0.01 W/(mK)$ must be inserted into the PHPP
For component quality recommendations see component requirements for certification according to component standard, below

Mandatory Envelope Performance - EnerPHit and EnerPHit+i - All regions

Draft-free $\leq 1.0h^{-1}@50Pa^{\S}$
External building envelope should be thermal bridge free $\Psi \geq 0.01 W/(mK)$ must be inserted into the PHPP
For component quality recommendations see component requirements for certification according to component standard, below

§ This is a limiting value in recognition of the greater difficulties associated with existing buildings, however the target remains $\leq 0.6h^{-1}@50Pa$

Mandatory requirements for certification according to the component standard - EnerPHit/ EnerPHit+i - Cool temperate regions only*
(recommendations for Passive House and EnerPHit/ EnerPHit+i according to heating demand)

Exterior building elements U value external insulation	$f_t \cdot U \leq 0.15 W/m^2K$ †
Exterior building elements U value internal insulation	$f_t \cdot U \leq 0.35 W/m^2K$ †
Window installed U value ($U_{W,installed}$)	$\leq 0.85 W/m^2K$ ‡ (vertical)
	$\leq 1.00 W/m^2K$ ‡ (rooflights)
Window g and U_g-value of glazing	$g \cdot 1.6 W/(m^2K) \geq U_g$
Door installed U value ($f_t \cdot U_{D,installed}$)	$\leq 0.80 W/m^2K$ §

> *Note: In exceptional circumstances where it is not possible to meet all of these criteria in renovation projects the PHI has provided a set of absolute minimum thermal comfort requirements. These can be downloaded from http://www.passiv.de/downloads/03_enerphit_criteria_en.pdf*

* For all other regions refer to Table 2 'EnerPHit criteria for the building component method' on page 8 of the 'Criteria for the Passive House, EnerPHit and PHI Low Energy Building Standard' document, which can be seen at - http://www.passiv.de/downloads/03_building_criteria_en.pdf)

† With temperature factor f_t: in contact with the outdoor air $f_t = 1$ in contact with the ground "ground reduction factor" from the PHPP "Ground" Sheet
‡ This is based on a design temperature for the coldest day in winter for Central European climates which is -10°C. When certifying through means other than by the component standard there is flexibility in this value in the UK due to the milder winters.
§ Door $f_t \cdot U_{D,installed}$ with temperature factor f_t in contact with the outdoor air $f_t = 1$ or in contact with the unheated basement: $f_t =$ "ground reduction factor" from the PHPP "Ground" Sheet

Recommended Services Performance (Mandatory for component standard)		Recommended Thermal and Acoustic Performance	
MVHR system efficiency	$\geq 75\%$†	Overheating frequency	>25°C$\leq$10%of yr (target >25°C$\leq$5% of yr)
MVHR unit electrical efficiency	$\leq 0.45 Wh/m^3$	Maximum sound from MVHR unit	35 dB(A)
		Maximum transfer sound in occupied rooms	25dB(A)

† MVHR unit efficiency must be calculated according to Passive House standards not manufacturer's rating, if Manufacturer's rating is used 12 percentage points must be deducted

Note: designers working with the imperial system can refer to a converted version of this table at the back of the book, Table 9.1, p. 259.

2.3 The new Passive House Classes

PHPP9 saw the introduction of a series of new Passive Houses classes: Classic, Plus and Premium. The PHI developed these new classes based on renewable energy supplies and an assessment of the energy that a building generates.

It is helpful to take a little time to understand the rationale for these new classes, as this update represents one of the most significant changes to the Evaluation Criteria since the inception of the standard in the 1990s.

Across the world today we are seeing a significant shift towards sustainable energy supplies. In the UK, Scotland met nearly 60% of its electricity consumption from renewable sources in 2015; with overall energy produced from renewable sources rising 14% since 2014.* This puts Scotland on track to meet 100% of its electricity demand from renewables by 2020. This scenario, which is being repeated in many counties around the world, sits within the wider

* Energy Statistics Summary – December 2016, http://www. gov.scot/Topics/Statistics/Browse/Business/Energy/ energysumdec2016

context of the Paris Agreement that came into effect in November 2016. The Paris Agreement provides a framework for governments as well as business and investors to keep global warming below 2°C, pursuing efforts to limit the temperature increase to 1.5°C. The Paris negotiations have set us on an irreversible route towards low-carbon growth and the updated PHPP now performs assessments of buildings within the context of this future of fully renewable energy supplies. This is important, as most of the energy demand over the life-cycles of today's buildings will be consumed at a time when renewable energy supplies will dominate.

What is the same in the new Classes?

If there is one figure designers talk about when it comes to the Passive House standard it is 15kWh/(m^2a) and this remains unchanged in the new Classes. This value is the specific space heating demand, which is the total energy required to heat the building for a year (explained in detail on p. 48). It is this figure (or the alternative criterion $10W/m^2$ heating load) that designers use as the key benchmark for all early design decisions. Whether using the SketchUp plugin, *design*PH, or inputting data manually into the PHPP, designers are looking to see at an early stage if their designs can meet this challenging energy figure. In all of the new Classes this figure remains the starting point, as it provides a limiting value for the amount of energy required for heating (or cooling in hot climates) purposes and is inexorably linked with high quality and draught-free qualities of Passive House buildings.

Useful energy demand for cooling, airtightness, and all criteria for comfort and hygiene also remain the same.

What is new in the new Classes?

A building's total energy demand – including the energy needed to provide the building with final energy – needs to be taken into account. This was previously referred to as the Primary Energy demand (PE) and was based on the existing and historic non-renewable energy supplies. However, our energy supplies are increasingly coming from renewable sources and this is where the new Passive House Classes come in. They divide buildings into categories based on renewable primary energy demand and their own renewable primary power production.

Generation and demand remain separated and clear targets and limits are provided for both. Passive House buildings are first and foremost highly energy efficient, requiring very little heat energy to keep them warm (or cool in hot climates). Importantly, it remains impossible to disguise an inefficient building behind many renewable technologies.

Another important feature of the new PHPP, which sets it aside from many other methodologies for calculating renewable contribution, is that it takes into account the balance of when the energy is produced and when it is actually needed.

For example, solar power generated in the summer should not be treated as though it directly offsets heating energy in the winter because energy from the summer would need to be stored seasonally for the winter, a process that entails additional losses. If this factor is not taken into consideration during planning, buildings are not properly optimised and the true energy consumption is not understood.

By contrast, in the UK designers often refer to buildings as being Zero Energy Buildings, if they produce about as much energy as residents consume.

When used in this way the Zero Energy title may be slightly misleading, as the calculations are net calculations over the year, and do not take into account the balance of when the energy is produced and when it is actually required. The methodology introduced in PHPP9 is more robust in this sense.

PHPP9 also introduces a new methodology for determining how much renewable energy a building should contribute. This calculation uses the building's footprint rather than its treated floor area. This is an important differentiation as a building's ability to create energy is linked more closely to its footprint than its internal floor area. This can be easily visualised if designers think about a building's ability to support Photovoltaic (PV) panels to produce electricity. So in PHPP9, energy generation is stated relative to the projected building footprint, defined as the area of the vertical projection of the thermal envelope on ground (see **Figure 3.17**).

This new evaluation system consists of three Passive House classes, all of which start with the same core principles for space heating demand/load and airtightness but introduce varying limits for the primary energy of the whole building, and renewable energy generation. These three new classes are:

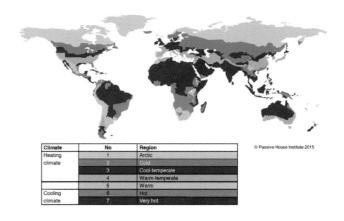

Climate	No	Region
Heating climate	1	Arctic
	2	Cold
	3	Cool-temperate
	4	Warm-temperate
	5	Warm
Cooling climate	6	Hot
	7	Very hot

© Passive House Institute 2015

Figure 2.3 *Climate zones*

- The **Passive House Classic**, for those familiar with the Passive House Standard, this is the traditional Passive House.

- The **Passive House Plus**, in which the whole building primary energy demand is lower and additional energy is generated, such as from photovoltaics (PV).

Figure 2.4 *PHI classes*

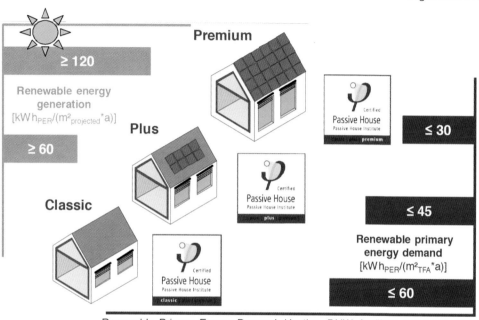

Renewable Primary Energy Demand: Heating, DHW, Auxiliary and Appliances

- In a **Passive House Premium** building, even less energy is consumed by the building and even more energy is produced, more in fact than is needed. It is therefore a goal for the particularly ambitious building owners and designers. PHI is working to make the Passive House Standard more attractive for these innovative projects.

2.4 Four Key Evaluation Criteria for New Builds

There are four key Evaluation Criteria for new builds – Specific Space Heating Demand, Specific Renewable Primary Energy Demand, Renewable Energy Generation and Airtightness. The 'Verification' worksheet of the PHPP facilitates easy monitoring of these requirements. **Important note:** The Frequency of Overheating is a key consideration, covered in Section 2.7.

Designers working with the imperial system can refer to **Table 9.1** at the back of this book, page 259, for some key Evaluation Criteria Conversions.

2.4.1. Specific Space Heating Demand

What is the Specific Space Heating Demand?
The specific space heating demand is the total energy required to heat the building for a year. It is

measured in kilowatt-hours (kWh) per metre squared (m^2) of treated floor area per year (a).

What value is required for a new build Passive House?
≤15 kWh/(m^2a)

How does this compare to UK regulations?
As part of the move towards zero carbon standards, the new edition of the UK Building Regulations Part L, released 6 April 2014, incorporates an aggregate 6% improvement on the 2010 Part L for homes and 9% improvement on aggregate for non-residential buildings. The new Part L also introduced evaluation criteria for dwellings known as the Fabric Energy Efficiency Standard (FEES). These focus on the energy demand of the building, in line with the Passive House approach, rather than mitigating CO_2 through building systems and renewable technologies. The calculation is bespoke to the dwelling plot, so it is not possible to provide a direct comparison with the Passive House Evaluation Criteria. The UK had planned to introduce zero carbon standards in 2016, however this has been delayed (except for housing developments in London: see page 54, 'Renewable Energy Generation') and no current date has been given for their introduction. While there remains a policy vacuum in the UK, we

> The word 'specific' refers to a specific unit of area of the building (per m^2 of treated floor area). 'Space heating demand' without the word specific is technically referring to the total figure.

Specific building characteristics with reference to the treated floor area

						Criteria	Alternative criteria		Fullfilled?[2]
	Treated floor area	m²	0.0						
Space heating	Heating demand	kWh/(m²a)	≤15	OR	≤	15	-		YES
	Heating load	W/m²	≤10		≤	-	10		
Space cooling	Cooling & dehum. demand	kWh/(m²a)	-		≤	-	-		-
	Cooling load	W/m²	-		≤	-	-		
	Frequency of overheating (> 25 °C)	%			≤	10			
	Frequency of excessively high humidity (> 12 g/kg)	%			≤	20			
Airtightness	Pressurization test result n₅₀	1/h			≤	0.6			
Non-renewable Primary Energy (PE)	PE demand	kWh/(m²a)			≤	-			-
Primary Energy Renewable (PER)	PER demand	kWh/(m²a)			≤	60	-		
	Generation of renewable energy (in relation to pro-jected building footprint area)	kWh/(m²a)	-		≥	-	-		

[2] Empty field: Data missing; '-': No requirement

I confirm that the values given herein have been determined following the PHPP methodology and based on the characteristic values of the building. The PHPP calculations are attached to this verification.

Passive House Classic?

Task: First name: Surname: Signature:

Issued on: City:

Figure 2.5 *Extract from the PHPP 'Verification' worksheet, with annual heating demand highlighted*

can look to wider EU policy. The Energy Performance of Buildings Directive was adopted in 2002, and recast in 2010, by the European Parliament and the Council. It is designed to improve the energy efficiency of buildings and thus reduce carbon emissions, and lessen the impact of climate change. Among other requirements, it necessitates all new buildings developed from 2021 to be nearly zero energy buildings, with an earlier target date of 2019 where the building will be owned and occupied by a public authority. Each European country must establish what a Nearly Zero Energy building is in their own country. Without clear guidance on this in the UK, the new Passive Houses classes provide an excellent framework to follow; not only setting out clear standards but also providing a proven methodology to follow.

> Passive House certification requires one or the other of the heat demand or heat load values to be met, not both. But if the heating is to be supplied exclusively via the air, the heat load requirement must be met.

What is the Specific Heat Load?

This is the maximum heat load required on the coldest day of the year to heat the building. Two scenarios are calculated, the first is calculated for a cool and cloudy day and the second for a cold, but sunny day, as the different conditions impact performance. The worse case scenario is displayed. It is measured in watts (W) per metre squared (m^2) of treated floor area. It is important to understand this is not the same as the heating demand which is measured in kilowatt hours per metre squared per year, as explained on page 48.

What value is required for a new build Passive House?
$\leq 10 W/m^2$

How does this compare to UK regulations?

No limiting values are given in UK regulations. The reason this figure is important in a Passive House is that this is the limiting value for heating through the air supply. However, in practice ability to heat via the ventilation depends on ventilation requirements, and in many cases there are more efficient and practical ways to provide the very small amount of heat required by a Passive House.

2.4.2. Primary Energy Renewable

The term Primary Energy Renewable (PER) is new to PHPP9 and to the Certification Criteria. PER is an alternative to the previously used evaluation method based on the non-renewable primary energy factors (PE). As explained above PER is the preferred evaluation method as it is based on the future scenario of fully renewable energy supplies. While the PE method can still be used, this is not a long-term solution and will eventually be phased out by PHI. As explained in section 2.3, PHPP9 introduced new Passive House classes resulting from this new PER assessment.

Figure 2.6 *Extract from the PHPP 'Verification' worksheet, with primary energy and Renewable Energy Generation highlighted*

Primary Energy Renewable (PER) is new to PHPP9. This is the most significant update to the Passive House Certification Criteria since its introduction. PER demand should be used for all projects now as reflects our future energy supplies. In some cases, designers may choose to use the old PE demand; while this is still acceptable for certification this should no longer be the first choice.

Note: All specific values in the PHPP relate to the TFA except the new value for the generation of renewable energy. This figure is kWh/(m²a) where m² is projected building footprint not TFA. Full definitions of the projected building footprint and the TFA are included in Chapter 3.

Specific building characteristics with reference to the treated floor area					Criteria	Alternative criteria	Fullfilled?[2]
	Treated floor area	m²	0.0				
Space heating	Heating demand	kWh/(m²a)		≤	15	-	
	Heating load	W/m²		≤	-	10	
Space cooling	Cooling & dehum. demand	kWh/(m²a)		≤	-	-	
	Cooling load	W/m²		≤	-	-	
	Frequency of overheating (> 25 °C)	%		≤	10		
	Frequency of excessively high humidity (> 12 g/kg)	%		≤	20		
Airtightness	Pressurization test result n₅₀	1/h		≤	0.6		
Non-renewable Primary Energy (PE)	PE demand	kWh/(m²a)	≤120*	≤	-		YES
Primary Energy Renewable (PER)	PER demand	kWh/(m²a)	≤30,45,60	≤	VARIES by Class	±15 kWh/(m²a) deviation	YES
	Generation of renewable energy (in relation to pro-jected building footprint area)	kWh/(m²a)	≥0,60,120	≥			

OR

¹ Empty field: Data missing; '-': No requirement

I confirm that the values given herein have been determined following the PHPP methodology and based on the characteristic values of the building. The PHPP calculations are attached to this verification.

| Task: | First name: | | Surname: | Passive House Classic? |
| Issued on: | | City: | | Signature: |

* Passive House (non-renewable) ≤ 120kWh(m²a) base value, to be adjusted up or down to accommodate the varying PE factor of electricity in the country you are building. In the UK, at the time of writing, this value is adjusted to ≤135kWh(m²a), adjustments are made automatically by the PHPP.

What is Specific Primary Energy Renewable Demand?

Primary Energy (PE), the previous evaluation criteria, included not only the energy content of the raw material but also the losses from distribution, conversion and delivery to the end-user. So, PE is distinguished from energy used in the building (final energy), measured by the utility's gas or electric meter on the building. Similarly, for Primary Energy Renewable (PER), where the energy is supplied solely by renewable energy (RE) sources, all losses are included, although now the most notable losses are through storage. The calculations are based on climate data from various sources; the resulting PER factors describe how much more renewable energy must be supplied in order to cover the final energy consumed at the building. And as implied by the link to the climate data, the PER is location specific, so varies depending on the energy demand profile of the building based on its location and the renewable energy supply profile for that location.

$$PER = \frac{Energy\ supply\ from\ renewable\ sources}{Final\ energy\ demand\ at\ the\ building}$$

Determining the PER factor is far more complex than determining the previous PE factor, as the PER factor is determined not only by the energy demand but also by the availability of renewable energy resources to meet the demand at particular times. The time when energy demand occurs is important. There are three scenarios to consider:

• Direct use
• Short-term storage which can technically be achieved fairly efficiently
• Longer term seasonal storage, which will always cause higher energy losses.

Heating demand is highest when solar energy supply is lowest. Therefore heating – which occurs only during seasons with low renewable energy (RE) availability – requires much more source renewable energy in the envisioned future renewable energy supply chain because of conversion losses for seasonal energy storage. For cooling, on the other hand, a larger proportion of the associated energy demand can be used directly without need for temporary or seasonal energy storage and losses. For example, cooling demand correlates with sunny days when PV production is high. Load profiles that occur throughout the year (domestic electricity use, hot water) lie within these two extreme scenarios. The PHPP makes all of these calculations for designers, but it is important to understand the basis of these, so designers can make informed decisions and optimise their designs. Further reading on this topic can be found on Passipedia with a number of interesting and informative papers: https://passipedia.org/certification/passive_house_categories#per_factors

One important aspect of the new PER factors is how biomass is accounted for in energy generation. It may seem like an easy win to power a building with biomass, which could be claimed as completely renewable, however biomass is actually a limited resource. And as explained on Passipedia, there is a clear usage hierarchy for biomass: 1) food production, 2) materials, and 3) energy[*].

Taking this into account the new PHPP limits the contribution of biomass for renewable primary energy to 20 kWh/(m²a), and the PER factor is set for biomass at 1.10. To put this in context, if a building has a traditional gas boiler (PER factor 1.75 for gas), the first 20 kWh/(m²a) will be assumed to be created with biomass and have a reduced PER factor of 1.1. In a Passive House

the heating demand will be less than 20 kWh/(m²a), so any surplus can be set against hot water use and then if there is any left, household electricity. Because biomass can be stored without energy expenditure in conversion or storage, it is perfect to use in winter when other renewable energy production is lowest. So it makes sense to prioritise the use of the biomass budget as follows: heating, hot water in the winter, and then household electricity. Further reading on this topic can be found on Passipedia.

The Specific Primary Energy Renewable Demand is the sum of all of the energy demands for the building: heating and cooling, domestic hot water (DHW), auxiliary and household electricity including all losses divided by the floor area. As with specific space heat demand it is measured in kilowatt-hours per metre squared of floor area per year (kWh/(m²a)).

What value is required for a New Build Passive House?
Specific Primary Energy Renewable (PER) demand:
Passive House Classic ≤ 60kWh(m²a)
Passive House Plus ≤ 45kWh(m²a)
Passive House Premium ≤ 30kWh(m²a)

The PHPP does allow for ±15 kWh/(m²a) deviation from these criteria, as long as this is compensated for

---

[*]   https://passipedia.org/certification/passive_house_categories/classic-plus-premium#using_biomass_budgets_efficiently

in the renewable energy generation. This is referred to as the Alternative Criteria.

In addition, at the time of writing it is still possible to certify a home under the previous Primary Energy (PE) factors, non-renewable energy supply, with the Specific Primary Energy (PE) limit:
Passive House (non-renewable) ≤ 120kWh(m²a) base value, to be adjusted up or down to accommodate the varying PE factor of electricity in the country in which you are building.

It is important to note here that the PHI specify other national values based on national PE factors. In the UK, at the time of writing, the PE value for electricity was 3.07, so this value is automatically adjusted in the PHPP to ≤135kWh(m²a).

2.4.3. Renewable Energy Generation

What is Specific Renewable Energy Generation?
The Specific Renewable Energy Generation is the sum of all of the energy created. In this case divided by the Projected Building Footprint rather than the TFA. The projected building footprint is defined as the vertical projection of the thermal envelope towards ground. See **Figure 3.17**.

Specific Renewable Energy Generation is renewable energy produced either on the site or offsite by newly-built renewable energy facilities owned by the building owner including a fractional share in a community-owned renewable energy production facility.

What value is required for a New Build Passive House?
Renewable energy generation (see **Figure 2.6**)
Passive House Classic – no requirement to produce energy
Passive House Plus ≥ 60kWh(m²a)
Passive House Premium ≥ 120kWh(m²a)
If the Alternative Criteria has been used in the PER values ±15 kWh/(m²a) deviation from these criteria may be necessary to compensate for this. It's important to note here that the ±15 kWh/(m²a) is referenced to the TFA as relates to the PER value.

How does this compare to UK regulations?
No targets or minimum values are given under the current regulations. The UK delayed the introduction of its 2016 zero carbon standard, with no current date for its introduction. However, from October 2016 all new

housing schemes in London, with more than 10 homes, have to meet a tough new zero carbon requirement.* This requires all new homes to reduce their carbon emissions by 35% more than the Part L minimum. If a new home fails to achieve net zero carbon emissions either through its building fabric or on-site renewables, the developer will have to make an offset payment. There remain concerns in the UK about the current methodology for calculation of both energy demands and generation. Once again the PHPP provides an excellent tried and tested tool for these calculations.

How does this compare to UK regulations?

No general limiting values are given under the current regulations, which focus only on 'regulated' loads, i.e. space heating, hot water, fixed lighting, and pumps and fans. All energy consumption associated with the user, i.e. appliances and consumer electronics, are 'unregulated' and therefore the designer does not have to account for them.

Under the current system, targets are worked out on a project-by-project basis. Without going into too much depth, the UK standards for new build dwellings are covered by the government's Standard Assessment Procedure (SAP) and new build, non-residential projects are covered by the Simplified Building Energy Model (SBEM).

---

* In England, the government definition of a zero carbon home is one where CO_2 emissions from regulated energy use, i.e. heating, DHW, ventilation and lighting, are reduced to zero. This does not account for unregulated emissions such as plugin appliances, i.e computers and TVs.

   In London, showing compliance with this requirement for zero carbon emissions requires a minimum 35% reduction below Building Regulations Part L 2013 on site, with any remaining carbon shortfall accounted for with an offset payment of £60 per tonne of CO_2 per year for a period of 30 years.

   'Zero carbon' is achieved using a combination of three factors: fabric, on-site measures and off-site measures (which could include the offset payment to the local authority). In this definition a zero-carbon home is not limited to renewable energy. This is certainly a limit of this methodology, as surplus energy from renewables generated on site, eg PV cells during summer, could be used to offset non-renewable energy taken off site from the National Grid in the winter, without the need to account for any additional storage losses.

2.4.4. Airtightness

What is Airtightness?
Airtightness is the measurement of how much air leaks through the fabric of a building (eg through the floor, walls, and roof). To test the airtightness of a building it must be pressurised and depressurised, giving an accurate basis for comparison with other buildings. Airtightness is the number of air changes per hour of the total building volume (n50).* This must be tested at pressurisation and depressurisation of 50 pascals (50Pa).

What value is required for a new build Passive House?
$\leq 0.6h^{-1}$ @50Pa (n50 test).

How does this compare to UK regulations?
Limiting values in the UK are given in m^3/m^2h @50Pa, as required for the q50 test. In England and Wales the limiting value is $\leq 5m^3/m^2h$ @50Pa. In Scotland the recommended value is $\leq 7m^3/m^2h$ @50Pa for residential and $\leq 10m^3/m^2h$ @50Pa for non-residential. Additionally, in Scotland if a design value of $\leq 5m3/m2h$ @50Pa is being used, planned

* Refer to Key Principle 2 (page 14) for further information on the n50 standard.

COMMON MISTAKES

Calculating the internal volume wrong.

It is very important to calculate the Vn50 correctly. This is often calculated incorrectly including service routes, suspended ceilings etc. Once corrected this can lead to failed pressure test results.

ventilation must be implemented to avoid problems with internal air quality and condensation.

The n50 (the Passive House measurement) and q50 (the standard UK measurement) readings cannot be compared directly as there is no direct relationship between the values, and they vary both for building size and form.

An n50 of $0.6h^{-1}$ @ 50Pa is approximately equal to a q50 result of $1.0m^3/h/m^2h$@50Pa for small buildings; in larger buildings the n50 and q50 values will be similar. The air test carried out for building regulations can be used to give PHPP data, but must include pressurisation and depressurisation, and use the Vn50 according to PHPP, not the air testers standard internal volume.

Value is the average of pressurisation and depressurisation test results – this is essential for certification

Specific building characteristics with reference to the treated floor area					Criteria	Alternative criteria	Fullfilled?[2]
	Treated floor area	m²	0.0				
Space heating	Heating demand	kWh/(m²a)		≤	15	-	
	Heating load	W/m²		≤	-	10	
Space cooling	Cooling & dehum. demand	kWh/(m²a)		≤	-	-	
	Cooling load	W/m²		≤	-	-	
	Frequency of overheating (> 25 °C)	%		≤	10		
	Frequency of excessively high humidity (> 12 g/kg)	%		≤	20		
Airtightness	Pressurization test result n_{50}	1/h	≤0.6	≤	0.6		YES
Non-renewable Primary Energy (PE)	PE demand	kWh/(m²a)		≤	-		
Primary Energy Renewable (PER)	PER demand	kWh/(m²a)		≤			
	Generation of renewable energy (in relation to pro-jected building footprint area)	kWh/(m²a)		≥			

[2] Empty field: Data missing; '-': No requirement

I confirm that the values given herein have been determined following the PHPP methodology and based on the characteristic values of the building. The PHPP calculations are attached to this verification.

Passive House Classic?

Task:	First name:		Surname:	Signature:
	Issued on:		City:	

Figure 2.7 *Extract from the PHPP 'Verification' worksheet, with airtightness highlighted*

2.5 Key Evaluation Criteria for Retrofits

It is often difficult to achieve the Passive House Standard in older buildings. Buildings that have been retrofitted with Passive House components and, to a great extent, with exterior wall insulation, can achieve the EnerPHit certification where the energy demand limits are higher than the Passive House Standard as evidence of both building quality and fulfilment of specific energy values.
The EnerPHit+i designation is applied if more than 25% of the opaque exterior wall surface has interior insulation.

Unlike the new build criteria, the EnerPHit criteria varies by climatic region. Figures in the following pages relate to cool temperate regions.

In addition, a new feature of PHPP9 is staged EnerPHit certification. This new process for certification opens the EnerPHit standard up to many more retrofit projects. It encourages designers to plan and certify the full retrofit designs but allows for the work to be carried out in stages. This may be over the course of many years. By planning the full retrofit in advance designers ensure that work carried out in early stages supports future improvement work. This process is covered in detail in Chapter 8, with the 'Variants' Worksheet and the EnerPHit Retrofit Plan (ERP).

There are two ways to achieve these retrofit standards:

Method 1 – Certification based on three key Evaluation Criteria; these are Specific Space Heating and Cooling Demand, Specific Primary Energy Demand and Airtightness. The 'verification' sheet of the PHPP facilitates easy monitoring of these requirements.

Important notes: If active cooling is used, not usually applicable in the UK, please refer to the additional certification requirements included in **Section 2.7**.

Method 2 – Certification based on requirements for individual building components.

Both these methods require the building to meet the airtightness criteria set out in the following pages.

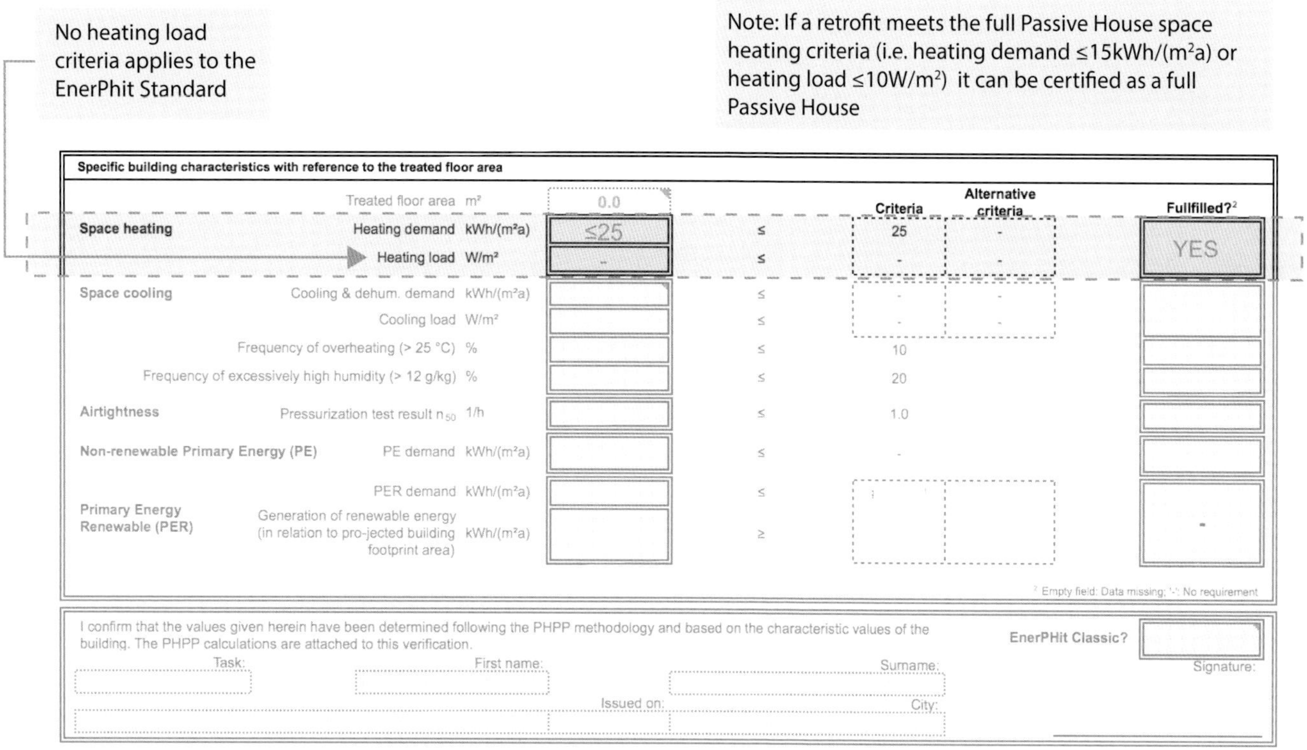

No heating load criteria applies to the EnerPhit Standard

Note: If a retrofit meets the full Passive House space heating criteria (i.e. heating demand ≤15kWh/(m²a) or heating load ≤10W/m²) it can be certified as a full Passive House

Figure 2.8 *Extract from the PHPP 'Verification' worksheet, with annual heat demand highlighted*

Method 1 – Specific Space Heating Demand

What is the Specific Space Heating Demand?

The specific space heating demand is the total energy required to heat the building for a year. It is measured in kilowatt-hours (kWh) per metre squared (m²) of treated floor area per year (a).

What value is required for an EnerPHit building in the UK?

≤25kWh/(m²a) in cool temperate regions or ≤20kWh/(m2a) in warm temperate regions (some of the UK falls within the warm temperate zone), for all other climatic regions refer to Table 3 'EnerPHit criteria for the building component method' on page 9 of the 'Criteria for the Passive House, EnerPHit and PHI Low Energy Building Standard' document, which can be seen at - http://www.passiv.de/downloads/03_building_criteria_en.pdf)

How does this compare to UK regulations?

No limiting value is given for renovation projects, although the government-funded Retrofit for the Future (RftF) projects aimed for 80% energy reductions, a target that is comparable with a typical EnerPHit standard upgrade.

The EnerPHit standard does not include heat load criteria. In general, in our climate, it is not possible to heat a building with supply air heating when the heat demand is around 25kWh/(m²a).

Method 1 and 2 – Primary Energy Renewable (PER)

Refer to description set out in 2.4.2 Primary Energy Renewable on Page 50.

What value is required for an EnerPHit Building?

See Figure 2.6 on page 51. However, note all values listed have to be adjusted for the greater heat demand of the EnerPHit building. Refer to the detailed explanation below.

Specific Primary Energy Renewable (PER) demand:
Passive House Classic $\leq$ 60kWh(m²a) + X
Passive House Plus $\leq$ 45kWh(m²a) + X
Passive House Premium $\leq$ 30kWh(m²a) + X

Where $X = (Q_H - Q_{H,PH}) \cdot f_{\varnothing PER,H} + (Q_C - Q_{C,PH}) \cdot \frac{1}{2}$
Q_H: heating demand
Q_C: Passive House criterion
$Q_{H,PH}$: Passive House criterion for the heating demand
$f_{\varnothing PER,H}$: weighted mean of the PER factors of the heating system of the building

Q_C: cooling demand (incl. dehumidification)
$Q_{C,PH}$: Passive House criterion for the cooling demand

Try not to be overwhelmed by these formulas, the figures are basically the same as the figures for new builds with an adjustment (X) to account for the extra heating/cooling that is allowed for in an EnerPHit project, all of which the PHPP calculates automatically.

As with new builds the PHPP does allow for ±15 kWh/(m²a) deviation from these criteria, as long as this is compensated for by the renewable energy generation. This is referred to as the Alternative Criteria.

In addition, at the time of writing it is still possible to certify a home under the previous Primary Energy (PE) factors, non-renewable energy supply, with the Specific Primary Energy (PE) limit:
Passive House (non-renewable) ≤ 120 kWh/(m²a) + X. As with new buildings this is only the base value and needs to be adjusted to accommodate the varying PE factor of electricity in the country in which you are building.

Where X = $(Q_H - 15\ kWh/(m^2a)) \cdot 1.2 + Q_C - Q_C$, Passive House criterion

In the formula above if the terms '$(Q_H - 15\ kWh/(m^2a))$' and '$Q_C - Q_C$, Passive House criterion' are smaller than zero, then zero will be adopted as the value.

It is important to note here that PHI specify other national values based on national PE factors. In the UK, at the time of writing, the PE value for electricity was 3.07, so this value is automatically adjusted in the PHPP to ≤135kWh(m²a).

3. Renewable Energy Generation

What is Specific Renewable Energy Generation?
Refer to description set out in 2.4.3 Primary Energy Renewable on page 54.

What value is required for an EnerPHit building?
Renewable energy generation
Passive House Classic – no requirement to produce energy
Passive House Plus ≥ 60kWh(m²a)
Passive House Premium ≥ 120kWh(m²a)
If the Alternative Criteria has been used in the PER values ±15 kWh/(m²a) deviation from these criteria may be required.

These figures apply to all regions.

How does this compare to UK regulations?

There is no limiting value in regulations.

Method 1 and 2 – Airtightness

What is Airtightness?

Airtightness is the number of air changes per hour of the total building volume (n50)*. It must be tested on site at a pressure of 50pascals (50Pa).

What value is required for an EnerPHit building?

Target ≤$0.6h^{-1}$ @50Pa with a limiting value of ≤$1.0h^{-1}$ @50Pa.

How does this compare to UK regulations?

No limiting value is given for renovation projects. The n50 (the Passive House measurement) and q50 (the standard UK measurement) readings cannot be compared directly as there is no direct relationship between the values, they vary both for building size and form. An n50 of $0.6h^{-1}$ @50Pa is approximately equal to a q50 result of $1.0m^3/h/m^2h$ @50Pa. The air test carried out for building regulations can be used to give PHPP data, but must include pressurisation and depressurisation, and use the Vn50 according to PHPP, not the air testers standard internal volume.

Method 2 – Component Quality

The component quality route is a particularly useful certification route if the existing building being upgraded has a poor area to volume (A/V) ratio and/or form factor, poor orientation, or excessive overshadowing by other buildings or features which would make certification by heating demand particularly difficult to achieve.

When certifying an EnerPHit or EnerPHit+i via the quality components route, full EnerPHit criteria should be met for the quality of the thermal bridge detailing, windows, doors and ventilation unit (refer to **Figure 2.2** on p. 43).

The standard EnerPHit+i is used when internal insulation (i) is required. The only variation in the certification criteria between EnerPHit and EnerPHit+i is in the U-values, as explained below. Due to the reduced performance of the internal insulation it is likely that Method 2 – Component Quality will be used, as achieving the Method 1 – Heat Demand criteria may not be possible.

---

* Refer to Key Principle 2 (p. 14) for further information on the n50 standard and the Vn50.

Value is the average of
pressurisation and
depressurisation test results –
this is essential for certification

Specific building characteristics with reference to the treated floor area					Criteria	Alternative criteria		Fullfilled?[2]
	Treated floor area m²		0.0					
Space heating	Heating demand kWh/(m²a)			≤	25	-		
	Heating load W/m²			≤	-	-		
Space cooling	Cooling & dehum. demand kWh/(m²a)			≤	-	-		
	Cooling load W/m²			≤	-	-		
	Frequency of overheating (> 25 °C) %			≤	10			
	Frequency of excessively high humidity (> 12 g/kg) %			≤	20			
Airtightness	Pressurization test result n₅₀ 1/h		≤1.0	≤	1.0			YES
Non-renewable Primary Energy (PE)	PE demand kWh/(m²a)			≤	-			
Primary Energy Renewable (PER)	PER demand kWh/(m²a)			≤				
	Generation of renewable energy (in relation to pro-jected building footprint area) kWh/(m²a)			≥				-

² Empty field: Data missing; '-': No requirement

I confirm that the values given herein have been determined following the PHPP methodology and based on the characteristic values of the building. The PHPP calculations are attached to this verification.

EnerPHit Classic?

Task: First name: Surname: Signature:

Issued on: City:

Figure 2.9 (above) Extract from the PHPP 'Verification' worksheet, with Airtightness highlighted

Unprotect the worksheet and click on the small '+' sign next to row 57, this will change to a '−' sign as shown here and the EnerPHit component criteria will now be displayed in the main body of the worksheet. Once done remember to reprotect the worksheet.

Refer to table 2.2 for a summary of the limiting values for these components in EnerPHit buildings in cool temperate regions ie UK. For all other regions refer to Table 2 'EnerPHit criteria for the building component method' on page 8 of the 'Criteria for the Passive House, EnerPHit and PHI Low Energy Building Standard' document, which can be seen at – http://www.passiv.de/downloads/03_building_criteria_en.pdf)

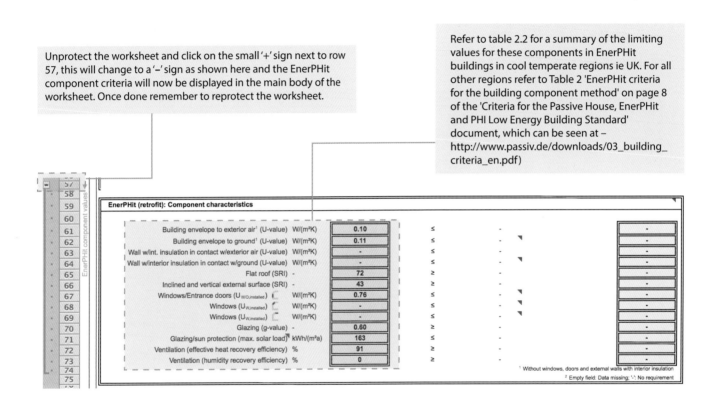

Figure 2.10 *(above) Extract from the PHPP 'Verification' worksheet, with the EnerPHit Component characteristics expanded*

Opaque building envelope:

- For exterior insulation: $f_tU \leq 0.15W/(m^2K)$ for walls/roofs, $\leq 0.25W/(m^2K)$ to the ground
- For interior insulation: $f_tU \leq 0.35W/(m^2K)$ applicable to EnerPHit+i only[*]

Use of interior insulation is advised only if exterior insulation is structurally impossible, not permitted by planning, or clearly uneconomical with regard to life cycle costs. If interior insulation is used with the higher U-value option, the certification will be under EnerPHit +i.

---

[*] Further details on the EnerPhit+i criteria can be found in the technical manual and on Passipedia

Note: Some exemptions apply to EnerPHit buildings; the full list of exemptions can be read in on page 11 of the 'Criteria for the Passive House, EnerPHit and PHI Low Energy Building Standard' document, which can be seen at - http://www.passiv.de/downloads/03_building_criteria_en.pdf)

2.6 Four Key Evaluation Criteria for Low-Energy Buildings

The PHI Low Energy Building Standard is new to PHPP9 and has been introduced to provide a certification standard for buildings, which have been built to the Passive House build quality, but do not quite meet the limits for one or more of the Key Evaluation Criteria: Specific Space Heat Demand, Specific Primary Energy Renewable (PER), Renewable Energy Generation and Airtightness.

This could be due to a number of reasons, such as a particularly complex form resulting in a poor Form Factor/difficulty in achieving the airtightness criteria/errors on site/unavailability of components for a particular climate/an unfortunate orientation and/or shading situation making the Space Heating Demand difficult to achieve. In these cases the extra fabric improvements required to meet the Passive House Standard may have been uneconomical. Or, in the case of failing to meet the airtightness requirement or site errors, the rectification work on site may have been uneconomical.

If certifying to this PHI Low Energy Criteria it is important to first read through section '2.4 Four Key Evaluation for New Builds'. As all of the Criteria topics are the same, the only variation is in the limiting values, as listed below.

Specific Space Heating Demand: ≤ 30 kWh/(m^{2}a)
Specific Primary Energy Renewable Demand (PER): ≤ 75 kWh/(m^{2}a)

As with the full Passive House Standard, there is an allowance for the ± 15 kWh/(m^{2}a) deviation from this criteria, as long as this is compensated for by the renewable energy generation. And the same note applies regarding the transitional allowance for Specific Primary Energy (PE) to be used.

Passive House Low Energy (non-renewable) $\leq$ 120kWh(m^{2}a) base value, to be adjusted up or down to accommodate the varying PE factor of electricity in the country in which you are building.

It is important to note here that PHI specify other national values based on national PE factors. In the UK, at the time of writing, the PE value for electricity was 3.07, so this value is automatically adjusted in the PHPP to ≤ 135kWh(m^{2}a).

Renewable Energy Generation – none unless the

No heating load criteria applies to the Low Energy Standard

Specific building characteristics with reference to the treated floor area					Criteria	Alternative criteria	Fullfilled?[2]
	Treated floor area	m²	0.0				
Space heating	Heating demand	kWh/(m²a)	≤30	≤	30	-	YES
	Heating load	W/m²	-	≤	-	-	
Space cooling	Cooling & dehum. demand	kWh/(m²a)	-	≤	-	-	-
	Cooling load	W/m²	-	≤	-	-	
	Frequency of overheating (> 25 °C)	%		≤	10		
	Frequency of excessively high humidity (> 12 g/kg)	%		≤	20		
Airtightness	Pressurization test result n50	1/h		≤	1.0		
Non-renewable Primary Energy (PE)	PE demand	kWh/(m²a)		≤	-		-
Primary Energy Renewable (PER)	PER demand	kWh/(m²a)		≤	75	-	
	Generation of renewable energy (in relation to pro-jected building footprint area)	kWh/(m²a)	-	≥	-	-	

[2] Empty field: Data missing; '-': No requirement

I confirm that the values given herein have been determined following the PHPP methodology and based on the characteristic values of the building. The PHPP calculations are attached to this verification. PHI Low Energy Building?

Task: First name: Surname: Signature:

Issued on: City:

deviation has been applied to the PER Airtightness – ≤1.0h-1 @50Pa (n50 test). For cooling requirements refer to section 2.7. As with all of the Passive House Standards and Classes, buildings that are certified as PHI Low Energy buildings, will have a high level of thermal comfort and a high degree of user

Figure 2.11 *Extract from the PHPP 'Verification' worksheet, with annual heat demand highlighted*

satisfaction. However, because lower performing components may have been used this Low Energy

Note: All specific values in the PHPP relate to the TFA expect the new value for the generation of renewable energy, this figure is kWh/(m²a) where m² is projected building footprint not TFA. Full definitions of the projected building footprint and the TFA are included in Chapter 3.

Primary Energy Renewable (PER) is new to PHPP9. This is the most significant update to the Passive House Certification Criteria since its introduction. PER demand should be used for all projects now as reflects our future energy supplies. In some cases, designers may choose to use the old PE demand, while this is still acceptable for certification this should no longer be the first choice.

Specific building characteristics with reference to the treated floor area					Criteria	Alternative criteria	Fullfilled?²
	Treated floor area	m²	0.0				
Space heating	Heating demand	kWh/(m²a)		≤	30	-	
	Heating load	W/m²		≤	-	-	
Space cooling	Cooling & dehum. demand	kWh/(m²a)		≤	-	-	
	Cooling load	W/m²		≤	-	-	
	Frequency of overheating (> 25 °C) %			≤	10		
	Frequency of excessively high humidity (> 12 g/kg) %			≤	20		
Airtightness	Pressurization test result n₅₀	1/h		≤	1.0		
Non-renewable Primary Energy (PE)	PE demand	kWh/(m²a)	≤120*	≤	-		YES
Primary Energy Renewable (PER)	PER demand	kWh/(m²a)	≤75	≤		±15 kWh/(m²a) deviation	YES
	Generation of renewable energy (in relation to pro-jected building footprint area)	kWh/(m²a)	0	≥			

² Empty field: Data missing; '-': No requirement

OR

I confirm that the values given herein have been determined following the PHPP methodology and based on the characteristic values of the building. The PHPP calculations are attached to this verification.

PHI Low Energy Building?

Task:	First name:		Surname:	Signature:
		Issued on:	City:	

* Passive House (non-renewable) ≤ 120kWh(m²a) base value, to be adjusted up or down to accommodate the varying PE factor of electricity in the country in which you are building. In the UK, at the time of writing, this value is adjusted to ≤135kWh(m²a); adjustments are made automatically by the PHPP.

Figure 2.12 *Extract from the PHPP 'Verification' worksheet, with the primary energy demand highlighted*

Standard cannot guarantee the optimum standard of thermal comfort guaranteed by the other Passive House Standards; as well as protection against fabric damage caused by condensation.

Value is the average of pressurisation and depressurisation test results – this is essential for certification

Figure 2.13 *Extract from the PHPP 'Verification' worksheet, with airtightness highlighted*

Specific building characteristics with reference to the treated floor area					Criteria	Alternative criteria	Fullfilled?[2]
	Treated floor area m²	0.0					
Space heating	Heating demand kWh/(m²a)		≤		30	-	
	Heating load W/m²		≤		-	-	
Space cooling	Cooling & dehum. demand kWh/(m²a)		≤		-	-	
	Cooling load W/m²		≤		-	-	
	Frequency of overheating (> 25 °C) %		≤		10		
	Frequency of excessively high humidity (> 12 g/kg) %		≤		20		
Airtightness	Pressurization test result n₅₀ 1/h	≤1.0	≤		1.0		YES
Non-renewable Primary Energy (PE)	PE demand kWh/(m²a)		≤		-		
Primary Energy Renewable (PER)	PER demand kWh/(m²a)		≤				
	Generation of renewable energy (in relation to pro-jected building footprint area) kWh/(m²a)		≥				

[2] Empty field: Data missing; '-': No requirement

I confirm that the values given herein have been determined following the PHPP methodology and based on the characteristic values of the building. The PHPP calculations are attached to this verification.	**PHI Low Energy Building?**	
Task:	First name:	Surname:	Signature:
	Issued on:	City:

2.7 Active Cooling Energy Demand

If active cooling is used, not usually applicable in the UK, additional certification requirements must be met. In order to achieve Passive House certification reduction of summer solar heat loads and minimisation of summer internal heat loads are particularly important. The result of designing to these principles is that active cooling in residential buildings in the UK is not required. As long as the overheating limits are not exceeded, further entries of cooling data are not necessary.

It is not just in the UK where designing to the Passive House Standard should mean active cooling for residential buildings is unnecessary – the technical manual states that this applies to all climate zones where night-time temperatures drop to around 20°C.

There are three cooling worksheets in the latest version of PHPP. The Cooling worksheet calculates the useful cooling demand where active cooling is used. Similar to the heating demand, the specific cooling demand represents the amount of heat that must be removed from the building to create a comfortable internal environment. As with the heating requirements, either the specific total cooling demand or the specific cooling load must be met.

What is the specific total cooling demand?
The specific total cooling demand is the energy required to meet the cooling demand excluding the energy used for dehumidification and cooling system losses. It is measured in kilowatt-hours (kWh) per metre squared (m^2) of treated floor area per year (a).

What value is required for a new build Passive House?
$\leq 15 kWh/(m^2 a)$ + dehumidification contribution.

The dehumidification contribution is not a set figure as it varies depending on the selected climate data, necessary air change rate and internal moisture loads. This is automatically calculated within the PHPP.

What value is required for a PHI low-energy building?
$30 kWh/(m^2 a)$ + dehumidification contribution

How does this compare to UK regulations?
No limiting value is given for space cooling demand in UK building regulations.

Passive House certification requires that one or other of the cooling demand or cooling load values are met, not both.

Specific building characteristics with reference to the treated floor area

				Criteria	Alternative criteria	Fullfilled?[2]
	Treated floor area m²	0.0				
Space heating	Heating demand kWh/(m²a)		≤	15	-	
	Heating load W/m²		≤	-	10	
Space cooling	Cooling & dehum. demand kWh/(m²a)	≤15*	≤	-	-	YES
	Cooling load W/m²	≤10*	≤	-	-	YES
	Frequency of overheating (> 25 °C) %	≤10	≤	10	Target ≤5%	YES
	Frequency of excessively high humidity (> 12 g/kg) %	≤20	≤	20		YES
Airtightness	Pressurization test result n₅₀ 1/h		≤	0.6		
Non-renewable Primary Energy (PE)	PE demand kWh/(m²a)		≤	-		-
Primary Energy Renewable (PER)	PER demand kWh/(m²a)		≤	60	-	
	Generation of renewable energy (in relation to pro-jected building footprint area) kWh/(m²a)	-	≥	-	-	

[2] Empty field: Data missing; '-': No requirement

I confirm that the values given herein have been determined following the PHPP methodology and based on the characteristic values of the building. The PHPP calculations are attached to this verification.   **Passive House Classic?**

Task: First name: Surname: Signature:

Issued on: City:

* These values relate to active cooling and dehumidification only; in residential buildings in the UK active cooling should not normally be required to maintain comfortable summer temperatures.

Figure 2.14 *Extract from the PHPP 'Verification' worksheet, with space cooling highlighted*

What is the specific cooling load?

The specific cooling load is the maximum energy required to maintain a comfortable internal temperature, on the hottest day of the year. As that

> If supply air-cooling is being used it is important to remember that the cooling capacity of the supply air is not equivalent to a standard AC system. The maximum cooling load that can be met by the supply air in residential buildings is around $10W/m^2$ (technical manual, p. 174).

day can vary depending on the solar declination, two calculations are completed in the PHPP and the worst-case scenario is then displayed. It is measured in watts (W) per metre squared (m^2) of treated floor area (a). Refer to Chapter 4 for further information.

What value is required for a new build Passive House?
The cooling load must be $\leq 10W/m^2$

There is a variable limit value for cooling and dehumidification demand, which vary depending on the chosen climate data, necessary air change rate and internal heat and moisture loads. These values are calculated within the PHPP. If the cooling demand limit is not met then the cooling load limit of $\leq 10W/m2$ must be met.

What value is required for a PHI low-energy building?
$30W/m^2$. Refer to the technical manual for further details.

How does this compare to UK regulations?
As with the cooling demand, there is no limiting value given in the UK building regulations.

What is the frequency of overheating?
The frequency of overheating is the percentage of hours in a given year that the temperature exceeds 25°C. For Passive House certification this must not exceed 10% of the year. The technical manual provides a useful table to refer to when making an assessment of the overheating (p. 167). Although 10% is the upper limit for certification this is given a 'poor' rating; 5–10% is 'acceptable', but it is not until the overheating is down to 5% that this is considered a 'good' design in terms of overheating. Therefore consider it best practice to aim for <5%, although this is not a requirement of certification. In practice, I find even less is better, i.e. 1%. Designing for a lower overheating percentage will create a more robust design.

Overheating is covered in detail in Chapter 4.

2.8 The Flow Chart

The flow chart depicted overleaf is an adaptation of the chart from the technical manual. This can be referred to, to keep track of which Excel sheets to fill in. Each subsection in the following chapters refers back to this chart to maintain a clear reference point.

This guide is focusing on the residential inputs for PHPP, as it is recommended that users input a small, simple residential project the first time they use the program. It is assumed that by the time users are working with non-residential projects in the PHPP they will be familiar with the program, terminology and technical manual. The non-residential chart has some minor variations and can be seen in the technical manual.

The next five chapters walk through inputting data into the PHPP. The chapters are split into:

Chapter 3, PHPP Heating Demand Basics – covering basic inputs required for a provisional annual heat demand and heat load result (key requirements for a Passive House project).

Chapter 4, PHPP Cooling Basics – covering basic inputs required for PHPP to assess the summer conditions in the building. This touches on active cooling but does not cover it in detail, as active cooling is not normally required for residential buildings in the UK.

Chapter 5, PHPP Primary Energy Basics – covering the basic M&E inputs.

Chapter 6, designPH – written by designPH creater Dave Edwards, covering what a designPH model is, its primary aims and how to create and manage energy models with this SketchUp plugin.

Chapter 7, PHPP Heating Demand Details – increasing the detail of the information entered in Chapter 3 to obtain a more accurate result, specifically focusing on thermal bridging.

Chapter 8, New PHPP9 worksheets and Staged Retrofits – covers these new tools in PHPP9 which assist in testing design options and cost optimisation in all of the Passive House Standards and Classes. This chapter will also touch on staged EnerPHit projects and the new EnerPHit Retrofit Plan (ERP).

The book closes with a glossary of new terms.

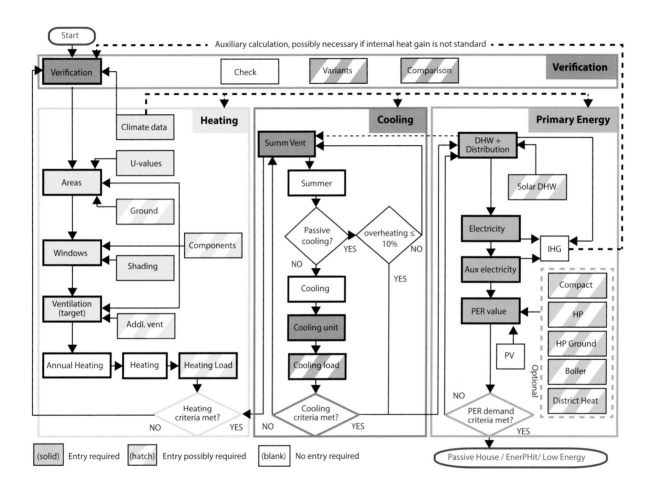

Figure 2.15 *Flow chart*

Chapter 3

PHPP Heating Demand Basics

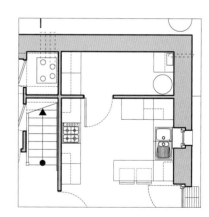

This chapter walks through inputting initial data to obtain a provisional heat demand/heat load result. This provisional result will demonstrate whether the project is able to achieve the Passive House Standard without major revisions. This can and should be completed early in the schematic design process. Some assumptions with regard to the building components may be required if this information is unknown.

Remember this guide is an accompaniment to the full technical manual and not a replacement for it. At various points in this chapter the reader is directed to the full technical manual for more detailed information. Every purchaser of PHPP is also given an English example PHPP fully completed, which can be a useful reference tool.

Completing this section, with a bit of practice, for a medium-sized single dwelling is likely to take one or two hours. Thus it is a good investment to complete the task early in the design process to minimise abortive design work.

There are a couple of choices of PHPP workbook. Most designers will want to start with the standard PHPP file (xlsx). If designers are using the variants worksheet (explained further in chapter 8) the Variants PHPP (xlsm) should be used. The PHPP import tool makes it easy to convert a normal PHPP into a Variants PHPP, if required. In addition, if a staged retrofit is being planned PHPP9 introduces for the first time the EnerPHit Retrofit Plan (ERP), an additional excel workbook that is to be used alongside the PHPP file.

Before starting to make inputs into the PHPP, copy and re-save it, so there is always an original blank version for new projects. As users become familiar with using PHPP they may wish to create a slightly modified 'blank' PHPP for new projects, which has components they commonly use pre-entered.

Open the workbook and read the PHPP worksheet titled 'Brief Instructions', then work through the Heating Demand Basics entry requirements set out in the following sections. As a beginner to PHPP it is recommended that a small, simple residential project be used to gain familiarity with the program. The case study house is used throughout this chapter to illustrate various inputs. Some reference is made to inputs that are required for non-residential buildings, but it is assumed that by the time readers are modelling non-residential buildings they are familiar with the PHPP and technical manual.

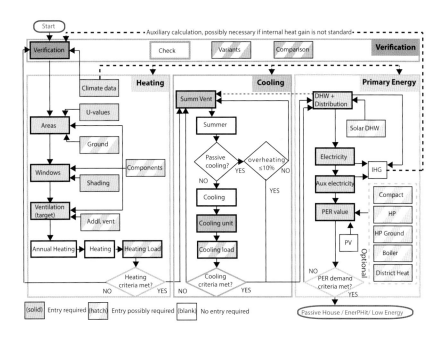

Figure 3.1 *Heating Demand Basics, worksheets*

Note to International Readers:
A (SI) metric PHPP has been used throughout this book. Two tables are included at the end of the book to assist designers working with the imperial system. In addition the (IP) imperial PHPP comes with a 'Conversions' worksheet at the end of the workbook, making it easy for designers to convert between the two systems.

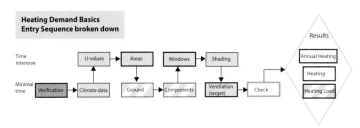

Figure 3.2 *Heating Demand Basics, Entry Sequence*

77

3.1 Verification

The 'Verification' worksheet:

- records general project information

- selects which level of Passive House certification the project is aiming for.

This page is the main point of reference to confirm if the project is meeting the Passive House Evaluation Criteria. Refer to Chapter 2 for a full explanation of these criteria.

The 'Verification' worksheet in PHPP9 has been redesigned and expanded. This is largely to accommodate the introduction of the PER

assessment method and the new Passive House Classes this has created.

There are tools inbedded in this worksheet, which are new to PHPP9, highlighted in the image opposite. These tools are hidden when a new PHPP file is started; to view these the worksheet must first be unprotected (refer to figure 2.1 for guidance on how to do this). Then press the '+' sign next to row 43. This will provide details on the thermal performance requirements for the building based on the selected climate data.

The second tool is only for Renovation, EnerPHit, projects. To view this tool press the '+' in row 57. If designers are certifying an EnerPhit project via the Component Method, refer to Chapter 2, then this tool provides a comprehensive summary of the recommended component values. To see these recommendations the certification method must be set to '1-Compenent method' in cell R85.

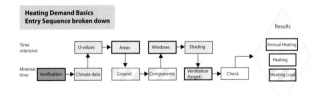

Figure 3.3 *Heating Demand Basics – Verification*

Figure 3.4 *(opposite) 'Verification' worksheet PHPP9*

To insert an image, unprotect the workbook. This is normally locked to prevent accidental alterations of formula and links. Make sure to re-protect as soon completed.

Set temps. should not be altered, unless through agreement with PHI.

Number of units to be modelled in this PHPP, this is an important input as affects the winter internal heat gains.

New tool in PHPP9

For the 'spec. capacity' see fig. 3.4

New tool in PHPP9

Check this box only if mechanical cooling is required (not normally required in the UK)

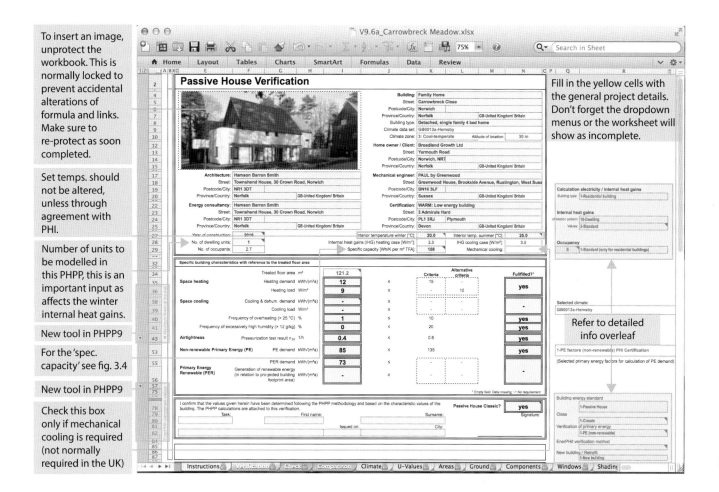

Fill in the yellow cells with the general project details. Don't forget the dropdown menus or the worksheet will show as incomplete.

Refer to detailed info overleaf

The thermal mass or effective thermal storage capacity of the building is input into this worksheet. The thermal mass does not have a very significant effect on the heating, cooling and comfort of Passive House buildings when compared with other parameters. But that is not to say it has no effect so it is important that the input is accurate and reflects what is being designed.

The PHPP only models overheating as a single zone, which is an acceptable simplification for a dwelling, so the algorithm only needs a single parameter to describe thermal mass without any detailed analysis.

A standard value can be used for lightweight, mixed or massive buildings – these values can be seen by hovering over cell C26, or a project-specific value can be calculated using the given formula (see **Figure 3.5**).

For the case study house 108Wh/(m²K) has been used, meaning it is neither a fully lightweight or massive construction but sits between these two extremes. There are some massive elements such as the ground floor slab, which is exposed to the inside of the building with below slab insulation; and to some extent the external walls where the lime rendered clay block is exposed to the inside

of the building, again with the insulation to the outside. However, the internal walls and ground floor ceilings are plastered metal stud/posi-joists with no significant thermal mass contribution. The second-floor ceilings similarly have limited thermal storage capacity as they are plaster-boarded OSB panels with recycled newspaper insulation.

As summarised in figure 3.5, when calculating the specific thermal capacity in PHPP all buildings start with 60Wh/(m²K); 24Wh/(m²K) is then added for massive elements and 8Wh/(m²K) in the case of partially massive elements.
The 108Wh/(m²K) was arrived at as follows:
60+(1*24) slab +(3*8) contribution from the exterior walls and double boarded ceilings = 108Wh/(m²K).

The technical manual provides more detailed information on calculating this value (p. 31).

Figure 3.5 *(opposite) Specific thermal capacity*

Typical room

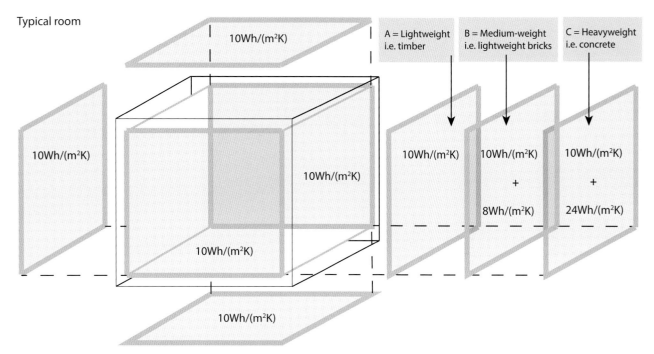

10Wh/(m²K)

10Wh/(m²K)

10Wh/(m²K)

10Wh/(m²K)

10Wh/(m²K)

A = Lightweight
i.e. timber

B = Medium-weight
i.e. lightweight bricks

C = Heavyweight
i.e. concrete

10Wh/(m²K)

10Wh/(m²K)

10Wh/(m²K)

+

+

8Wh/(m²K)

24Wh/(m²K)

Each surface is given a value to represent its capacity to store heat.

All surfaces start with a value of 10Wh/(m²K), giving a starting value for ALL projects of 60Wh/(m²K).

24Wh/(m²K) is then added to each surface which is massive or heavy construction (brick, concrete etc) and 8Wh/(m²K) to each surface which is partially massive (porous concrete, lightweight blocks etc.). Note double plasterboarded surfaces can only be counted as 4Wh/(m²K). Refer to the technical manual p. 31 for more details

PHI summarise this in a formula: $c = 60 + n_{tm} * 8 + n_m * 24$ [Wh/(m²K)], where $0 \leq (n_{tm} + n_m) \leq 6$

Once the relevant selections have been made from the drop-down menus (see **Figure 3.6**), no further information needs to be inserted into this worksheet at this stage. As progress through this chapter is made the green cells will start to display figures. When the end of this chapter is reached some preliminary results will be ready for viewing on this worksheet.

The next worksheet in the PHPP, labelled 'Overview', is hidden when a new PHPP file is started. Refer to **Figure 2.1** on p. 41 to unhide this worksheet.

The 'Overview' worksheet has been added to provide an overview of the project. It is self-explanatory to complete. Project details are added here but no new data relevant to the energy performance calculations. Part of the rationale behind this new worksheet is to provide a template for transferring details on to the Passive House database where details of, at the time of writing, 3,912 completed projects can be found (www.passivehouse-database.org). This is a great resource for finding out about other Passive House projects.

Many PHPP users prefer to leave this worksheet hidden while working on the PHPP and simply unhide and complete this worksheet when the project is ready for certification.

Figure 3.6 *(opposite) 'Verification' worksheet PHPP9, drop-down menus in detail*

Calculation electricity / Internal heat gains

Building type: 1-Residential building

Allows the PHPP to make assumptions re. electricity use and Internal Heat Gains (IHG).

Internal heat gains

Utilisation pattern: 10-Dwelling

Values: 2-Standard

Allows PHPP to make assumptions re. the IHG. The PHPP has a number of pre-set utilisation patterns for homes, schools etc. For example, if the project is a standard residential project, i.e our Case Study home, '10-Dwelling' should be selected in the fist box, and '2-Standard' in the second box. 'PHPP calc.' can be selected in the second box if there are special requirements or design feature which mean the IHG are non standard. It is then necessary to complete the PHPP 'IHG' worksheet, covered in Chapter 5.

Occupancy

5   1-Standard (only for residential buildings)

For dwellings the number of occupants should be left as 'standard' to calculate automatically. If the occupancy is going to be significantly different from that shown (in cell F29) variations can be tested by changing to 'user-determined' and entering the number manually in the yellow cell. However, for certification this should be left to calculate automatically. The reason for this requirement is that it is not possible to know how future owners will occupy the space. The automatic calculation is based on the average square meterage provided per person. For non-domestic buildings 'user-determined' must be selected and the occupancy entered manually.

Building energy standard

1-Passive House

Class

1-Classic

Verification of primary energy

1-PE (non-renewable)

EnerPHit verification method

New building / Retrofit

1-New building

Select the Energy Standard for the building, there are four options:
1. Passive House – for projects aiming for full Passive House Certification
2. EnerPHit – for retrofit projects only
3. Low Energy – for projects not quite meeting one or more of the full Passive House criteria
4. Other – for projects not meeting any of the three Standards listed above (i.e non-certifiable)

If 1 (Passive House) or 2 (EnerPHit) above have been selected the Class has to selected, there are three options:
Classic, Plus or Premium, refer to Chapter 2 for full details on these Classes, new to PHPP9

This cell only needs to be completed for retrofit, EnerPHit, projects, chapter 2 explains when each of these certification types may be appropriate.

The method of calculating the energy used in the house is selected here. Primary Energy (PE) values are based on non-renewable energy supplies. This is the original calculation method and cannot be used with the new Classes Plus and Premium. Primary Energy Renewable (PER) is the new methodology based on renewable energy supplies and is suitable to be used with all of the new Classes. Refer to Chapter 2 for full details on the PER, new to PHPP9.

3.2 Climate Data

The local climate certainly has a big impact on the performance of a Passive House. A project that meets the Passive House Evaluation Criteria in southern England will be highly unlikely to meet the same criteria if situated in northern Scotland, where mean temperatures and solar radiation are likely to be lower. It is important that the correct climatic region is selected for the building. The chosen climate data set will determine if the building is in a warm or cool temperature climate zone. This in turn effects the Passive House criteria (component performance and heat demand), particularly for EnerPHit projects.

Additionally, in PHPP9, the climate data sets have been supplemented with information about the regional availability of renewable energy sources (PER factors). Refer now to the 'Climate data' worksheet.

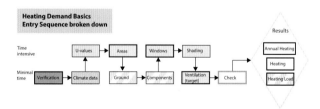

Figure 3.7 *Heating Demand Basics – climate data*

The 'Climate data' worksheet provides the opportunity to:

(a) select climate data from data sets stored within the PHPP, including utilising a new tool which searches for the closest climate data set to the buildings location, or

(b) insert data obtained from an outside source such as iPHA's Climate Data Tool, Meteonorm or a local weather station.

Once set, the climate data will automatically update on the 'Verification' page.

COMMON MISTAKES

Forgetting to take into account altitude
The UK data is collected from weather stations that are based at between 0 and 50m. A subtraction of 0.6°C is therefore required for every 100m increase in altitude. All altitude-related adjustments are made automatically from PHPP8 onwards when the building altitude is inserted into the 'Climate data' worksheet, cell D18.

This map indicates the 22 climate regions for the UK that are included in the PHPP.

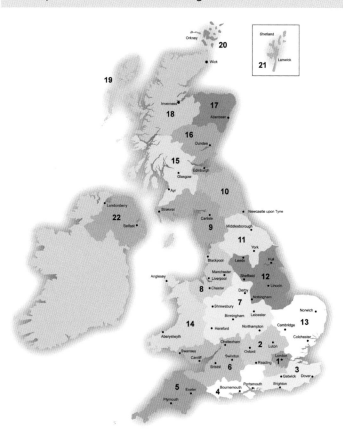

Due to the London Heat Island effect, use data set 'London (Central)' within PHPP for the London boroughs listed below:

- Hammersmith and Fulham
- Kensington and Chelsea
- Westminster
- Islington
- City of London
- Hackney
- Tower Hamlets
- Newham
- Lewisham
- Southwark
- Lambeth
- Wandsworth
- Camden

Figure 3.8 *BRE climate regions*

(a) Select climate data from data sets stored within the PHPP.
There is now a good selection of UK data, which has been prepared jointly by the PHI and the Building Research Establishment (BRE).

(b) Insert data obtained from an outside source such as iPHA's Climate Data Tool, Meteonorm or a local weather station.

Firstly, if a non-standard data set is being proposed it needs to be checked with the certifier at a very early stage (as finding that it is not accepted later on could jeopardise a scheme).

For most projects in the UK it will be accurate enough to use the BRE data sets. If more specific climate data is deemed necessary it is possible to add new data sets. It is important that the weather data is correctly prepared for insertion into the PHPP. For more information on how to prepare data for insertion please refer to the technical manual, pp. 55–6. It's important to note that designers cannot certify their buildings using their own climate data sets without special permission from PHI. And PHI is the only organisation which can supply PER factors for use in buildings being certified under the new Passive House Classes.

iPHA has a Climate Data Tool, which provides PHPP ready data for any location in the UK; this can be found on Passipedia. This uses satellite data from the NASA Langley Research Center Atmospheric Sciences Data Center POWER Project. However, the data is only complete enough to be used for orientation calculations (due to the limited resolution of the original data – one degree latitude by one degree longitude – which means that local micro-climatic effects are not reflected correctly).

Alternatively, the BRE can provide bespoke weather data for any site in the UK; for further information please visit **www.passivhaus.org.uk**. The BRE can provide this as a separate Excel document with instructions for how to insert it easily into the PHPP.

It can be interesting to see how the building would perform in neighbouring climate regions or even elsewhere in the world; this can be done at any time, by simply selecting a different climatic zone in this worksheet.

If no entry is made on this spreadsheet the standard German climate data is used. This is not recommended for UK projects.

Select GB - United Kingdom/Britain to access the UK climate sets

Select the local region; refer to image 3.8, BRE map.

Select the climate data set. PHPP9 provides new a tool (cell FC20), which advises on the data set based on the site latitude and longitude. Note: this may not provide the most appropriate data set. For certification in the UK, refer to the maps shown on the PHI website and confirm the chosen data set with your certifier.

It is particularly important that the building altitude is included here if it varies significantly from the weather station. But even if the site altitude is the same as the weather stations it should still be inserted.

The climate data will auto-fill in here

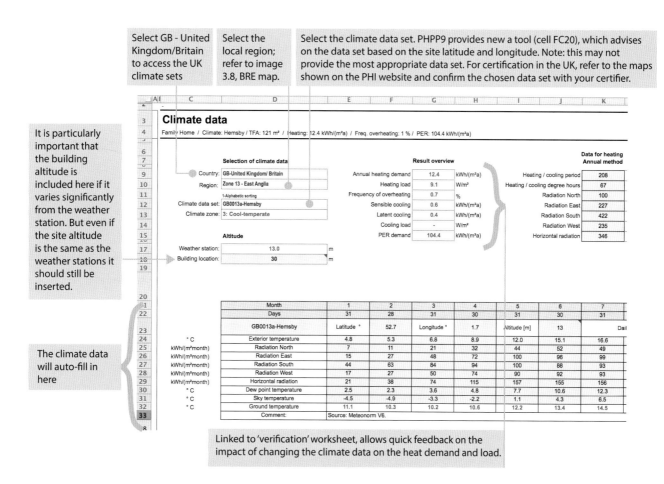

Linked to 'verification' worksheet, allows quick feedback on the impact of changing the climate data on the heat demand and load.

Figure 3.9 'Climate data' worksheet PHPP9

87

3.3 U-values

The 'U-value' worksheet:

- calculates U-values for each building assembly

- includes tools for calculating air voids and wedge-shaped insulation.

It is useful to enter the U-values before moving on to the area entries. Thinking about the different U-values the building has helps to set out how many areas will have to be set up separately on the next worksheet. Also, remember that the U-values affect the thickness of the walls and hence affect the area entries. This is another good reason to complete this worksheet first.

It is important to enter:

- all components that have different build-ups separately

- the correct surface heat transfer resistances; refer to **Figure 3.12**

- all elements and their respective thermal conductivities

- accurate thermal conductivities for still air spaces and wedge-shaped insulation/components by using the tools to the right of the worksheet (these tools should be easy to use by referring to the embedded notes – if anything remains unclear refer to the technical manual).

- only elements that are to the warm side of any ventilated air space (a ventilated air space is defined as an opening exceeding 1,500mm^2 per m length for vertical layers and per m^2 for horizontal layers)

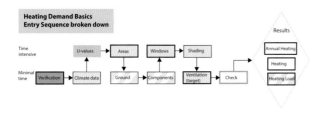

Figure 3.10 *Heating Demand Basics – U-values*

Figure 3.11 *(opposite) Heating Demand Basics – U-values extract PHPP9*

New to PHPP9, once selections are made from the drop-down menu, the heat transmission resistances are auto-filled to the right. Refer also to fig. 3.12. (Alternatively designers can enter their own values directly)

Start inside

To outside

Refer to note in fig. 3.13 on p. 93

U-value of building assemblies

Passive House with PHPP Version 9.6a

Family Home / Climate: Hemsby / TFA: 121 m² / Heating: 12.4 kWh/(m²a) / Freq. overheating: 1 % / PER: 104.4 kWh/(m²a)

Very useful additional tools for calculating thermal conductivities are included to the right of the worksheet (beyond the errors/warnings columns)

Secondary calculation: Equivalent thermal conductivity of still air spaces -> (on the right)
Wedge-shaped assembly layer -> (on the right)
Unheated / uncooled attic -> (on the right)

Assembly no.	Building assembly description	Interior insulation?
01ud	**Exterior Wall - Porotherm Render**	

Orientation of building element	**2-Wall**	Heat transmission resistance [m²K/W]		
Adjacent to	**1-Outdoor air**	interior R$_{si}$	0.13	
		exterior R$_{se}$	0.04	Refer embedded note

Area section 1	λ [W/(mK)]	Area section 2 (optional)	λ [W/(mK)]	Area section 3 (optional)	λ [W/(mK)]	Thickness [mm]
parge - lime plaster	0.250					22
Clay blocks	0.090	mortar	0.700			300
Adhesive	0.700					10
Baumit Open EPS	0.031					220
Render	0.700					6

Percentage of sec. 1	Percentage of sec. 2	Percentage of sec. 3	Total
99%	**1.0%**		**55.8** cm

U-value supplement [   ] W/(m²K)

U-value: **0.094** W/(m²K)

This provision allows for a second and even third material to be included in one layer. In this example the thin joint mortar within the clay block layer has been accounted for at 1%. More commonly, these additional materials will be regular structural elements within insulation layers i.e timber stud-work in an insulated wall. It is important not to under-estimate the percentage of the poorer performing material.

This is the important result, values from 0.10–0.15W/(m²K) are normally required for a new build in the UK. For more details refer to the Component Performance Criteria in Chapter 2, fig 2.2.

COMMON MISTAKES

Thermal conductivity entered is not to the Lambda 90/90 standard

- The PHI accept national standards for thermal conductivity values. In the UK this means all values must comply with the Lambda 90/90 standard.

- Before European product standards, UK manufacturers for the most part based their claims on typical or mean values. The 90/90 values are subject to strict analysis to provide a value which, among other things, is representative of 90% of production within a 90% confidence level.

- In the UK it is now BBA policy to quote only λ90/90 values in all new certificates. From the 30 June 2012 all insulation certificates should either state the λ90/90 value, note that a standard adjustment has been made, or note that no λ90/90 adjustment has been made. In this case it must be adjusted before being entered into the PHPP using 0.005 W·m-1.K-1.

- Although SAP assessors often do not check stated thermal conductivities, Passive House certifiers do. If in doubt, check with the manufacturer or certifiers.

The heat transfer resistance is the value given to the surface thermal resistance. It varies depending on the direction of the heat movement and the location of the surface, either internal or external (see **Figure 3.12**). PHPP9 now automatically sets the correct heat transfer resistances based on information selected from the drop-down menus (in column M).

The outside above ground (ambient air) heat transfer resistance of $0.04m^2K/W$ is not used if there is a rain screen cladding that has been excluded from the U-value calculation. In this case the exterior value should be the same as the interior surface value.

Remember, for Passive House certification U-values should meet the requirements set out in Chapter 2, **Figure 2.2**. If they do not this should be discussed early with the certifier and compensation will have to be made elsewhere.

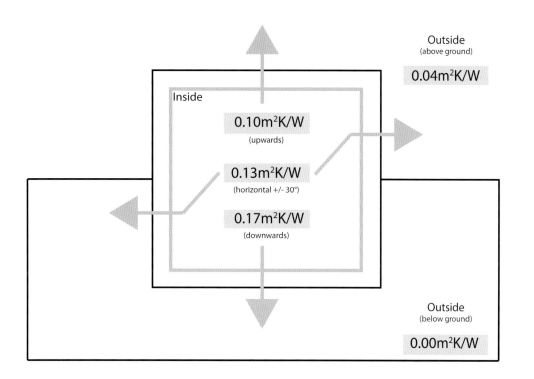

Outside
(above ground)

0.04m²K/W

Inside

0.10m²K/W
(upwards)

0.13m²K/W
(horizontal +/- 30°)

0.17m²K/W
(downwards)

Outside
(below ground)

0.00m²K/W

Figure 3.12 *Heating Demand Basics – heat transfer resistances*

Figure 3.13 *(overleaf) Carrowbreck U-values explained with extracts from PHPP9*

Surface resistance values refer to EN ISO 6946 which describes values according to direction of heat flow. In hot climates, where heat flow would be from outside to inside through the roof, the value would be 0.17m²K/W.

In the case of rain screen claddings or, for example, attics or unheated basements, the interior value equals the external value i.e for a rain screen cladding the external surface resistance is 0.13m²K/W.

Assembly 05ud — Roof Terrace - flat

Assembly no.	05ud	Roof Terrace - flat				Interior insulation?	

Heat transmission resistance [m²K/W]

| Orientation of building element | 1-Roof | interior R_{si} | 0.10 |
| Adjacent to | 3-Ventilated | exterior R_{se} | 0.10 |

Area section 1	λ [W/(mK)]	Area section 2 (optional)	λ [W/(mK)]	Area section 3 (optional)	λ [W/(mK)]	Thickness [mm]
Single layer plasterboard with skim	0.210					15
Batten Zone	0.150	Timber	0.130			25
OSB	0.130					18
Rockwool	0.038	Joist Flange	0.130	Joist Flange	0.130	39
Rockwool	0.038			Web	0.130	322
Rockwool	0.038	Joist Flange	0.130	Joist Flange	0.130	39
Ventilated void						

Percentage of sec. 1	73%	Percentage of sec. 2	24.0%	Percentage of sec. 3	3.0%	Total	45.8	cm

U-value supplement		W/(m²K)			U-value:	0.101	W/(m²K)

A separate calculation is required to quantify the thermal conductivity of the air void that forms the service zone - the PHPP provides a tool for this calculation to the right hand side of the worksheet

Assembly 01ud — Exterior Wall - Porotherm Render

Assembly no.	01ud	Building assembly description	Exterior Wall - Porotherm Render			Interior insulation?	

Heat transmission resistance [m²K/W]

| Orientation of building element | 2-Wall | interior R_{si} | 0.13 |
| Adjacent to | 1-Outdoor air | exterior R_{se} | 0.04 |

Area section 1	λ [W/(mK)]	Area section 2 (optional)	λ [W/(mK)]	Area section 3 (optional)	λ [W/(mK)]	Thickness [mm]
parge - lime plaster	0.250					22
Clay blocks	0.090	mortar	0.700			300
Adhesive	0.700					10
Baumit Open EPS	0.031					220
Render	0.700					6

Percentage of sec. 1	99%	Percentage of sec. 2	1.0%	Percentage of sec. 3		Total	55.8	cm

U-value supplement		W/(m²K)			U-value:	0.094	W/(m²K)

No calculation or allowance is required for the special thermally broken fixings used to secure the insulation. If designers are unsure if their fixings are classed as thermal bridge free they should speak to their certifier.

Terrace Construction
- Plasterboard and skim — 15mm
- Service zone — 25mm
- OSB3 = Airtight Layer — 18mm
- Insulation between I-joists — 400mm
- Ventilated void with furrings — 50mm
- WEP plywood decking — 22mm
- Waterproofing (single ply) — —
- Decking pedestals — 50mm
- Decking slabs — 20mm

Rendered Wall Construction
- Finishing lime plaster — 2mm
- Parge lime plaster = Airtight Layer — 20mm
- Hollow Clay Blocks — 300mm
- Adhesive/external parge layer — 10mm
- Vapour Open EPS insulation — 220mm
- Render system with mesh layers — 6mm

Ground Slab Construction
- Zone for floor finishes — 20mm
- Reinforced concrete slab = Airtight layer — 250mm
- Separating layer — —
- Insulation — 300mm
- Damp proof membrane — —
- Sand blinding — 25mm
- Compacted hardcore — 150mm

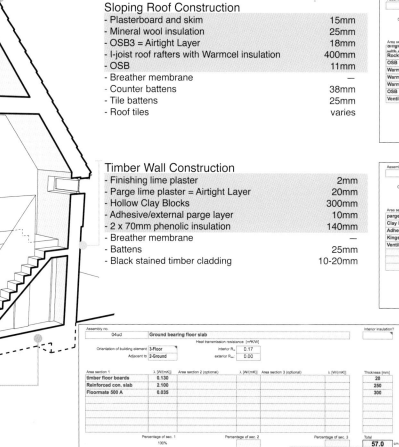

Sloping Roof Construction

- Plasterboard and skim	15mm
- Mineral wool insulation	25mm
- OSB3 = Airtight Layer	18mm
- I-joist roof rafters with Warmcel insulation	400mm
- OSB	11mm
- Breather membrane	—
- Counter battens	38mm
- Tile battens	25mm
- Roof tiles	varies

Timber Wall Construction

- Finishing lime plaster	2mm
- Parge lime plaster = Airtight Layer	20mm
- Hollow Clay Blocks	300mm
- Adhesive/external parge layer	10mm
- 2 x 70mm phenolic insulation	140mm
- Breather membrane	—
- Battens	25mm
- Black stained timber cladding	10-20mm

Assembly no. 06ud — Roof Sloping - Metsawood UK

Interior insulation?

Heat transmission resistance [m²K/W]
Orientation of building element: 1-Roof — interior Rsi 0.10
Adjacent to: 3-Ventilated — exterior Rse 0.10

Area section 1	λ [W/(mK)]	Area section 2 (optional)	λ [W/(mK)]	Area section 3 (optional)	λ [W/(mK)]	Thickness [mm]
Single layer plasterboard with skim	0.210					15
Rockwool RWA45 Slabs	0.035	timber battens	0.130			25
OSB	0.130					18
Warmcel	0.038	Kerto Flange	0.130	flange	0.130	39
Warmcel	0.038			Kerto Web	0.130	322
Warmcel	0.038	Kerto Flange	0.130	flange	0.130	39
OSB	0.130					11
Ventilated void						

Percentage of sec. 1: 92% Percentage of sec. 2: 6.0% Percentage of sec. 3: 2.0% Total: 46.9 cm

U-value supplement: ___ W/(m²K)   **U-value: 0.090** W/(m²K)

Assembly no. 02ud — Exterior Wall - Porotherm Boarded

Interior insulation?

Heat transmission resistance [m²K/W]
Orientation of building element: 2-Wall — interior Rsi 0.13
Adjacent to: 3-Ventilated — exterior Rse 0.13

Area section 1	λ [W/(mK)]	Area section 2 (optional)	λ [W/(mK)]	Area section 3 (optional)	λ [W/(mK)]	Thickness [mm]
parge - lime plaster	0.250					22
Clay blocks	0.090	mortar	0.700			300
Adhesive	0.035					6
Kingspan K5	0.020					140
Ventilated void						

Percentage of sec. 1: 99% Percentage of sec. 2: 1.0% Percentage of sec. 3: Total: 46.8 cm

U-value supplement: 0.01 W/(m²K)   **U-value: 0.100** W/(m²K)

Assembly no. 04ud — Ground bearing floor slab

Interior insulation?

Heat transmission resistance [m²K/W]
Orientation of building element: 3-Floor — interior Rsi 0.17
Adjacent to: 2-Ground — exterior Rse 0.00

Area section 1	λ [W/(mK)]	Area section 2 (optional)	λ [W/(mK)]	Area section 3 (optional)	λ [W/(mK)]	Thickness [mm]
timber floor boards	0.130					20
Reinforced con. slab	2.100					250
Floormate 500 A	0.035					300

Percentage of sec. 1: 100% Percentage of sec. 2: Percentage of sec. 3: Total: 57.0 cm

U-value supplement: ___ W/(m²K)   **U-value: 0.111** W/(m²K)

A separate calculation is required for the metal fixings that fix the timber battens through the insulation layer and into the Porotherm wall. WARM: Low Energy Building Practice published a tool for this calculation 'U-Value Corrections Calculator' free to download – http://www.peterwarm.co.uk/resources/downloads/ Refer also to BS EN ISO 6946, section D.3: Correction for Mechanical Fasteners and speak to the PH certifier.

KEY

Components to be included in U-value calculation

93

3.4 Areas

The 'Areas' worksheet:
- records information about the envelope of the building
- assigns U-values to each heat transfer area of the building
- assigns environment conditions to each heat transfer area of the building
- assigns orientation and radiation balance information to each heat transfer area of the building
- records information regarding thermal bridging (covered in Chapter 7)
- provides information on average building envelope performance and the proportion of the performance of each building component compared to the total building envelope in order to detect weak points.

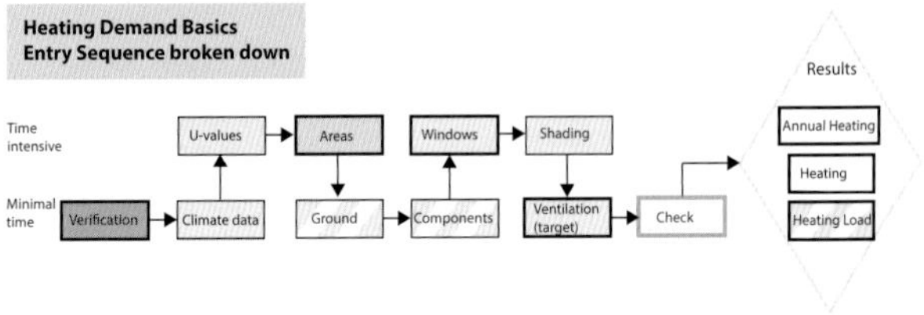

The Passive House Institute also provides *design*PH, a SketchUp plugin, as an additional Passive House planning tool, which can be purchased as part of a bundle with the PHPP. This tool can potentially save time as it calculates all of the heat loss areas and provides a preliminary energy balance calculation directly from a SketchUp model. *design*PH is particularly useful in the early design stages when the form of the building is subject to change and especially so if SketchUp already forms part of the design workflow. However, it is not mandatory to use this new plug-in for Passive House planning and certification, so this chapter will first set out how to enter area data manually. If this is being done manually it is likely to take less than an hour to complete for a medium-sized dwelling. If *design*PH is being used please refer also to Chapter 6.

Correctly defining the heat transfer areas is critical to obtaining an accurate result in the PHPP, making this one of the most important sections of the PHPP. The more accurate the input the more accurate the output.

Figure 3.14 *Heating Demand Basics – areas*

Figure 3.15 *(opposite) PHPP and SAP measurements*

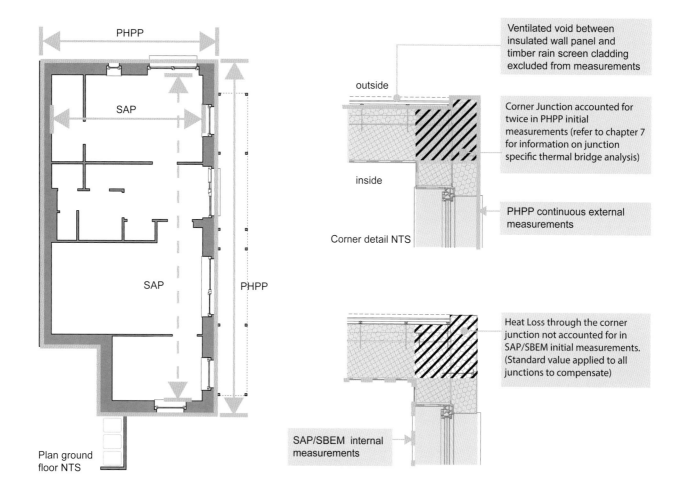

PHPP

SAP

SAP

PHPP

Plan ground
floor NTS

Ventilated void between
insulated wall panel and
timber rain screen cladding
excluded from measurements

outside

inside

Corner detail NTS

Corner Junction accounted for
twice in PHPP initial
measurements (refer to chapter 7
for information on junction
specific thermal bridge analysis)

PHPP continuous external
measurements

Heat Loss through the corner
junction not accounted for in
SAP/SBEM initial measurements.
(Standard value applied to all
junctions to compensate)

SAP/SBEM internal
measurements

The measurements input at this stage are very important as they represent the surface area of the building through which heat can be lost (or gained in hot climatic regions). We will refer to these as heat transfer areas.

The surface area of the thermal envelope is calculated based on the external dimensions of the conditioned (heated and/or cooled) area of the building envelope when carrying out PHPP modelling. This differs from the convention used by SAP and SBEM in the UK, which require the envelope area to be calculated based on internal dimensions. This is one of the key differences in how data is prepared for input into PHPP and SAP/SBEM.

The result of this difference is that PHPP slightly overestimates the heat loss and heat gain from the building elements (wall, roof, floor), thus it has already taken into account heat loss from most geometrical thermal bridges and in some instances over-accounts for them. SAP and SBEM may apply a standard value (known as a y value in SAP) by means of a slight reduction in the overall performance of the building fabric in order to

account for heat loss from thermal bridges. The y value in the SAP model can be reduced from the default by using accredited construction details. Alternatively the psi value* and length of each bridge can be entered in the SAP and SBEM, but this is not mandatory. The Passive House Standard requires thermal bridge free detailing to be used.

3.4.1 Heat transfer areas

Manual inputs

When preparing the areas it is important to maintain an accurate record of all measurements inputted into the PHPP. The certifier will probably require this information. It can be a good idea to set up a new CAD file for the PHPP areas or set up a new CAD layer just used for PHPP inputs.

Here is our case study house broken down ready for inputting into the PHPP. The CAD drawing essentially creates an external net of the house. Another useful method can be to create a simple SketchUp block model. Even if *design*PH is not being used, this can save a lot of time.

* Psi values are explained in Chapter 7.

Figure 3.16 *(opposite) Case study house CAD heat transfer areas*

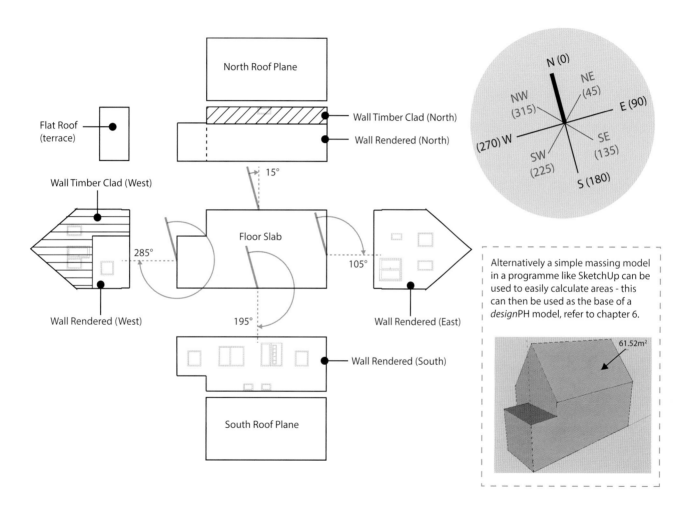

North Roof Plane

Flat Roof
(terrace)

Wall Timber Clad (North)

Wall Rendered (North)

Wall Timber Clad (West)

15°

Floor Slab

285°

105°

Wall Rendered (West)

Wall Rendered (East)

195°

Wall Rendered (South)

South Roof Plane

N (0)
NE (45)
E (90)
SE (135)
S (180)
SW (225)
(270) W
NW (315)

Alternatively a simple massing model in a programme like SketchUp can be used to easily calculate areas - this can then be used as the base of a designPH model, refer to chapter 6.

61.52m²

COMMON MISTAKES

The external measurements do not join up, so some areas are not accounted for

It is good practice to draw a line on the plan and sections for where the external measurements will be taken. This line must be continuous. If unsure of where the line should be, refer to the U-values. The line should be on the outside of the outer element in the U-value calculation, including to the base of any insulation under the floor slab. Remember, this measurement will be inside any ventilated rain screen cladding.

These areas are then inputted into the 'Areas' worksheet, making sure each element with different material qualities and/or orientation is inputted separately. Make sure each element is appropriately titled, ideally using notation used in the CAD file and referencing notation from the 'U-value' worksheet for clarity. This will make it much easier to return to the PHPP at a later date to make edits.

For additional accuracy, the PHPP requires information on the shading, absorptivity and emissivity for each external surface.

For entry requirements refer to **Figure 3.25**. (p. 105)

3.4.2 Projected Building Footprint

One of the first figures you are requested to input into the 'Areas' worksheet is the projected building footprint. This figure is only required if you are certifying the building using the new Passive House Classes, which use renewable primary energy factors, referred to in the PHPP as Primary Energy Renewable (PER).

This projected building footprint is representative of the area available on the building for harvesting renewable energy (if you imagine many buildings will have the harvesting equipment mounted on their roofs).

All renewable energy generated in the building will then be divided by this figure. This prevents there being a penalty for designing multi-story buildings which have a large internal floor area (TFA – see 3.4.3) but limited roof space to generate renewable energy, compared to, for example, a bungalow with a much smaller internal floor area but the same roof area for mounting renewable technologies.

To calculate the projected building footprint, the external extent of the heated (or air-conditioned) building envelope is projected to a horizontal plane. In many cases, such as in the Case Study home, the projected building footprint area is the same as the input for the floor slab. This would not be the case if there were elements which cantilevered over the ground floor; in these cases the projected building footprint would be greater than the area of the floor slab. *DesignPH* (since v1.5) now includes a function to calculate the projected footprint area. See **Figure 3.17** and refer to the technical manual pp. 76–7.

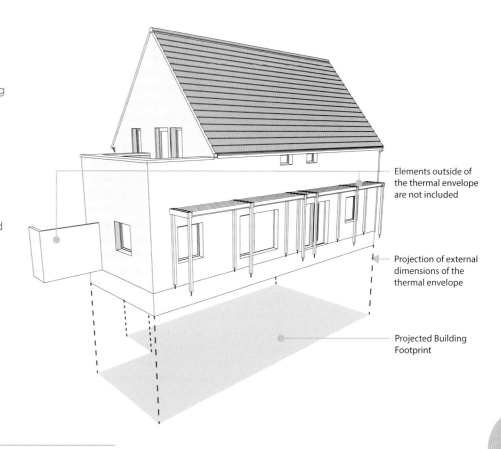

Elements outside of the thermal envelope are not included

Projection of external dimensions of the thermal envelope

Projected Building Footprint

Figure 3.17 *Case study house Projected Building Footprint*

3.4.3 Treated floor area

The next figure you are requested to input on the 'Areas' worksheet is the treated floor area (TFA). This is possibly the most important figure in the entire PHPP, as all energy demands are calculated with reference to this number.

The TFA is based on a German standard called WofIV for residential buildings and DIN 277 for non-residential buildings. The simplest definition of it is that it is all of the useful floor area within the thermal envelope of the building.

The TFA includes some areas at 100% of their area, others at a lesser percentage and some areas cannot be included at all. These rules incentivise designing efficient plans, which make maximum use of space within the thermal envelope.

In a non-residential building the TFA calculation is slightly different from the

residential. For demonstration purposes the Mayville Community Centre Passive House is used as the case study project.

The following applies for all areas: clear height 1–2 m ⇒ the TFA is reduced by 50%.

Note: If you are using *design*PH, the plug-in allows you to draw and assign the TFAs directly, automatically applying the reduction factors to the areas that are exported. For very quick analysis of a form, there is also a simple TFA estimation tool which uses the building footprint as the basis and makes a number of adjustments (based on a method originally provided by WARM: Low Energy Building Practice).

Figure 3.18 *TFA residential table, based on WofIV*

Include at 100% (if within thermal envelope and ≥ 2m high)	Include a percentage only	Not included
Living and circulation space	Areas between 1–2m high can be counted at 50% (if usable)	Areas < 1m high (for example under staircases)
Window reveals which are floor to ceiling and ≥ 130mm deep	If habitable rooms occupy <50% of a floor, i.e. basement, then all adjoining rooms and circulation can only be included at 60% (the habitable room may be included at 100%)	Doorways
Stair landings and heads		Window reveals that are not floor to ceiling or window reveals which are floor to ceiling but not ≥ 130mm deep
Built-in baths, storage, plinths, skirting boards		
Basements if they have habitable rooms occupying > 50% of the total basement		Stairs or steps with more than three rises
		Areas outside of the thermal envelope
Walls/elements < 1.5m high		Floor area taken up by walls/elements >1.5m high

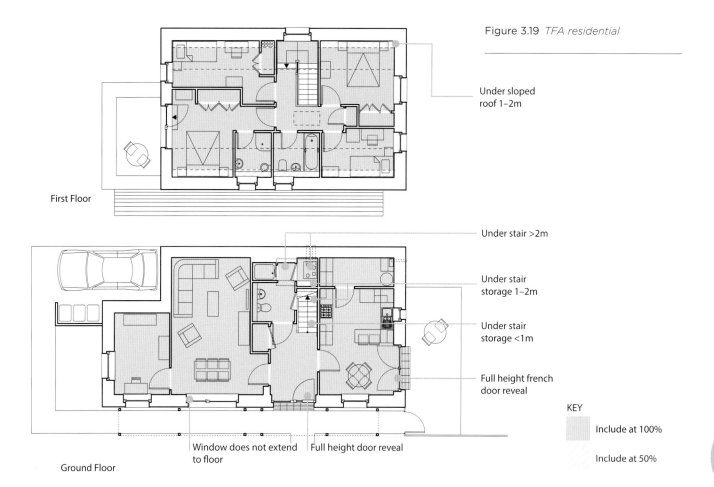

Figure 3.19 *TFA residential*

Under sloped
roof 1–2m

First Floor

Under stair >2m

Under stair
storage 1–2m

Under stair
storage <1m

Full height french
door reveal

Window does not extend
to floor

Full height door reveal

Ground Floor

KEY

Include at 100%

Include at 50%

101

The 'Areas', worksheet, **Figure 3.24**, provides for entries on the surface properties of the building elements or, as we are referring to them, heat transfer areas (columns AJ – shading, AK – absorptivity, AL – emissivity). These inputs lead to some solar gain via the opaque fabric being included in the monthly method heating demand sheet. These inputs are straightforward to complete with the extra help provided by passing the mouse over the cells with the red corners.

The worksheet also records the orientation information. It is very important to input this data accurately as this data is used to establish the window orientations.

Refer to figure 3.16 for clarification on the calculation of the orientation figure.

Below the main area table, shown in **Figure 3.24**, there is a table for recording the thermal bridges. This table can be left blank at this stage; thermal bridges are covered in Chapter 7.

Figure 3.20 *(above left) Mayville, south elevation*
Figure 3.21 *(above right) Mayville, main community hall*

Figure 3.22 *(opposite) TFA non-residential plans*

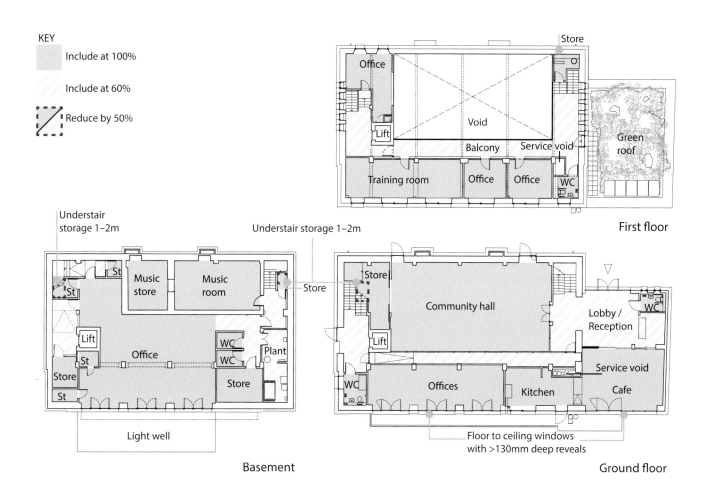

KEY

Include at 100%

Include at 60%

Reduce by 50%

First floor

Store
Office
Void
Balcony
Service void
Green roof
Lift
Training room
Office
Office
WC

Understair storage 1–2m

Understair storage 1–2m

Store

Basement

St
Music store
Music room
St
St
Lift
St
Store
St
Office
WC
WC
Store
Plant

Light well

Ground floor

Store
Community hall
Lift
WC
WC
Offices
Kitchen
Lobby / Reception
Service void
Cafe

Floor to ceiling windows with >130mm deep reveals

Include at 100% (if within thermal envelope and ≥2m high)	Include at 60% only	Not included
Living, office and recreational space	Technical functional areas:	Areas <1m high (for example under staircases)
Washrooms	– House installations room	Doorways
Classrooms, common rooms	– Plant room for electrical system, ventilation technology, heating, cooling, telecommunications	Window reveals that are not floor to ceiling or window reveals which are floor to ceiling but not ≥130mm deep
Storage and cloakrooms		
Kitchens	Access areas:	Stairs or steps with more than three rises
Laboratories	– corridors	Areas outside of the thermal envelope
Swimming pools and poolside areas	– foyers	Floor area taken up by Walls/elements >1.5m high
Access and transit areas with additional uses (except emergency exits)	– stairheads and landings	Lift shafts
Built-in baths, storage, plinths, skirting boards		Installation/service shafts
Window and door reveals that are floor to ceiling and ≥130mm deep		Air spaces

Figure 3.23 *TFA non-residential table based on DIN 277*

Figure 3.24 *(opposite) 'Areas' worksheet entries PHPP9*

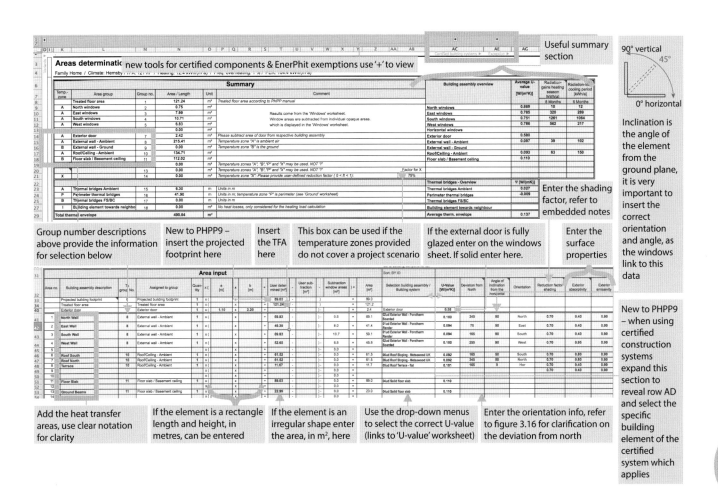

90° vertical
45°

0° horizontal

Inclination is the angle of the element from the ground plane, it is very important to insert the correct orientation and angle, as the windows link to this data

Useful summary section

new tools for certified components & EnerPhit exemptions use '+' to view

Group number descriptions above provide the information for selection below

New to PHPP9 – insert the projected footprint here

Insert the TFA here

This box can be used if the temperature zones provided do not cover a project scenario

If the external door is fully glazed enter on the windows sheet. If solid enter here.

Enter the surface properties

Enter the shading factor, refer to embedded notes

New to PHPP9 – when using certified construction systems expand this section to reveal row AD and select the specific building element of the certified system which applies

Add the heat transfer areas, use clear notation for clarity

If the element is a rectangle length and height, in metres, can be entered

If the element is an irregular shape enter the area, in m², here

Use the drop-down menus to select the correct U-value (links to 'U-value' worksheet)

Enter the orientation info, refer to figure 3.16 for clarification on the deviation from north

105

3.5 Ground

The 'Ground' worksheet:

• provides the opportunity to calculate more precisely the heat losses through the ground
• allows the PHPP to take into account both the building geometry and the seasonal storage effects.

Although not a mandatory requirement, the worksheet does not take long to complete so is recommended. If not completed, the PHPP calculates a reduction factor from standardised values and the interpreted geometry of the floor slab.

Before completing this worksheet it is important to understand the difference in how SAP and PHPP treat the ground. The UK convention, as used in SAP, is to quote floor U-values including the effect of the ground. Users may encounter UK manufacturers quoting floor U-values including the ground effect.

In PHPP the U-value entered excludes the effect of the ground ('ground reduction factor'). This is worked out separately in this worksheet. Because of this the boundary condition to the ground is set as zero: any resistance provided by the ground is worked out separately. This worksheet considers perimeter/area ratio, floor type, etc.

The PHPP does not display the U-value of the floor including the effect of the ground. If users would like this (SAP floor U-value) figure they must multiply the ground U-value, from the 'U-value' worksheet, by the ground reduction factor, in this worksheet.

To complete this sheet, specific information about the site is required. A site-specific geotechnical survey will provide the most accurate data for insertion in the PHPP. Online resources can be used if a geotechnical survey is not available but the results will be less accurate.

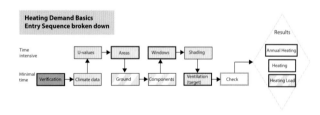

Figure 3.25 *Heating Demand Basics – ground*

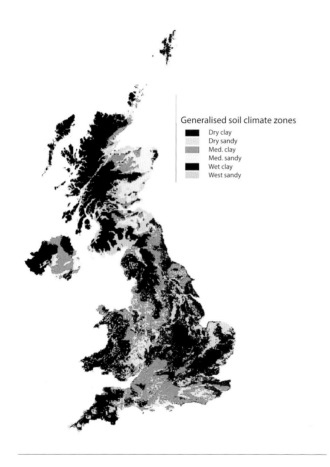

Figure 3.26 *Generalised UK soil type map*

First find out what type of soil exists on the site (see Figures 3.26 and 3.27).

Refer to Figure 3.28 (overleaf) for details on the inputs for this worksheet.

Enter the properties of the soil in the 'Ground Characteristics' box. This is not critical, and if not known, the default can be used. The height of the water table is input towards the end of the worksheet, which if <3m deep with a velocity >0.2m/d, can have an effect on the insulation so should be entered. As with the soil type, in most cases this does not need to be considered.

Soil type	Thermal conductivity W/(mK)	Heat capacity MJ/(m³K)
Silt/clay	1.5	3
Peat	0.4	3
Dry sand/gravel	1.5	1.5
Wet sand/gravel/moist clay	2	2
Saturated clay	3	3
Rock	3.5	2

Figure 3.27 *Soil thermal properties table*

107

Perimeter insulation (i.e insulation which extends out from the slab either vertically or horizontally) is used when there is not sufficient insulation of the floor slab. This is a common scenario in EnerPHit projects where it is not practical to insulate the existing slab to an acceptable level. If perimeter insulation is used for a slab on grade complete the section.

Suspended floors are an interesting condition. They are not recommendable due to moisture problems that can occur within the void/crawl space. However, it may be necessary to model a suspended floor in an existing construction. The data should be inserted here.
U_{crawl}: This is the U-value of the floor under the crawl space, in most cases this is not insulated. In these cases the heat transfer coefficient of 5.9W/(m²K) must be used.
h: Average height of the crawl space walls
U_w: Average U-value of the crawl space walls
εP: Total area of the ventilated openings of the crawl space
v: Average wind velocity at 10m height on the site
f_w: Wind shield factor. The technical manual provides a table with values for various site conditions.

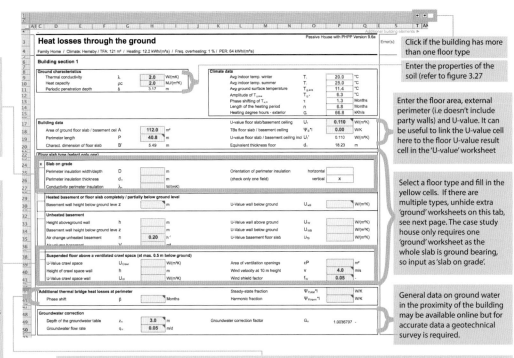

Click if the building has more than one floor type

Enter the properties of the soil (refer to figure 3.27

Enter the floor area, external perimeter (i.e doesn't include party walls) and U-value. It can be useful to link the U-value cell here to the floor U-value result cell in the 'U-value' worksheet

Select a floor type and fill in the yellow cells. If there are multiple types, unhide extra 'ground' worksheets on this tab, see next page. The case study house only requires one 'ground' worksheet as the whole slab is ground bearing, so input as 'slab on grade'.

General data on ground water in the proximity of the building may be available online but for accurate data a geotechnical survey is required.

Perimeter thermal bridges result in heat loss and should be accounted. State-steady thermal bridges should be entered on the 'Areas' worksheet; harmonic thermal bridges should be entered here. The technical manual provides a lot of information about the additional thermal bridge heat losses at the ground, refer to pp. 93–4 of the technical manual. Refer also to chapter 7 in this guide.

Figure 3.28 *'Ground' worksheet*

Only one floor slab type can be selected on the 'Ground' worksheet; if the building has more than one floor slab type a second 'Ground' worksheet must be activated (there are three 'Ground' worksheets available in total). This is easy to do – unprotect the worksheet (see **Figure 3.4**) then click the small '+' sign at the top of the worksheet, refer to **Figure 3.28**. Remember to re-protect the sheet once the new sheet has been added. The ground reduction factor is then calculated taking into account the aggregated results over all of the 'Ground' worksheets. This aggregated figure is then inserted automatically into the 'Annual heating' worksheet. The ground reduction factor is also used in the 'Areas' worksheet, for the calculation of any below ground building components.

Our case study house required only one 'Ground' worksheet.

The results are displayed at the bottom of the 'Ground' worksheet. The results are split into three parts, the Ground Reduction Factor, the Monthly Average Designed Ground Temperatures and the Designed Ground Temperature for use in the heat and cooling load worksheets, see **Figure 3.29**.

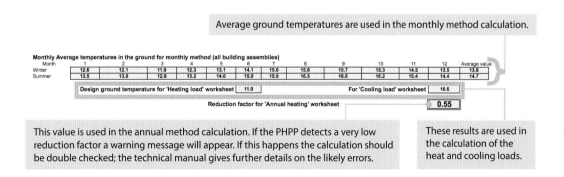

Figure 3.29 *'Ground' worksheet results*

3.6 Components

This worksheet was new to PHPP8, bringing together information that was previously spread over a number of different worksheets.

The 'Components' worksheet:

- provides a summary of U-values
- records the detailed data for the glazing
- records the detailed data for the window frames
- records the installation thermal bridges for the windows (this is covered in Chapter 6).
- records detailed data for the ventilation system being used, either standard heat recovery ventilation or compact unit with exhaust air heat pump.

In PHPP9 it has been supplemented with:

- thermal bridges of connection details in certified systems
- values for entry doors are now contained within the 'glazing' table
- a new section for shower drain heat recovery systems

The 'Components' worksheet is not normally time-consuming to complete as the PHPP has many certified components pre-entered. It is only necessary to add components if the ones being used are not listed. At an early stage in the design process it is acceptable to select components from those provided. But remember to update these as soon as project specifications are determined. It is also worth remembering that the highest performing components are often the most expensive. If the highest performing components are relied on to meet the Passive House Evaluation Criteria this will have a budget implication.

3.6.1 Components – windows

The quality of a window depends on two essential characteristics – the U-value of the window (glass and frame combined), U_w, and the g-value, which

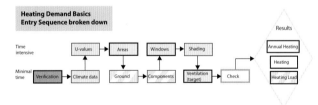

Figure 3.30 *Heating Demand Basics – components*

COMMON MISTAKES

Using the same frame dimensions for fixed and opening windows

Fixed and opening windows will have different frame dimensions. Therefore two separate window types should be added to the 'Components' worksheet, allowing accurate frame dimensions to be utilised by the PHPP for each scenario.

is a measurement of how much solar heat gain is admitted through the glass. Refer to Chapter 2, Key Principles for further explanation.

For the PHPP to calculate the U_w, information about the window glazing U_g and frame U_f must be inputted in the 'Components' worksheet.

The frame-to-glazing ratio and individual glazing unit sizes, when taken in conjunction with the U_f/U_g and glazing g-value, are what affect window performance.

If the exact make and manufacturer of the window is unknown at this stage, the example certified window types (already in the PHPP) can be used.

These should then be updated as soon as the exact specification is known.

Remember, as explained in Key Principle 3, certified window frames are often the most expensive option and a lot of certified Passive House projects use cheaper uncertified windows, which, with good installation details, can meet performance requirements. Window data is calculated to agreed universal metrics so certification is not needed for data to be valid for use in PHPP. However, getting accurate glazing data for non-certified products can be harder – data is normally quoted to one decimal place, but PHPP requires two defining positions, for values <1 this requires two decimal places eg 0.62, for values >1, one decimal place is sufficient eg 1.2.

Note also that laminated glass is common in the UK and has a higher U-value and lower g-value than equivalent toughened glass units.

For curtain walls where a glazing unit is surrounded on all sides by other glazing units, the frame should be included at half its total width. Note: this does not apply to units which have at least one side (right, left, head or sill) adjacent to the building. For more details on curtain walling refer to the technical manual.

g-Value

This value is a measure of the solar heat energy that the glazing allows through. This is a percentage value. Common g-values are around 0.5, meaning 50% of the solar heat hitting the outer surface of the glass penetrates the glass and enters the building.

U_g-Value

This value is a measure of heat transfer (loss or gain) through the glass only. This is not the same as a whole window U-value (U_w).

U_f-Value

This value is a measure of the heat transfer (loss or gain) through the frame. This is not the same as a whole window U-value (U_w). If unsure contact the window manufactures.

Glazing				Glazing
	Recommended glazing type to start planning:			
	Triple thermally insulated glazing (Please consider the comfort criterion!)			
ID	Description		g-Value	U_g-Value
				W/(m²K)
01ud	All Internorm KF410 Glazing		0.62	0.51
02ud	Laminated Glazing		0.59	0.54
03ud				
10ud				
	Certified Passive House components:			
	(gl: glazing) Glazing, certified:			
0665gl03	AGC - iplus Advanced 1.0 (4:/10/4/10/:4 Kr 90%)		0.42	0.51
0666gl03	AGC - iplus Advanced 1.0 (4:/12/4/12/:4 Kr 90%)		0.42	0.44
0667gl03	AGC - iplus Advanced 1.0 (4:/14/4/14/:4 Ar 90%)		0.42	0.59

Alternatively PHPP provides lists of certified glazing and frames which, if applicable, or early in the design process (and this information is not known), can be selected. Be careful here not to select the best performing glazing and frames if it is unlikely these can be included in the project budget. This will just cause problems when the lower performing components are substituted.

Window frames

ID	Description	U_f-Value				Frame width				Glazing edge thermal bridge				Installation thermal bridge				Curtain wall facades:
		left	right	bottom	above	left	right	bottom	above	$\Psi_{Glazing\,edge}$ left	$\Psi_{Glazing\,edge}$ right	$\Psi_{Glazing\,edge}$ bottom	$\Psi_{Glazing\,edge}$ top	$\Psi_{installation}$ left	$\Psi_{installation}$ right	$\Psi_{installation}$ bottom	$\Psi_{installation}$ top	χ_{GC} -value Glass carrier
		W/(m²K)	W/(m²K)	W/(m²K)	W/(m²K)	m	m	m	m	W/(mK)	W/(mK)	W/(mK)	W/(mK)	W/(mK)	W/(mK)	W/(mK)	W/(mK)	W/K
01ud	Render Opening (blind) Internorm KF410	0.85	0.85	0.85	0.85	0.113	0.113	0.113	0.113	0.031	0.031	0.031	0.031	0.011	0.011	0.023	0.076	
02ud	Render Opening Internorm KF410	0.85	0.85	0.85	0.85	0.113	0.113	0.113	0.113	0.031	0.031	0.031	0.031	0.011	0.011	0.023	0.013	
03ud	Timber Opening (blind) Internorm KF410	0.85	0.85	0.85	0.85	0.113	0.113	0.113	0.113	0.031	0.031	0.031	0.031	0.014	0.014	0.011	0.109	
04ud	Timber Opening Internorm KF410	0.85	0.85	0.85	0.85	0.113	0.113	0.113	0.113	0.031	0.031	0.031	0.031	0.014	0.014	0.011	0.043	
05ud	Render FIXED (blind) Internorm KF410	0.85	0.85	0.85	0.85	0.076	0.076	0.076	0.076	0.031	0.031	0.031	0.031	0.011	0.011	0.023	0.076	
06ud	Render FIXED Internorm KF410	0.85	0.85	0.85	0.85	0.076	0.076	0.076	0.076	0.031	0.031	0.031	0.031	0.011	0.011	0.023	0.013	
07ud	Timber FIXED (blind) Internorm KF410	0.85	0.85	0.85	0.85	0.076	0.076	0.076	0.076	0.031	0.031	0.031	0.031	0.014	0.014	0.011	0.109	
08ud	Timber FIXED Internorm KF410	0.85	0.85	0.85	0.85	0.076	0.076	0.076	0.076	0.031	0.031	0.031	0.031	0.014	0.014	0.011	0.0	
09ud																		
10ud																		
	Certified Passive House components:																	
	(wi: window) Windows, certified:																	
0719wi	ACO Severin Ahlmann GmbH & Co. KG - AC	0.80	0.80	0.80	0.80	0.125	0.125	0.125	0.125	0.028	0.028	0.028	0.028	0.040	0.040	0.040	0.040	
0784wi	Alcoa Architectuursystem an - Alcoa RT 82 H	0.79	0.79	0.79	0.79	0.116	0.116	0.116	0.116	0.027	0.027	0.027	0.027	0.040	0.040	0.040	0.040	
0777wi	Alumil S.A. - S91 - SWISSPACER Ultimate	0.78	0.78	0.78	0.78	0.178	0.178	0.178	0.178	0.025	0.025	0.025	0.025	0.040	0.040	0.040	0.040	

Window frames

Frame Dimensions (m)
The accuracy of these is important.

There are two thermally weak points in a window, one is where the glazing unit meets the window frame (Ψ_{spacer}) and the second is where the window frame meets the building ($\Psi_{installation}$). The Ψ_{spacer} must be obtained from the window manufacturer. The $\Psi_{installation}$ must be assessed from the detailed project drawings. In the first instance this can be set at 0.040W/(mK), with the understanding it will be corrected later in the process. This is covered in detail in chapter 5.

Figure 3.31 *'Components' worksheet PHPP9, windows*

3.6.2 Components – standard heat recovery ventilation

There are two different options for how to provide ventilation in a Passive House building. The first option is through a stand-alone heat recovery ventilation unit (MVHR). The second option is as part of a compact unit that also provides heating and hot water. Only one of these options will be used in a project. Therefore, the user is only required to complete either the table labelled 'Ventilation units with heat recovery' or 'Passive House compact unit with exhaust air heat pump'.

Most UK Passive Houses use the stand-alone option. Many of the PHI-certified compact units are not approved for UK unvented hot water regulations, so not available to us. Also at the time of writing, stand-alone units are a more cost-effective option in the UK.

As with the windows, PHI has supplied data for a large number of certified units, covering a variety of capacities, and this data is pre-entered into this worksheet. The user only has to provide additional information if the unit being used is not on the list provided.

Here the situation is different from windows because non-certified MVHR units are corrected by a 12

percentage point reduction on efficiency – therefore it is normally the case that certified units are used.

3.6.3 Components – compact unit with exhaust air heat pump

As with the standard units, the PHPP has a number of compact units pre-entered into the worksheet. If adding in a new unit, follow the instructions provided in the technical manual. It can be useful to send the PHPP worksheet to the manufacturer and ask them to insert the relevant data into the worksheet, or the project M&E consultant may be happy to help with this. If a third party is inserting data, it is important to check this and make sure it complies with the PHI requirements. If in doubt send the details to the certifier for clarification.

3.6.4 Shower drain-water heat recovery

This new section in PHPP9 contains data on systems that recover heat from drain-water, usually from a shower. There are pre-entered systems or users can enter their own, using data from the manufacturer. Once the system is in this worksheet, it will be available for selection in the 'DHW+Distribution' worksheet, covered in Chapter 5.

3.7 Windows

The 'Windows' worksheet:

- records information about the geometry of the windows
- records the relationship of each window within the building
- assigns windows to heat loss areas recorded in the 'Areas' worksheet
- orientation is taken from the 'Areas' worksheet, making it very important that this information is entered accurately
- allows each window to be assigned properties from the 'Components' worksheet.
- provides a graphical summary of the energy balance (losses and gains) for each facade orientation of the building

- provides recommended installed window U-values based on the certification comfort criteria
- provides confirmation of compliance with the comfort criteria for each window

As explained in the Key Principles, windows have a huge influence on the energy balances in a Passive House. Making accurate inputs in this section is extremely important.

COMMON MISTAKES

Entering multiple casement windows in a single row

The PHPP needs to understand the proportion of frame to glass for every window. If a single opening is made up of more than one window, enter each window in a new row. If there are multiple windows that are exactly the same and experience the exact same shading, each window does not need its own row, as there is the provision for listing the quantity of each window type. But remember windows with the same aspect on different floors will experience different shading so must be entered in separate rows.

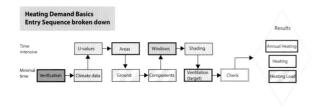

Figure 3.32 *Heating Demand Basics – windows*

In new buildings dimensions should be actual window dimensions.
In renovations (EnerPHits) dimensions can be taken to structural openings.

Unlike SAP, each individual window light must be entered separately. So a single "window" with a fixed light and opening light has to be entered into PHPP as two windows.

Note the g-value and u-value of safety glass is likely to differ from standard glass

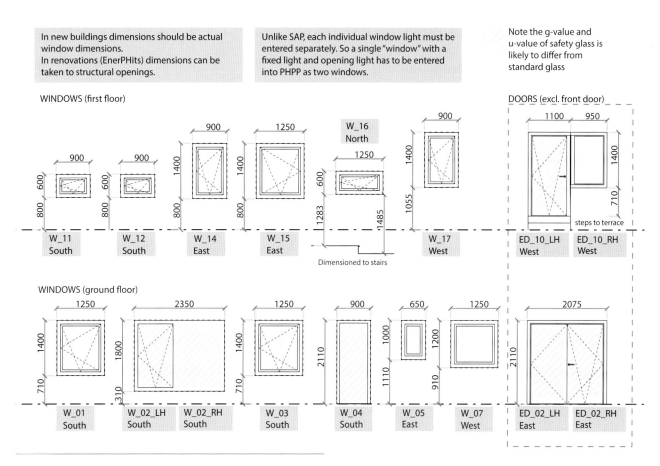

Figure 3.33 *Case study house PHPP window schedule*

Quantity will be '1' unless there are multiple windows with same dims and shading.

Use a clear labeling method that matches an annotated drawing file as this helps both the user and the assessors.

Orientations are listed as a deviation from north (refer to figure 3.13) – this information is auto-filled based on entries on the 'Areas' worksheet once the 'Installed In' column is completed.

These cells auto-fill based on the data inserted into the 'Components' worksheet.

90° vertical

45°

Inclination is the angle of the window in the building, as above this is auto-filled based on the entries on the 'Areas' worksheet.

0° horizontal

Window dimensions (m) (refer to figure 3.33).

Select the building (heat transfer) element where the window is installed.

The glazing and frame types are assigned from these drop-down menus, which link to the 'Components' worksheet (refer to figure 3.31).

Go to glazing list   Go to window frames list

Quantity	Description	Deviation from north	Angle of inclination from the horizontal	Orien- tation	Window rough openings		Installed in	Glazing	Frame	g-Value	U-Value		Ψ Glazing edge
					Width	Height	Selection from 'Areas' worksheet	Selection from 'Components' worksheet	Selection from 'Components' worksheet	Perpendicular radiation	Glazing	Frames (avg.)	$\Psi_{Glazing\,ed}$ (Avg.)
		°	°		m	m		Sort: AS LIST	Sort: AS LIST	-	W/(m²K)	W/(m²K)	W/(mK)
	Ground Floor												
1	W_4A_01	165	90	South	1.250	1.400	3-South Wall	07ud All Internorm KF410 Glazing	02ud Render Opening Internorm KF410	0.62	0.51	0.85	0.031
1	W_4A_02_LH	165	90	South	1.250	1.800	3-South Wall	08ud Laminated Glazing	02ud Render Opening Internorm KF410	0.59	0.54	0.85	0.031
1	W_4A_02_RH	165	90	South	1.100	1.800	3-South Wall	08ud Laminated Glazing	06ud Render FIXED Internorm KF410	0.59	0.54	0.85	0.031
1	W_4A_03	165	90	South	0.900	2.110	3-South Wall	08ud Laminated Glazing	02ud Render Opening Internorm KF410	0.59	0.54	0.85	0.031
1	W_4A_04	165	90	South	1.250	1.400	3-South Wall	07ud All Internorm KF410 Glazing	02ud Render Opening Internorm KF410	0.62	0.51	0.85	0.031
1	ED_4A_02_LH	75	90	East	1.038	2.110	2-East Wall	08ud Laminated Glazing	01ud Render Opening (blind) Internorm KF410	0.59	0.54	0.85	0.031
1	ED_4A_02_RH	75	90	East	1.038	2.110	2-East Wall	08ud Laminated Glazing	01ud Render Opening (blind) Internorm KF410	0.59	0.54	0.85	0.031
1	W_4A_05	75	90	East	0.600	1.000	2-East Wall	07ud All Internorm KF410 Glazing	06ud Render FIXED Internorm KF410	0.62	0.51	0.85	0.031

Heating degree hours [kKh/a]:   66.8

This section allows the PHPP to understand the position of each window in the opening. '0' means the window is adjacent to another window, '1' means it is adjacent to part of the building.

These cells auto-fill based on the data inserted into the 'Components' worksheet

This new PHPP9 tool provides recommended installed Uw values for four different window positions based on the climate data and comfort criteria.

This is the design temperature the PHPP is basing its recommendations above on, taken from the climate data.

Figure 3.34 *'Windows' worksheet PHPP9*

New section in PHPP9

This section will mark red any windows that do not meet the comfort criteria.

It makes it possible to quickly evaluate the contribution a window is making to heat gains or losses in the 'Energy Balance' column.

Note: if the window is exempt from meeting the comfort criteria, select the 'x' from the drop-down menu in the 'Exemption' column. Refer to the technical manual for further details on why a window would be exempt.

This results section provides a useful summary of the key properties for each individual window.

Design temperature [°C] (from location *)
-6 °C
[°C] User defined

recommendation for $U_{W,installed}$ [W/(m²K)]

| 0.85 | 1.00 | 1.10 | 0.64 |

Installation situation					Results				Window surface temperature indicator		
user determined value for $\Psi_{installation}$ or '1': $\Psi_{installation}$ from 'Components' worksheet '0': in the case of abutting windows											
left	right	bottom	top	$\Psi_{Installation}$ (Avg.)	Window Area	Glazing area	U_w installed	Glazed fraction per window	Comfort		Energy balance
W/(mK) or 1/0				W/(mK)	m²	m²	W/(m²K)	%	Exemption		kWh/a
1	1	1	1	0.014	1.8	1.20	0.74	69%			80
1	0	1	1	0.015	2.3	1.61	0.73	72%			118
0	1	1	1	0.015	2.0	1.56	0.72	79%			124
1	0	1	1	0.014	1.9	1.27	0.76	67%			78
1	1	1	1	0.014	1.8	1.20	0.74	69%			38
1	0	1	1	0.030	2.2	1.53	0.77	70%			-60
0	1	1	1	0.030	2.2	1.53	0.77	70%			-48
1	1	1	1	0.014	0.6	0.38	0.84	63%			-20

Entering the windows into the PHPP is easy but does take a little time. If *design*PH, the SketchUp plug-in, is being used the windows will be entered automatically. These should still be carefully checked once imported into the PHPP.

First set up a logical naming convention for the windows. **Figure 3.35** shows the schedule of windows input into the PHPP for the case study house.

It is very important to enter every glazing unit separately. Do not group windows made up of multiple casements into one window entry – this may seem like a sensible shortcut but it will result in the PHPP using a much higher glazing-to-frame ratio than is going to be possible in the final design. As the triple glazing has a higher performance than the frame, this will cause problems when the correct information is input, resulting in higher heat loses and therefore a higher heat demand.

Once the 'Components' worksheet has been completed and these properties have been assigned to the windows, this worksheet is complete. At the top of the 'Windows' worksheet there is a table with useful summaries, giving average window U-values, g-values, total glazed

COMMON MISTAKES

Over-reliance on solar gains

It can be tempting to simply increase the size of south-facing windows to lower the overall heat demand. However, this may not be a good idea as this approach can result in overheating problems. In addition, over-reliance on the solar gains puts a lot of pressure on the specification of the windows and, if late in the process a specification needs to be updated with laminated glass for example, this will reduce the solar gains and can mean the building misses the heat demand target. The energy balance charts on the 'Annual Heating' and 'Heating' worksheets help assess the balance of the solar gains (see **Figure 3.51 on p. 143**).

Also solar heat via windows is 10–20 times more expensive than gas unless that area of glass was needed for daylight or views to the south; refer to Key Principle 3.

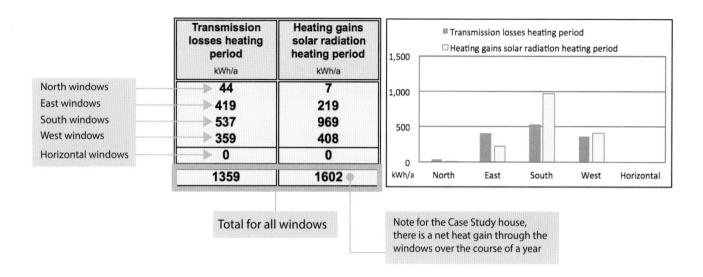

	Transmission losses heating period kWh/a	Heating gains solar radiation heating period kWh/a
North windows	44	7
East windows	419	219
South windows	537	969
West windows	359	408
Horizontal windows	0	0
	1359	1602

Total for all windows

Note for the Case Study house, there is a net heat gain through the windows over the course of a year

Figure 3.35 *'Windows' worksheet PHPP9, summary*

area, etc. There is also a helpful table and graph summarising the heating degree hours (see **Figure 3.35**). This gives the total transmission (heat) losses and solar (heat) gains for each façade orientation in the building. This is a good reference point when assessing the proportion of glazing in the building.

For example, if the space heating demand/heat load for the building does not achieve Passive House levels, it is easy and quick to understand which windows are contributing to overall gains or to overall losses by referring to these tools.

3.8 Shading

The 'Shading' worksheet:

* records elements that shade the glazed areas of the building

The following shading elements are considered by the PHPP:

1. horizontal obstructions in front of a glazed unit such as landscape, buildings, etc. (Horizontal Shading r_H)
2. vertical window reveals or protrusions from the building (Vertical Shading r_R)
3. overhangs such as balconies (Overhang Shading r_O)

4. additional (Other) shading elements, including, for example, partial shading from balcony railings, screens, trees, etc. (Other Shading r_{other})
5. temporary shading (z) i.e. retractable blinds.

The shading factor is representative of the percentage of solar radiation reaching the glazed surface past the shading element, not the percentage of shading. So a shading factor of 100% means there is no shading, i.e. 100% of the solar radiation is reaching the window. A shading factor of 0% means there is complete shading, i.e. no solar radiation is reaching the glazed surface. This can be a little confusing so refer back to this note the first few times shading data is entered (or hover over the PHPP cells with the red tabs). If no entry is made in this worksheet the PHPP assumes a default figure of 75% – so when a small amount of shading is inserted the shading can actually reduce from the PHPP default position, with the result that the heating demand figure will go down.

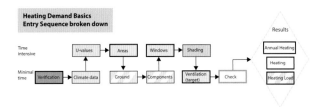

Figure 3.36 *Heating demand basics – shading*

Figure 3.37 *(opposite) With shading horizontal obstructions*

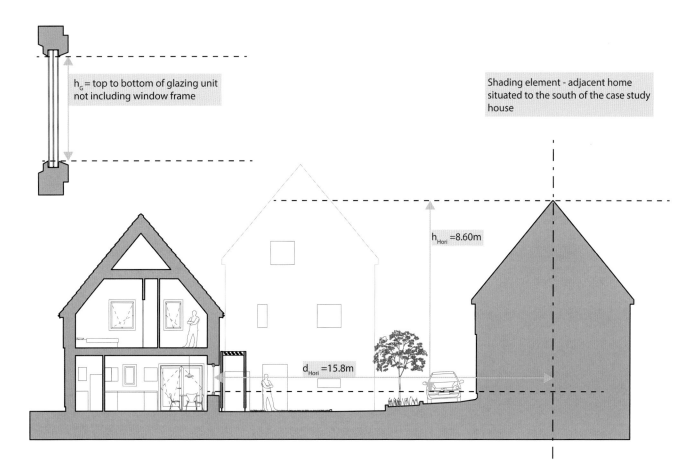

h_G = top to bottom of glazing unit not including window frame

Shading element - adjacent home situated to the south of the case study house

h_{Hori} =8.60m

d_{Hori} =15.8m

Winter/heating period shading

Items 1–4 above provide the information for the PHPP to calculate the total shading factor during the heating period, referred to by the PHPP as the r_S.

If *design*PH is being used the heating period shading elements will automatically be transferred into the PHPP. But remember, all shading elements must be modelled in the SketchUp file for this to work. The shading has to be inputted manually if *design*PH is not being used.

1. Horizontal obstructions in front of a glazed unit such as landscape, buildings, etc. (Horizontal Shading r_H)

For this shading element the PHPP requires three measurements:

(i) the height of the shading objects (h_{Hori}) (this is measured from the bottom edge of the glazing unit, not from the external ground level)
(ii) the distance of the shading objects from the glazed unit (d_{Hori})
(iii) the height of the glazed unit (h_G), (PHPP takes this automatically from the 'Windows' worksheet).

The evaluation of the shading objects is open to some interpretation. Here is an explanation for the methodology used for the Case Study house. To establish what to include in the calculation, lines were extended at 45° from either side of the windows.

2. Vertical window reveals or protrusions from the building (Vertical Shading r_R)

For this shading element the PHPP requires two measurements:

(i) the average reveal depth (o_{reveal}) (This is measured from the external glazed surface to the outer edge of the reveal)
(ii) the average frame depth (d_{reveal}) (this is measured from the edge of the glazing to the edge of the reveal. Note that this is an average measurement, and in a casement scenario the distance varies greatly to either side, as shown in **Figure 3.38**).

Figure 3.38 *(opposite) With shading vertical window reveal obstructions*

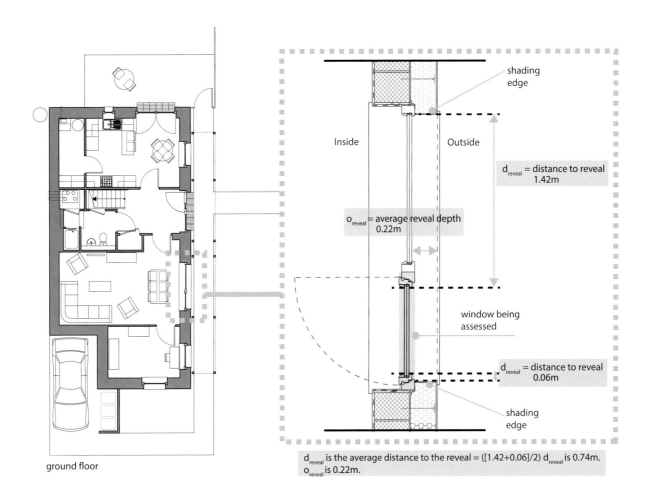

shading edge

Inside

Outside

d_{reveal} = distance to reveal 1.42m

o_{reveal} = average reveal depth 0.22m

window being assessed

d_{reveal} = distance to reveal 0.06m

shading edge

ground floor

d_{reveal} is the average distance to the reveal = ([1.42+0.06]/2) d_{reveal} is 0.74m. o_{reveal} is 0.22m.

3. Overhangs such as balconies (Overhang Shading r_O)

For this shading element the PHPP requires three measurements:

(i)   the distance over the glazing (d_{over}) (this is measured from the external glazed surface to the lower edge of the overhang)

(ii) the overhang length from the glazing (o_{over}) (this is measured from the edge of the glazing to the outside edge of the overhang)

(iii) the height of the glazing unit (PHPP takes this automatically from the 'Windows' worksheet).

4. Additional (Other) shading elements, including, for example, partial shading from balcony railings, screens, foliage, etc. (Other Shading r_{other})

This is a user-defined figure.

For the Carrowbreck home the following shading factors were added:

- brise soleil
- neighbouring trees, factoring in the shading contribution from these in the summer and winter for the east, south and west windows.

COMMON MISTAKES

It is difficult to get the shading 100% correct in the PHPP

It can be tempting to be overly conservative and overestimate the shading. However, this is not a good idea as it can hide potential overheating issues. It is recommended that careful attention is paid to the information provided in the technical manual on shading, in addition to the information provided here. As long as a reasonable assessment is made for the shading, it is likely that assessors will be in agreement.

The entry in the PHPP is a single percentage per window. If more than one shading element exists the percentage should account for all shading elements.

Figure 3.39 *(opposite) With shading overhangs such as window heads*

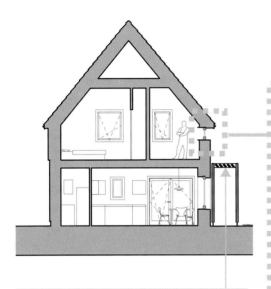

The brise soleil can be dealt with in two ways: it can be added to the overhang shading with an adjustment for the fact is it partially open, or it can be added under additional shading.

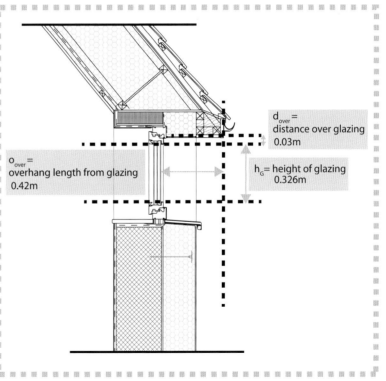

d_{over} = distance over glazing 0.03m

o_{over} = overhang length from glazing 0.42m

h_G = height of glazing 0.326m

125

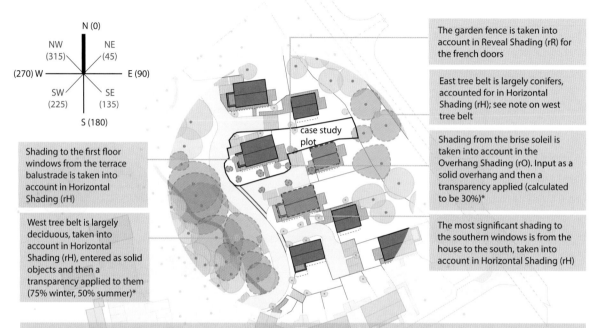

The garden fence is taken into account in Reveal Shading (rR) for the french doors

East tree belt is largely conifers, accounted for in Horizontal Shading (rH); see note on west tree belt

Shading from the brise soleil is taken into account in the Overhang Shading (rO). Input as a solid overhang and then a transparency applied (calculated to be 30%)*

Shading to the first floor windows from the terrace balustrade is taken into account in Horizontal Shading (rH)

The most significant shading to the southern windows is from the house to the south, taken into account in Horizontal Shading (rH)

West tree belt is largely deciduous, taken into account in Horizontal Shading (rH), entered as solid objects and then a transparency applied to them (75% winter, 50% summer)*

case study plot

*Trees and other shading objects with transparency – judgment is required here.

Some designers and certifiers use algorithms that can be copied into the PHPP to assist modeling shading objects with transparency (trees, fences, brise soleils). These algorithms allow designers to enter the shading objects in as if solid in the Horizontal Shading (rH) or Overhang Shading (rO) fields and then apply a transparency. This was the method used in the Case Study due to the significant impact of the trees on this heavily wooded site.

Alternatively, a cumulative shading reduction factor can be entered in the Additional Shading column. Certifiers will require a record of how this has been arrived at. Many designers will use additional software to aid in this assessment: designPH can be used for this, see chapter 6.

Figure 3.40 *Considerations for Additional (Other) shading elements*

Summer/cooling period shading

The PHPP has provision for two entries for the summer shading:

1. additional (Other) shading elements, including, for example, partial shading from balcony railings, screens, foliage, etc. (Other Shading r_{other})
2. temporary shading reduction factor (z). This allows the PHPP to consider temporary shading from blinds, shutters, etc.

1. Additional (Other) shading elements, including, for example, partial shading from balcony railings, screens, foliage, etc. (Other Shading r_{other})

Refer to the notes for the heating season. It is worth noting that the shading factor for the r_{other} summer column is often used to take into account shading from trees, which is more significant in the summer when deciduous trees are in full leaf, giving a lower reduction factor than in the r_{other} winter column. Remember, 100% is zero shading and 0% is total shading.

2. Temporary shading reduction factor (z). This allows the PHPP to consider temporary shading from blinds, shutters, etc.

Shading factors inserted here are for the shading devices in their closed position. As above, this is a user-defined figure. It is important that the shading is inserted here to prevent summer overheating. And it is important that this shading is practical and easy to use in reality. It can be worth looking at using automatic controls so that the building does not overheat when users are not available to control shading devices. If automatic systems are designed into the building, user overrides should be easy to operate, to give building users control over their environment.

The shading reduction factor varies depending on the position of the device; a shading device on the outside of the glazing will have a bigger effect on reducing solar gains and therefore overheating than a shading device positioned inside the glazing.

Some example temporary shading reduction factors (z) for triple low-e glazing taken from the technical manual are:

Roller blinds (internal)	60% (white) 80% (grey)
Roller blinds (external)	24% (white) 12% (grey)
Venetian blinds set at 45° (internal)	75%
Venetian blinds set at 45° (external)	10%

Remember 100% = no shading and 0% = total shading

In practice, solar shading devices are not always used by occupants. PHPP9 automatically makes an allowance for this. In previous versions of PHPP designers had to make this adjustment themselves. PHPP9 provides for two scenarios: the standard scenario assumes only a 70% use of shading devices; scenario two increases this to 80% for automatically controlled shading and/or where shading can be in use but views to the outside maintained. It is worth noting that manual shading is often preferred in residential buildings where occupants like to feel in control of their environment. To utilise scenario two, the 'x' must be selected from the drop-down menu in column AI on the 'Shading' worksheet.

For other less common shading scenarios refer to the technical manual for additional guidance.

In the Case Study house there are fixed brise soleil as well as external venetian blinds, which are controlled manually. Research has shown over a range of UK projects that occupants tend to use external blinds as privacy blinds and not for the control of overheating, significantly reducing their effectiveness. As a result of this, reliance on operable shading devices to control overheating in residential buildings is not always the best option in the UK. Whenever external blinds are provided, occupants must be given support to properly understand how to optimally use these.

Figure 3.41 *'Shading'*
worksheet PHPP9,
shading inputs and
results

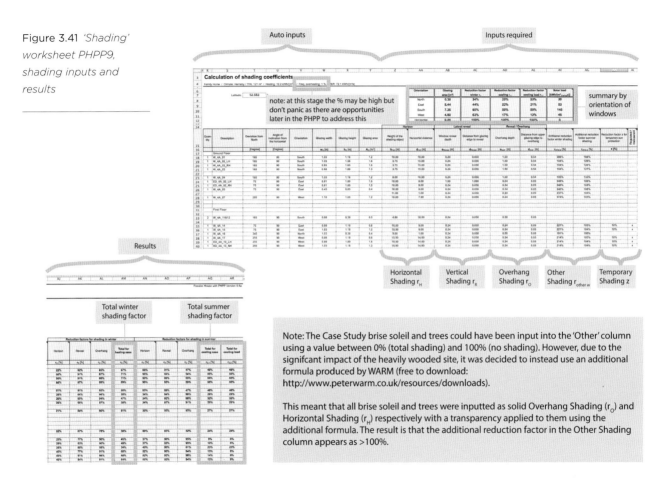

Note: The Case Study brise soleil and trees could have been input into the 'Other' column using a value between 0% (total shading) and 100% (no shading). However, due to the signifcant impact of the heavily wooded site, it was decided to instead use an additional formula produced by WARM (free to download: http://www.peterwarm.co.uk/resources/downloads).

This meant that all brise soleil and trees were inputted as solid Overhang Shading (r_O) and Horizontal Shading (r_H) respectively with a transparency applied to them using the additional formula. The result is that the additional reduction factor in the Other Shading column appears as >100%.

3.9 Ventilation

The 'Ventilation' worksheet:

- records details on the ventilation flow based on the extract and supply requirements

- calculates the MVHR efficiency including losses through the external supply and extract ductwork, based on designed ductwork

- records the airtightness of the building (if at design stage, this is assumed to be the maximum allowed for Passive House certification)

- records the exposure of the building on the site.

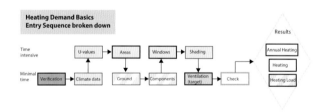

Figure 3.42 *Heating Demand Basics – ventilation*

It is essential to complete this worksheet before any results can be read on the 'Verification' worksheet. This worksheet can be filled in at an early stage in the design process using some generalised norms but it is necessary to return to this worksheet with more accurate data as soon as it becomes available.

For social housing projects it is important to base the ventilation rates on the expected occupancy as this will tend to be roughly 50% more than PHPP assumes. Certification is normally based on actual commissioned ventilation rates and higher ventilation rates increase the heating and cooling demand.

To complete this worksheet designers should first complete the 'Final Protocol Worksheet – Ventilation'. This worksheet is not part of the main PHPP file but can be found in the 'PHPP Tools' folder provided with all PHPP purchases. This is a good point for collaboration. If there is an energy consultant or services engineer working on the project they will be able to provide useful information here. They may also be able to complete this worksheet for the project. It should be noted that these worksheets provide only a rough assessment of the size of

Figure 3.43 *First half of 'Ventilation' worksheet, PHPP9*

Select the type of ventilation system from the drop-down menu

Insert wind protection coefficient e and f, refer to the table above

Air test result, assume 0.6 h⁻¹ unless the test result is available.

Select the type of ventilation system by typing an 'x' in the relevant box

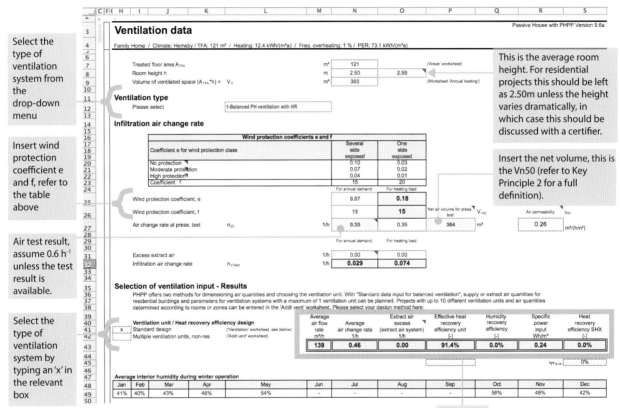

Passive House with PHPP Version 9.6a

Ventilation data

Family Home / Climate: Hemsby / TFA: 121 m² / Heating: 12.4 kWh/(m²a) / Freq. overheating: 1 % / PER: 73.1 kWh/(m²a)

Treated floor area A_{TFA}	m²	121		('Areas' worksheet)
Room height h	m	2.50	2.50	
Volume of ventilated space (A_{TFA}*h) = V_V	m³	303		(Worksheet 'Annual heating')

Ventilation type

Please select   1-Balanced PH ventilation with HR

Infiltration air change rate

Wind protection coefficients e and f		Several side exposed	One side exposed
Coefficient e for wind protection class			
No protection		0.10	0.03
Moderate protection		0.07	0.02
High protection		0.04	0.01
Coefficient f		15	20

			For annual demand:	For heating load:
Wind protection coefficient, e			0.07	0.18
Wind protection coefficient, f			15	15
Air change rate at press. test	n_{50}	1/h	0.35	0.35

Net air volume for press. test V_{n50} 364   m³

Air permeability q_{50} 0.26   m³/(hm²)

		For annual demand:	For heating load:
Excess extract air	1/h	0.00	0.00
Infiltration air change rate	$n_{V,Res}$ 1/h	0.029	0.074

Selection of ventilation input - Results

PHPP offers two methods for dimensioning air quantities and choosing the ventilation unit. With "Standard data input for balanced ventilation", supply or extract air quantities for residential buildings and parameters for ventilation systems with a maximum of 1 ventilation unit can be planned. Projects with up to 10 different ventilation units and air quantities determined according to rooms or zones can be entered in the 'Addl vent' worksheet. Please select your design method here:

Ventilation unit / Heat recovery efficiency design

		Average air flow rate m³/h	Average air change rate 1/h	Extract air excess (extract air system) 1/h	Effective heat recovery efficiency unit [-]	Humidity recovery efficiency [-]	Specific power input Wh/m³	Heat recovery efficiency SHX [-]
x	Standard design ('Ventilation' worksheet, see below)							
	Multiple ventilation units, non-res ('Addl vent' worksheet)							
		139	0.46	0.00	91.4%	0.0%	0.24	0.0%

η^*_{SHX} 0%

Average interior humidity during winter operation

Jan	Feb	Mar	Apr	May	Jun	Jul	Aug	Sep	Oct	Nov	Dec
41%	40%	43%	46%	54%	-	-	-	-	56%	48%	42%

Key results

This is the average room height. For residential projects this should be left as 2.50m unless the height varies dramatically, in which case this should be discussed with a certifier.

Insert the net volume, this is the Vn50 (refer to Key Principle 2 for a full definition).

131

COMMON MISTAKES

Ventilation rates can be set too low to meet Part F

In the UK there is some confusion over the requirements for Passive House certification and the requirements of Part F of the building regulations. PHPP frequently calculates a ventilation rate of around 0.3ACH, and warns you if the rate gets over 1.5x the supply air rate. UK building regulations requires 0.43ACH $(0.3l/s/m^2)$. The building regulations standard appears to have evolved from a natural ventilation scenario for control of VOCs.

In Passive House projects the MVHR has different settings and as long as the boost or highest setting can meet the building regulation requirement this is normally sufficient. The concern with designing for building regulations rather than the lower Passive House requirement is that the building can be over-ventilated and the air can become overly dry, especially in large (i.e. less densely occupied) buildings.

ventilation unit required for the building. A specialist should always be consulted regarding the final specifications.

The PHPP supplies a separate worksheet for more detailed analysis of the ventilation set-up; this is covered in detail in Chapter 7. This should be referred to now if the project uses more than one ventilation unit. Note that it is not acceptable to enter multiple MVHRs as a single unit even if they are identical and serving identical dwellings, a pair of semi-detached houses.

Figure 3.44 *(opposite) Second half of 'Ventilation' worksheet, PHPP9*

Inputs required:
Air supply per person
Quantities must be inserted for the extract rooms
Design air flow rate

This section allows the PHPP to understand how the ventilation system is likely to be used. In early design stages the pre-set values can be used.
The first column allows insertion of the modes for the ventilation system.
The second column allows for hours to be assigned to each mode, this must total 24 hours.
The third column rates the flow of each mode in relation to its maximum output.

Select the location of the unit

Select the unit from the drop down menu

The length of the supply and exhaust ducts is measured from the edge of the MVHR unit to the edge of the wall or roof insulation.

If being used, the efficiency of the subsoil heat exchanger must be insert in here. These are less common in the UK than on the continent due to our milder winters.

This calculation must be completed for both the outdoor (supply) and exhaust duct.
For the nominal width and insulation thickness see figure 3.40.
The reflectivity and thermal conductivity relate to the duct insulation material i.e. foil backed insulation is reflective, armaflex is not.

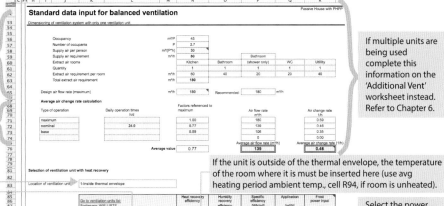

If multiple units are being used complete this information on the 'Additional Vent' worksheet instead. Refer to Chapter 6.

If the unit is outside of the thermal envelope, the temperature of the room where it is must be inserted here (use avg heating period ambient temp., cell R94, if room is unheated).

Select the power supply of the frost protection and insert the limit temperature, i.e the temperature at which the frost protection activates

Key result, the higher the better

If this is an outline PHPP the following generalised data can be used:

- Air supply per person: 30m³/(P*h) for residential projects, 15–20m³/(P*h) for schools and daycare projects, 60m³/(P*h) for a sports hall.
- Design airflow rate: this should as a minimum be equal to the sum of the extract requirements.

NB These figures relate to Passive House protocols and do not necessary comply with building regulations. All results should be cross-checked with the relevant section of building regulations.

When designing the ventilation system the duct running from the MVHR through the building fabric should be as short as possible to avoid further reductions in the efficiency of the ventilation system.

COMMON MISTAKES

MVHR details are incomplete

It is important to take into account the effect of heat loss from the MVHR's intake/exhaust ductwork. To do this the PHPP needs to know the duct length, diameter, insulation thickness and conductivity. If this information is missing the efficiency of the MVHR will be unrealistically high. Also, the assumptions sometimes made on duct insulation thickness are unrealistic and many modern MVHRs put the terminals so close together that 20mm is the maximum insulation thickness that can be installed.

Figure 3.45 *(opposite) Secondary ducting calculation for the Carrowbreck home*

MVHR units should be positioned to provide easy access for filter changes.

The PHPP is only interested in the ducts which lead from the unit through the thermal envelope. The ducts (shown dotted here) distributing the fresh air around the house and extracting the waste air back to the unit, do not need to be considered in this calculation. However, they do need to be carefully planned and installed in terms of the pressure loss of the overall system.

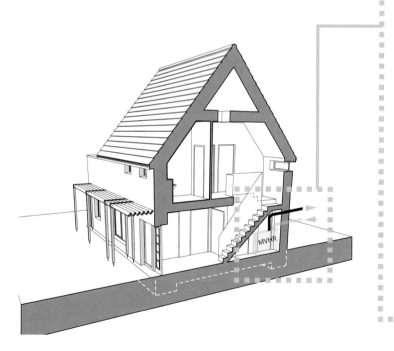

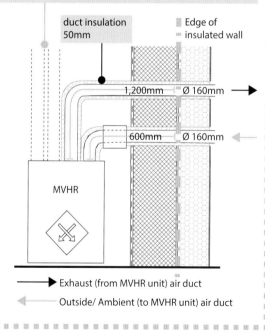

duct insulation 50mm

Edge of insulated wall

1,200mm   Ø 160mm

600mm   Ø 160mm

MVHR

MVHR

→ Exhaust (from MVHR unit) air duct

◄ Outside/ Ambient (to MVHR unit) air duct

135

3.10 Check

The 'Check' worksheet:

- is a new very helpful tool in PHPP9
- provides an overview of Error messages
- provides an overview of Plausibility warnings.

Error messages and Plausibility warnings are a couple of new and very useful tools in PHPP9, providing helpful additional guidance to both inexperienced and experienced users of PHPP. These messages and warnings allow for easy checking of the completeness and feasibility of data entries, and should now be the first port of call for designers checking through their PHPP files. They show up to the right hand side of PHPP worksheets, on the same row as the input being questioned. In addition a **red** '!' is displayed to the left hand side of the worksheet to prevent designers missing the notes to the right, as these are often off-screen. And a summary total of error messages is displayed in the top left corner of each worksheet.

The Error messages appear in **red** text; these must be addressed before the PHPP file can be completed. The Plausibility messages appear in blue text, highlighting inputs that should be double-checked before moving on. Certifiers, when evaluating the designer's PHPP, can also use these messages, as prompts for where data entries need to be questioned and justified.

The 'Check' worksheet provides one centralised location to review all of the Error and Plausibility warnings listed on the individual worksheets. Hyperlinks take you to the worksheet in question, making it easy to track down errors.

Care should be taken not to over-rely on the 'Check' worksheet to highlight errors, as it is only possible for this to pick up certain numerical errors and/

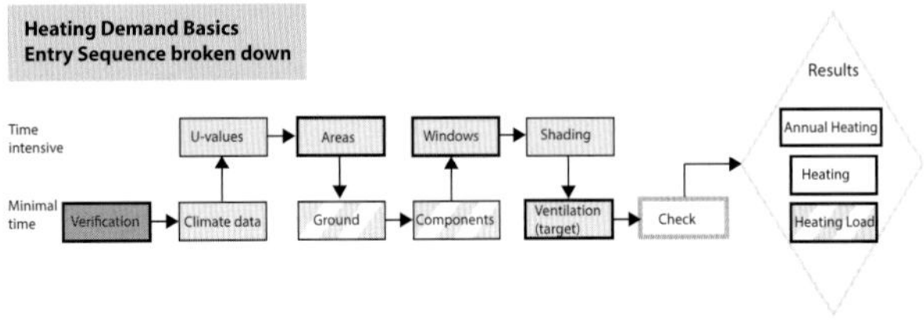

Figure 3.46 *Heating Demand Basics – check*

Figure 3.47 *(opposite) 'Check' worksheet, results PHPP9*

or omissions. In addition, to prevent all PHPP files starting with lots of Error messages the PHPP will not flag all missing data.

Error messages must be removed for a PHPP file to be certified, so when reviewing a PHPP file these messages should be addressed first. Once these Errors have all been cleared designers should work through all of the Plausibility warnings.

The 'Check' worksheet has a couple of other useful features. On row 37 there is a tool that troubleshoots why data may be missing specifically from the 'Verification' worksheet. And on row 58 there is a tool that summarises errors resulting from inputs over multiple worksheets and errors relating to the final energy balance results.

When working through the Plausibility warnings there is an opportunity to make notes against the warnings. If designers feel that their inputs are correct they should note the reasons for this to help the certifiers discharge the warnings.

Overview of errors by worksheet

Number of errors per worksheet

PHPP Check

Passive House with PHPP Version 9.6a

Family Home / Climate: Hemsby / TFA: 121 m² / Heating: 12.3 kWh/(m²a) / Freq. overheating: 1 % / PER: 64.2 kWh/(m²a)

Overview input errors

There are still 1 error message(s) in your PHPP.

Total number of errors in the PHPP workbook.

By clicking on a worksheet name designers will be taken directly to this worksheet, where they can find out more about the specific errors in the notes to the right hand side of the worksheet.

1 Error(s)

Example – one error has been found on the 'IHG' worksheet

Are results missing from 'Verification' worksheet? Possible causes can be found next

The following information is based on the energy balance calculation entered

Plausibility check

Additional tools. The Plausibility tool is particularly useful during the certification process as allows designers to make comments against the plausibility warnings that Certifiers can refer to.

'+' symbols indicate where sections can be expanded

3.11 Results

Major milestone, the preliminary results are ready! This section provides an introduction to the results worksheets.

A summary of the preliminary results can be seen on the 'Verification' worksheet.

In the results section, many of the green cells will now contain figures. The left column contains the result and the right column contains confirmation of whether the project currently meets the Passive House Evaluation Criteria (see **Figure 3.49**). It is likely (at this stage) that the overheating will be in excess of the 10% target figure. This is not yet a concern as Chapter 4 explains how to insert summer ventilation

options and how to account for windows being opened overnight for 'night purge' cooling.

If the space heating demand ($15kWh/m^2a$) and/or heat load ($10W/m^2$) is met then no major amendments are required to the design at this stage. Ideally, the space heating demand at this stage will be around $10-12kWh/(m^2a)$. If the space heating demand and/or heat load is not met at this stage it may be necessary to reconsider some of the key design moves.

If the project is very close to meeting the criteria but currently just misses the requirements, this may not be an insurmountable problem. In Chapter 7 we look at inserting thermal bridging details, windows installation details, etc. If the project is well detailed, inserting these can reduce the overall heating demand and load.

It may be worth highlighting at this stage that smaller dwellings can be harder to design to the space heating demand target than large ones because of the increased external area for a given floor area.

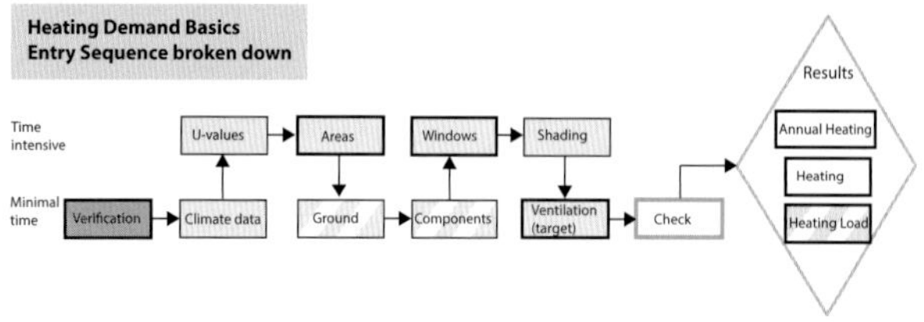

Figure 3.48 *Heating Demand Basics - results*

Figure 3.49 *(opposite) 'Verification' worksheet, results PHPP9*

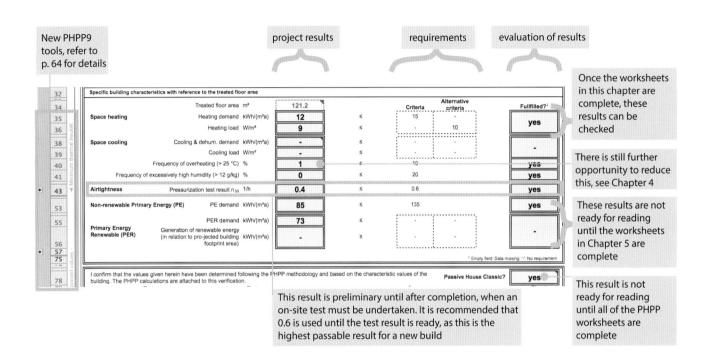

New PHPP9 tools, refer to p. 64 for details

project results

requirements

evaluation of results

Once the worksheets in this chapter are complete, these results can be checked

There is still further opportunity to reduce this, see Chapter 4

These results are not ready for reading until the worksheets in Chapter 5 are complete

This result is not ready for reading until all of the PHPP worksheets are complete

This result is preliminary until after completion, when an on-site test must be undertaken. It is recommended that 0.6 is used until the test result is ready, as this is the highest passable result for a new build

Specific building characteristics with reference to the treated floor area					Criteria	Alternative criteria		Fullfilled?[2]
	Treated floor area	m²	121.2					
Space heating	Heating demand	kWh/(m²a)	12	≤	15	-		yes
	Heating load	W/m²	9	≤	-	10		
Space cooling	Cooling & dehum. demand	kWh/(m²a)	-	≤	-	-		-
	Cooling load	W/m²	-	≤	-	-		
	Frequency of overheating (> 25 °C)	%	1	≤	10			yes
	Frequency of excessively high humidity (> 12 g/kg)	%	0	≤	20			yes
Airtightness	Pressurization test result n₅₀	1/h	0.4	≤	0.6			yes
Non-renewable Primary Energy (PE)	PE demand	kWh/(m²a)	85	≤	135			yes
Primary Energy Renewable (PER)	PER demand	kWh/(m²a)	73	≤	-	-		-
	Generation of renewable energy (in relation to pro-jected building footprint area)	kWh/(m²a)	-	≥	-	-		

² Empty field: Data missing; '-': No requirement

I confirm that the values given herein have been determined following the PHPP methodology and based on the characteristic values of the building. The PHPP calculations are attached to this verification.

Passive House Classic? **yes**

In PHPP9, for the first time the internal heat gains (IHG) reflect the increased density of power use in a small house, which helps to some extent to alleviate this problem. However, the IHG range of 2.1- 4.1 W/m2 may still be a little low for particularly small homes. This topic is covered more fully in Chapter 5.

To further understand the preliminary results now, refer to the 'Annual Heating' and 'Heating' worksheets. These two sheets provide analysis of the results. The technical manual will walk through all of the figures in more detail. These do not require further input of data; instead values are retrieved from other worksheets.

The 'Annual Heating' worksheet:

- calculates the energy balance using the annual climate data balance over the full heating period.

The 'Heating' worksheet:

- calculates the energy balance using monthly climate data to determine the sum of the monthly balances during the heating period
- takes into account the thermal storage capacity listed on the 'Verification' worksheet.

The results of the annual heating demand calculations in the two worksheets listed above are likely to be very similar. Exceptions to this do sometimes exist if the building has very high glazing percentages and/or a very low heat demand (much lower than the Passive House requirement). In these cases,

the verification method should be monthly, rather than the standard annual method. This should be discussed with the certifier.

One of the useful visual outputs is the specific heat loss, gain and heating demand graph from the 'Heating' worksheet. The graph from the case study house is copied here. The graph clearly illustrates the extent of the heating season – for this project it is from November to March (with additional tiny heat loads in October and April).

Finally, refer to the 'Heating Load' worksheet.

The 'Heating Load' worksheet:

- calculates the maximum building heat load
- provides a tool for calculating if a critical heating load situation exists for a specific room, which can be an issue when heating through the air
- this tool can only be used for Passive House buildings.

Figure 3.50 *(opposite) Energy balance from the 'Heating' worksheet, PHPP9*

From the Monthly method

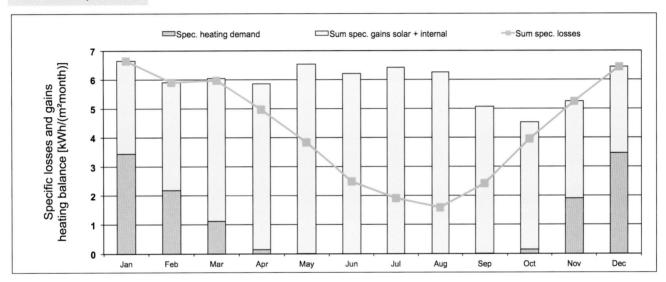

The maximum building heat load can occur in two different scenarios:

• on a cold, sunny (cloudless) day
• on a moderately cold, overcast day.

This worksheet is helpful for sizing the heating system in the building. It also comes with a tool that calculates the heating load of a particular room in a building, which is covered in Chapter 6. It is worth understanding at this point that the weather data does not account for unusually cold conditions and some scope for higher heat input should be designed in. For conventional heating system design, a room-by-room heat loss model is best used for heating sizing.

As explained in Chapter 2, if the heating load is over $10W/m^2$ then heating through the ventilation system will not be sufficient and a separate heating system will be required.

These three worksheets (Annual Heating, Heating and Heating Load) provide a huge amount of useful information about the energy balances of the building. It is important to read through the relevant sections of the technical manual (pp. 140–58) to get the most out of these PHPP worksheets.

Warm: Low Energy Building Practice, produced a useful graphical summary worksheet (PHPP WARM Results Sheet v6.06) available for free here – http://www.peterwarm.co.uk/resources/downloads/(this can added to any PHPP v8 or v9 file).

Figure 3.51 *(opposite) Losses and gains from the 'Heating' and 'Annual Heating' worksheets, PHPP9*

From the Annual method

From the Monthly method

Energy balance heating (annual method)

Energy balance heating (monthly method)

Legend:
- □ Non-useful heat gains
- □ External wall - Ambient
- ■ Roof/Ceiling - Ambient
- ■ Floor slab / Basement ceiling
- □ Windows
- □ Exterior door
- ■ Ventilation
- □ solar heat gains
- ■ internal heat gains
- ■ heating demand
- □ Heat gains TBs

Summary of the Annual Heat Demand results using each of the methods of calculation

Annual heating demand: Comparison

Monthly method	('Heating')	1505	kWh/a	12.4	kWh/(m²a) reference to treated floor area according to PHPP
Annual method	('Annual heating')	1692	kWh/a	14.0	kWh/(m²a) reference to treated floor area according to PHPP

What are these methods of calculation?

The 'monthly' method is the sum of all of the gains and losses month by month.

The 'annual' method is rather a 'heating period method', summing up the gains and losses over a period of several months, but not the whole year.

Apart from that, the sum of all gains over the respective months ('monthly' method) should closely equate to the gains in the 'annual' method, and correspondingly for the losses.

Why do they produce different results?

The reason why the heating demand differs is mainly the utilisation factor for the heat gains (briefly explained in the technical manual chapter about the annual method). The calculation of this utilisation factor can be more accurate if more information is available, as it is the case in the 'monthly' method (where the utilisation factor is calculated month by month).

In addition, there may be small differences caused by the calculation of heat losses to the ground.

143

Chapter 4

PHPP Cooling Basics

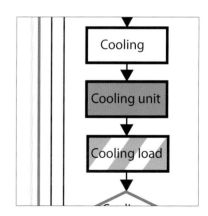

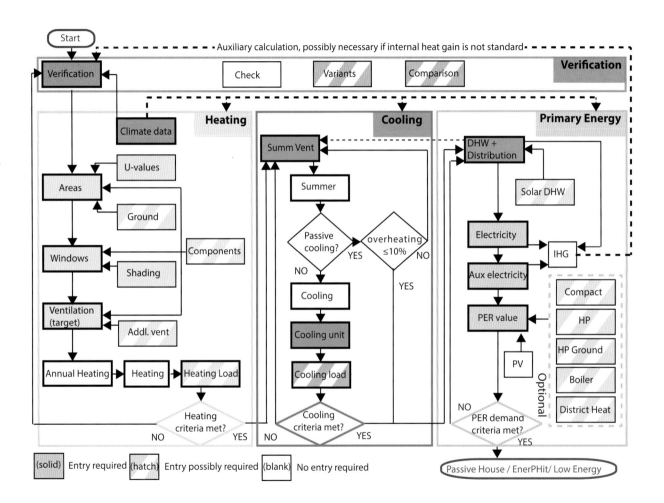

Start

Auxiliary calculation, possibly necessary if internal heat gain is not standard

Verification

Verification | Check | Variants | Comparison

Heating | **Cooling** | **Primary Energy**

Climate data

Summ Vent

DHW + Distribution

U-values

Summer

Solar DHW

Areas

Ground

Passive cooling?

overheating ≤10%

Electricity

IHG

Windows

Components

YES

NO

NO

Aux electricity

Shading

Cooling

YES

PER value

Ventilation (target)

Addl. vent

Cooling unit

PV

Compact

HP

HP Ground

Boiler

District Heat

Annual Heating | Heating | Heating Load

Cooling load

Optional

Heating criteria met?

NO   YES

Cooling criteria met?

NO   YES

PER demand criteria met?

NO   YES

Passive House / EnerPHit/ Low Energy

(solid) Entry required (hatch) Entry possibly required (blank) No entry required

This chapter explains how to input data that will allow PHPP to assess how the building performs in the summer. The chapter will inform users if the building has an overheating problem and if active cooling is required.

Residential buildings in the UK should not require active cooling. With night temperatures even in the middle of the summer dropping to around 20°C, a night-time ventilation strategy should be sufficient to remove excess warm air. The design should be reconsidered if the PHPP indicates that active cooling is required to meet the overheating criteria.

Non-residential buildings in the UK should not require active cooling unless they have specific programmatic requirements, such as laboratories. If a cooling unit is required, this chapter introduces the basics of how to add a cooling unit.

Dehumidification is often necessary in more humid climates, however this should not be a concern in the UK. For further information on dehumidification, please refer to the technical manual.

Figure 4.1 *(opposite) Cooling Basics, flow diagram worksheets*

In the UK the Passivhaus Trust published a useful guide 'Designing for Summer Comfort in the UK' (free to download here – http://howtopassivhaus.org.uk/pht-guidance-designing-summer-comfort-uk) and it is recommended that all UK designers familiarise themselves with this document when designing Passive House and other low energy buildings in the UK.

Note: The 'DHW+Distribution' worksheet (refer to Chapter 5) should be completed before a full understanding of the cooling demands is possible, as the DHW has a significant effect on overheating.

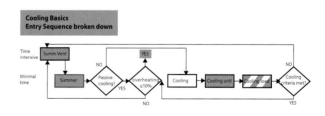

Figure 4.2 *Cooling Basics, Entry Sequence broken down*

Summer comfort without a cooling unit is normally met by following some simple guidelines (see **Figure 4.3**).

Completing the cooling section of PHPP for a medium-sized dwelling does not take long. Thus it is a good investment to complete the task early in the design process to minimise abortive design work.

COMMON MISTAKES

Over-reliance on shading and ventilation

Firstly, the overheating check in PHPP is designed around a standard building model. It is not suitable for basing design decisions for non-residential or unusual projects.

Secondly, it is important to understand that the PHPP distributes heat gains across the floor plan evenly. So when solar gains are concentrated in one area of the building it is possible that the PHPP will predict no overheating problems when some will exist.

Most importantly, the PHPP overheating check should not replace good common sense design!

Figure 4.3 *(opposite) Cooling Basics – three steps to Summer Comfort*

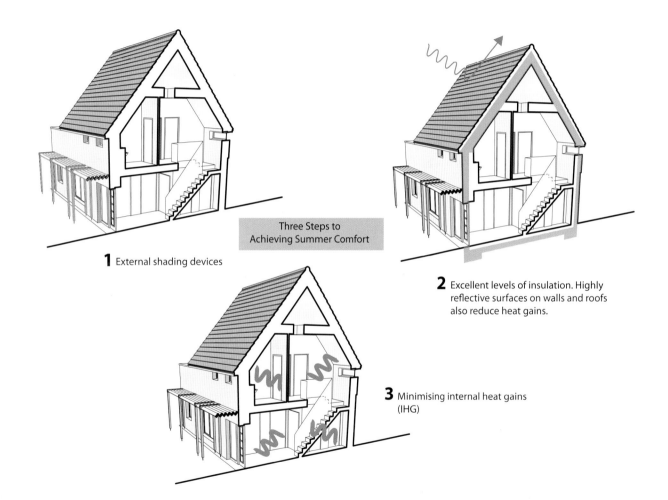

Three Steps to
Achieving Summer Comfort

1 External shading devices

2 Excellent levels of insulation. Highly reflective surfaces on walls and roofs also reduce heat gains.

3 Minimising internal heat gains (IHG)

4.1 Summer Ventilation

The 'SummVent' worksheet:

- provides PHPP with information regarding opening of windows both during the day and night

- calculates the airflow through different configurations of open windows

- calculates a daily average air change rate

- calculates the airflow through the MVHR during the summer.

This worksheet provides the user with the opportunity to test different ventilation strategies. It is important to consider how the occupants are expected to interact with these strategies and evaluate whether the planned interaction is realistic. Certain building types will be better suited to manual controls than others. Whatever strategies are incorporated into the design, it is critical that they are understood and implemented by the occupants for them to work as designed. This worksheet will confirm if a passive cooling strategy is sufficient or if a cooling unit is required.

The overheating limit should be left at 25°C. This value can be changed if the limit is known to be different for a particular building user, but for certification the limit should remain at 25°C unless otherwise agreed by the PHI.

The air change rate is an important figure. If an overly high figure is inserted it can hide potential overheating problems. This figure should be conservative. It is common that the MVHR has a summer mode that brings fresh air into the building, bypassing the heat recovery function. In this case the air change rate figure should be taken from the 'Ventilation' worksheet.

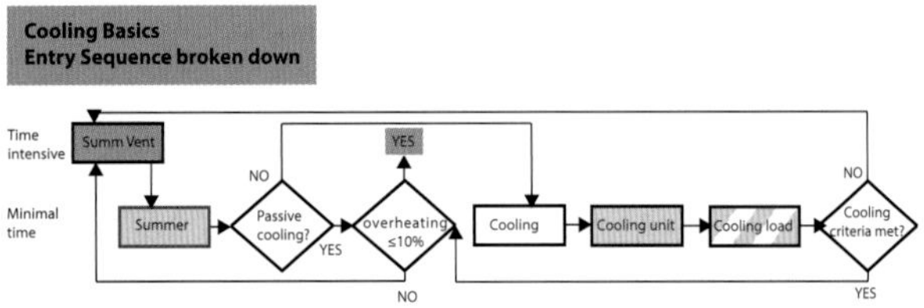

Figure 4.4 *Cooling Basics – summer vent*

Figure 4.5 *(opposite) 'Summ Vent' worksheet, PHPP9*

Typical humidity figures are provided. Use these unless the building has specific programmatic requirements that will result in non-typical humidity values.

The results section will update as progress is made through this chapter.

There are three ways to provide summer ventilation. These can be used exclusively or in combinations. This section is expanded on in figure 4.6.

This cell provides the opportunity to set a min indoor temp. for the summer. For certification set this to 22°C.

There are two ways to provide additional summer ventilation utilising the cooler temperatures at night. This section is expanded on in figure 4.6

Summer ventilation

Family Home / Climate: Hemsby / TFA: 121 m² / Heating: 12.2 kWh/(m²a) / Freq. overheating: 1 % / PER: 72.1 kWh/(m²a)

Building volume:	303	m³	Building type:	Detached, single family 4 bed home	
Max. indoor absolute humidity:	12	g/kg	Heat recovery efficiency:	91%	
Internal humidity sources:	100	g/(P*h)	Humidity recovery efficiency:	0%	
			Subsoil heat exchanger efficiency:	0%	

Results passive cooling

Frequency of overheating:	0.7%	at the overheating limit θ$_{max}$ = 25 °C
max. humidity:	12.6	g/kg
Frequency of exceeded humidity:	0.3%	

Results active cooling

Useful cooling demand:	0.6	kWh/(m²a)
Dehumidification demand:	0.0	kWh/(m²a)
Frequency of exceeded humidity:	0.3%	

Summer basic ventilation to ensure adequate air quality

1 Air change rate via vent. system with supply air: 0.35 1/h

HRV/ERV in summer (check only one field)
- None x
- Automatic bypass, controlled by temperature difference
- Automatic bypass, controlled by enthalpy difference
- Always

2 Air change rate via extract air system: 1/h   Specific power consumption (for extract air system) 0.20 Wh/m³

3 Window ventilation air change rate: 0.00 1/h

Effective air change rate

	$n_{V,system}$ 1/h		η^*_{SHX}		η_{HF}		$n_{V,equi,fraction}$ 1/h
Exterior n$_{V,e}$	0.350	*(1-	0%	)*(1-	0.91	) =	0.030
without HR	0.350	*(1-	0%	)		=	0.350
Ground n$_{V,g}$	0.350	*	0%	*(1-	0.91	) =	0.000
without HR	0.350	*	0%			=	0.000

Ventilation conductance

	V$_V$ m³		$n_{V,equi,fraction}$ 1/h		c_{Air} Wh/(m³K)			
exterior H$_{V,e}$	303	*	0.030	*	0.33	=	3.0	W/K
without HR	303	*	0.350	*	0.33	=	35.0	W/K
ground H$_{V,g}$	303	*	0.000	*	0.33	=	0.0	W/K
without HR	303	*	0.000	*	0.33	=	0.0	W/K
Infiltration, window, extract air system	303	*	0.029	*	0.33	=	2.9	W/K

Additional summer ventilation for cooling

Additional ventilation regulation
Minimum acceptable indoor temp. 22.0 °C

Type of additional ventilation

1 Window night ventilation, manual   Night ventilation value 0.10 1/h

2 Mechanical, automatically Controlled ventilation

Corresponding air change rate during operation, in addition to basic air change 1/h   Controlled by (please check)

Specific power consumption Wh/m³   Temperature diff.
Humidity diff. x

It is important to consider different user behaviour, as it is likely that the occupants will change over the lifetime of a building.

Consider whether windows should be inward or outward opening; inward opening windows with external shading can be one approach to secure night-time ventilation. Small opening sections within larger window units can be another approach to secure ventilation but this has to be carefully considered against the increased heat loss through the reduced glass-to-frame ratio.

The 'Summ-Vent' worksheet allows different strategies to be modelled and the overheating risks evaluated.

The occupants of the Case Study house did not want any windows open when the house was unoccupied. It was therefore decided to only use the background summer ventilation in combination with night purge, with no reliance on daytime window use. The house had an overheating percentage of 6.5% before the night purge window operation was added. Therefore, the implementation of additional purge ventilation was important to achieve the target of <5% overheating.

Figure 4.6 *(opposite) 'SummVent' worksheet, summer background ventilation PHPP9*

There are three ways to provide summer ventilation. These can be used exclusively or in combinations.

1. Ventilation system with supply air. In the UK this will be a supply and extract system (in warmer climates supply or extract only systems may be used, refer to the technical manual for details). The value to be entered here is the summer air change rate, see cell R76 on the 'ventilation' worksheet.

2. Extract air system. It is unlikely that this type of system would be used in the UK. If an extract only system is being used refer to the technical manual.

3. This section allows the user to incorporate daily window opening into the background ventilation strategy. The air exchange rate is calculated using the tool to the right hand side of the worksheet.

The PHPP needs to understand how the heat recovery function of the MVHR unit is regulated during the summer. Options are:

1. 'none' – heat recovery function is disabled in the summer. This is recommended for UK Passive House buildings.

2–3. If the heat recovery bypass is automatically triggered by the external and internal conditions one of these options should be selected. Refer to the technical manual for details.

4. If the heat recovery is never turned off, select this option. Note this is only recommended when the external temperature or humidity is higher than the internal all year.

Note: Most MVHR units with summer bypass used in the UK will switch automatically, always on temperature and not enthalpy.

Summer basic ventilation to ensure adequate air quality

1 — Air change rate via vent. system with supply air: 0.35 1/h

HRV/ERV in summer (check only one field)
None ... x ...1
Automatic bypass, controlled by temperature difference ...2
Automatic bypass, controlled by enthalpy difference ...3
Always ...4

2 — Air change rate via extract air system: 1/h

Specific power consumption (for extract air system) 0.20 Wh/m³

3 — Window ventilation air change rate: 0.00 1/h (cell L31)

Tools for calculating the effects of window opening to right of worksheet

This is a simple tool. For complex situations the user should either select only the most significant scenarios to include or use independent modeling software. The PHPP has two tools for calculating the effects of window opening, one for day and one for night operation.

In the UK it is good practice for the cooling strategy to work without day window opening, relying instead on the ventilation system (with heat recovery bypass) and if necessary some night purge ventilation.

However, to maintain a healthy air quality, the PHI recommend that window operation should be able to up the ventilation rate by 50% over the winter rate. So designers should test various window usage patterns to make sure this is feasible. But to prevent under-estimating any overheating it has been decided not to insert this additional ventilation into the overall calculations i.e cell L31 remains 0.

153

The additional summer ventilation in the Case Study house relies on the users opening windows manually. This was considered the most appropriate strategy, as the Case Study house is a small residential project.

Very complex ventilation scenarios can be difficult to calculate within this worksheet. Only the most significant (in terms of contribution to ventilation) combination of windows should be included in complex situations.

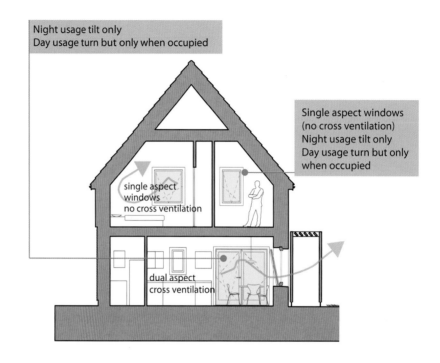

Night usage tilt only
Day usage turn but only when occupied

Single aspect windows
(no cross ventilation)
Night usage tilt only
Day usage turn but only when occupied

single aspect windows
no cross ventilation

dual aspect
cross ventilation

Figure 4.7 *(above) Case study house window airflow diagram*

Figure 4.8 *(opposite) Example window (W.1.3) clear opening diagram*

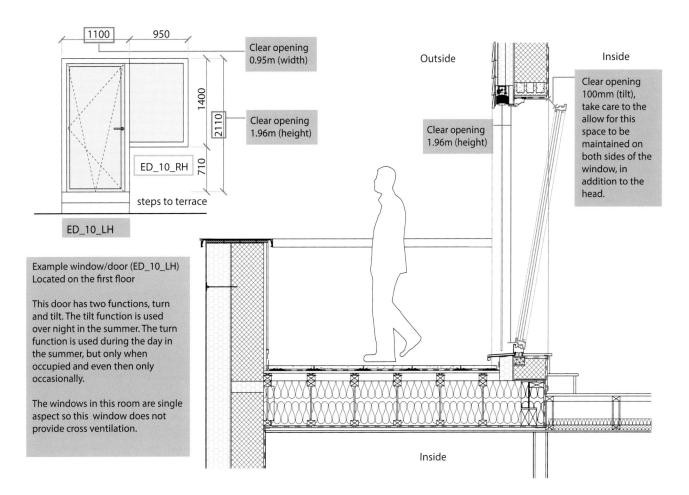

1100　　950

Clear opening
0.95m (width)

1400

2110

Clear opening
1.96m (height)

ED_10_RH

710

steps to terrace

ED_10_LH

Outside　　　　　　　　　Inside

Clear opening
100mm (tilt),
take care to the
allow for this
space to be
maintained on
both sides of the
window, in
addition to the
head.

Clear opening
1.96m (height)

Inside

Example window/door (ED_10_LH)
Located on the first floor

This door has two functions, turn
and tilt. The tilt function is used
over night in the summer. The turn
function is used during the day in
the summer, but only when
occupied and even then only
occasionally.

The windows in this room are single
aspect so this window does not
provide cross ventilation.

The external temperature drop at night in the summer can be utilised to provide thermal comfort and energy savings, instead of relying on active cooling systems. This worksheet looks at two ways to utilise this temperature drop:

1. Manual window opening
Use the secondary calculation, shown below, located to the right hand side of the worksheet to calculate this air flow. Remember that external factors such as weather, noise and security also contribute to an occupant's ability to utilise this type of cooling strategy.

2. Mechanical, automatically controlled ventilation (only consider this, if this ventilation has not already been accounted for within the summer background ventilation). Remember the ventilation system must have been designed to account for any additional summer usage. There are two ways this ventilation can be regulated, either by temperature or humidity difference.

Additional summer ventilation for cooling

Additional ventilation regulation
Minimum acceptable indoor temp. 22.0 °C

Type of additional ventilation

1 Window night ventilation, manual   Night ventilation value 0.10 1/h ◄— (cell P59)

2 Mechanical, automatically Controlled ventilation   Corresponding air change rate during operation, in addition to basic air change 1/h   Controlled by (please check)   Temperature diff.
Specific power consumption Wh/m³   Humidity diff. x

Relates to obstructions, eg an insect mesh, refer to technical manual

Defaults provided in PHPP by the PHI

Group 1 – windows on single facade

Refer to clear opening figure 4.8

Group 2 – windows located such that they result in cross ventilation with group 1

Refer to clear opening figure 4.8

Only needs completed when cross ventilation is being considered

Secondary calculation: Additional night ventilation for cooling
Air change value during additional window night ventilation

Description		Bedroom 1	Bedroom2	Bedroom 3	Bedroom 4			
Reduction factor		1	1	1	1	1	1	
Climate boundary conditions								
Temperature diff interior - exterior		1	1	1	1	1	1	K
Wind velocity		0	0	0	0	0	0	m/s
Window group 1								
Quantity		1	1	1				
Clear width		1.05	1.05	0.80				m
Clear height		1.25	1.25	1.00				m
Tilting window (check if appropriate)		x	x	x				
Opening width (for tilting windows)		0.050	0.050	0.050				m
Window group 2 (cross ventilation)								
Quantity								
Clear width								m
Clear height								m
Tilting window (check if appropriate)								
Opening width (for tilting windows)								m
Difference in height to window 1								m
Result: Night ventilation values		0.04	0.04	0.03	0.00	0.00	0.00	Total 0.10 1/h

Figure 4.9 *(opposite) 'Summ Vent' worksheet, summer additional ventilation PHPP9*

Once the 'Summ Vent' worksheet is completed, refer to the results section at the top of the worksheet to see the effect summer ventilation has had on the overall overheating percentage. If the overheating percentage is below 5% and ideally around 1% move on to the next worksheet. If the overheating is closer to, or over, 10% then some redesign is required or a cooling unit must be provided.

COMMON MISTAKES

Not taking into account actual occupancy

The summer overheating is very dependent on internal gains (IHG), which depend a lot on how many people are in the house. IHG is based on occupancy of 35m²/person. If occupancy is likely higher, e.g., only 20–30 m²/person, then check the overheating percentage with design occupancy rather than certification occupancy. To do this, insert the 'Planned Number of Occupants' on the 'Verification' worksheet (cell Q29) and select 'User-determined' from the drop-down menu.

4.2 Results – Summer Comfort

The 'Summer' worksheet:

- requires no inputs
- calculates the frequency of overheating
- provides detailed information about the summer comfort.

This worksheet provides data regarding the internal comfort conditions in the summer. No inputs are required here as this worksheet is for analysis. The result at the bottom of the worksheet, percentage of overheating, is carried over from the 'SummVent' worksheet. The table included in Figure 4.11 is adapted from the PHPP9 manual to better understand the impact this result has on occupant comfort.

COMMON MISTAKES

An overly optimistic assumption of how users will interact with the building

Consultants Warm: Low Energy Building Practice recommend running the following stress tests:

- minimum user-operated summer shading
- MVHR operating in summer at its background rate (summer bypass if fitted)
- no natural vent during the day
- 0.1ACH due to night ventilation.

If the design overheats frequently with these parameters it might be time to rethink or consider the future occupants' behaviour carefully.

It is important to consider the summer comfort at an early stage in the design as internal summer conditions are even more dependent on the size and orientation of windows, application of shading, internal heat gains and climatic region than the annual heating demand. Large east or west facing windows in particular can have a significant impact in

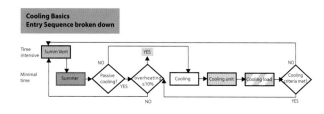

Figure 4.10 *Cooling Basics – summer*

Figure 4.11 *'Summer' worksheet*

Summer: Passive cooling

Passive House with PHPP Version 9.6a

Family Home / Climate: Hemsby / TFA: 121 m² / Heating: 12.2 kWh/(m²a) / Freq. overheating: 1 % / PER: 72.1 kWh/(m²a)

Building type:	Detached, single family 4 bed home		Treated floor area A_{TFA}:	121.2	m²
Upper temperature limit:	25	°C	Building volume:	303	m³
Nominal humidity:	12	g/kg	Internal humidity sources:	2.2	g/(m³h)
Spec. capacity:	108	Wh/(m²K)			

Building assembly	Temperature zone	Area m²		U-Value W/(m²K)		Red. factor $f_{T,summer}$		H_{summer} heat conductance
External wall - Ambient	A	215.4	*	0.097	*	1.00	=	21.0
External wall - Ground	B		*		*	1.00	=	
Roof/Ceiling - Ambient	A	134.7	*	0.093	*	1.00	=	12.5
Floor slab / Basement ceiling	B	112.0	*	0.110	*	1.00	=	12.3
	A		*		*	1.00	=	
	A		*		*	1.00	=	
	X		*		*	0.75	=	
Windows	A	26.3	*	0.773	*	1.00	=	20.3
Exterior door	A	2.4	*	0.580	*	1.00	=	1.4
Exterior TB (length/m)	A	6.3	*	0.027	*	1.00	=	0.2
Perimeter TB (length/m)	P	41.9	*	-0.009	*	1.00	=	-0.4
Ground TB (length/m)	B		*		*	1.00	=	

Exterior thermal transmittance, $H_{T,e}$	55.4	W/K
Ground thermal transmittance, $H_{T,g}$	11.9	W/K

Summer ventilation from 'SummVent' worksheet

Ventilation unit conductance			Ventilation parameter			Summer ventilation regulation	
exterior $H_{V,e}$	3.0	W/K	Temperature amplitude summer	10.2	K		HRV/ERV
without HR	35.0	W/K	Minimum acceptable indoor temperature	22.0	°C	None	x
ground $H_{V,g}$	0.0	W/K	Heat capacity air	0.33	Wh/(m³K)	Controlled by temperature	
without HR	0.0	W/K	Supply air changes	0.35	1/h	Controlled by enthalpy	
Ventilation conductance, others			Outdoor air changes	0.03	1/h	Always	
exterior	2.9	W/K	Window night ventilation air change rate, manual @ 1K	0.10	1/h	Additional ventilation	
			Air change rate due to mech. automatically controlled vent.	0.00	1/h	Controlled by temperature	
			Specific power consumption for	0.00	Wh/m³	Controlled by humidity	x
			η_{HR}	91%			
			η_{ERV}	0%			
			η^*_{ERV}	0%			

Orientation of the area	Angle factor Summer		Shading factor Summer		Shading dirt		g-Value (perp. radiation)		Area m²		Portion of glazing		Aperture m²
North	0.9	*	0.23	*	0.95	*	0.62	*	0.8	*	51%	=	0.0
East	0.9	*	0.21	*	0.95	*	0.60	*	8.0	*	68%	=	0.6
South	0.9	*	0.50	*	0.95	*	0.60	*	10.7	*	69%	=	1.9
West	0.9	*	0.13	*	0.95	*	0.60	*	6.8	*	70%	=	0.3
Horizontal	0.9	*	1.00	*	0.95	*	0.00	*	0.0	*	0%	=	0.0
Sum opaque areas													0.7

			m²/m²
Solar aperture		Total	3.6	0.03

	Specif. power q. W/m²		A_{TFA} m²		W	W/m²
Internal heat gains Q_I	3.5	*	121	=	426	3.5

Frequency of overheating $h_{\vartheta > \vartheta max}$	0.7%	At the overheating limit ϑ_{max} = 25 °C

If the "frequency over 25°C" exceeds 10%, additional measures to protect against the heat during the summer are necessary.

Daily internal temperature fluctuation

Transmission kWh/d		Ventilation kWh/d		Solar load kWh/d		1/k		Spec. capacity Wh/(m²K)		A_{TFA} m²		K
(6.8	+	6.3	+	11.3	)*	1000	/(	108	*	121	)=	1.9

For comfort it is good practice to keep the daily internal temperature fluctuation to around 2K

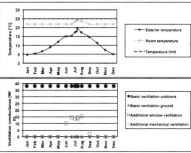

Comfort Graph

Summary of Ventilation used in project

Assessment of the Frequency of Overheating

Percentage of time temp. exceeds 25°C	Summer comfort
>15%	catastrophic
10–15%	poor
5–10%	acceptable
2–5%	good
0–2%	excellent

159

terms of overheating for UK projects and sun shading is essential for these orientations. South facing windows will generally also require some shading to ensure comfortable summer conditions.

If an active cooling unit is being added it must be designed to guarantee comfort conditions. Once mechanical cooling is selected on the 'Verification' work-sheet the overheating percentage will change to a blank cell and the cooling demand and load will be shown.

With the *Warm* stress test parameters set (on the 'Shading' and 'SummVent' worksheets) the Case Study house has an overheating percentage of around 0.7% depending on how little operation of the external blinds is assumed (increasing to 4.8% if no use is made of the external blinds). Therefore the

building should not suffer from overheating problems and does not require a cooling unit.

4.3 Cooling

The 'Cooling' worksheet:

- calculates the cooling demand (represents the heat that must be extracted from the building to obtain a comfortable temperature).

The 'Cooling' worksheet provides detailed information about the cooling demands of the building where a cooling system is to be installed. There are no inputs required on this worksheet. This worksheet is a good reference point for understanding more about the cooling requirements and how these vary over an annual cycle. Refer to the technical manual for a detailed look at the data provided on this worksheet.

The worksheet provides a useful visual aid to help users understand how their buildings perform over the course of an annual cycle. The Case Study house graph shown opposite illustrates a tiny cooling load in July and August. These months account for the 0.7% overheating. No active cooling system is required, as

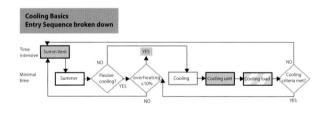

Figure 4.12 *Cooling Basics – Cooling*

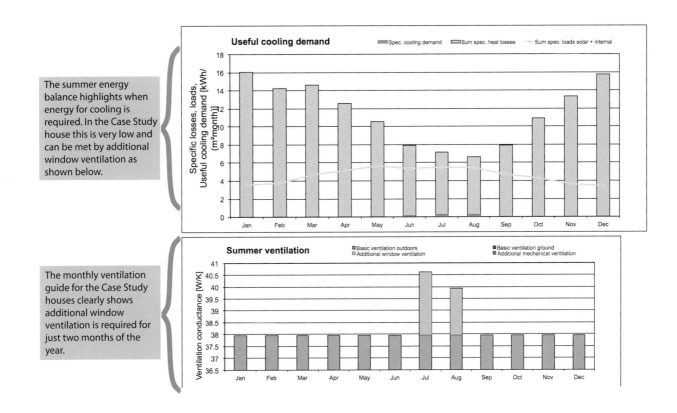

The summer energy balance highlights when energy for cooling is required. In the Case Study house this is very low and can be met by additional window ventilation as shown below.

The monthly ventilation guide for the Case Study houses clearly shows additional window ventilation is required for just two months of the year.

a 0.7% overheating figure is considered acceptable. It is important to understand that the monthly values in this graph do not necessarily correspond well with the actual in-use cooling demand due to thermal storage effects.

Figure 4.13 *(above) 'Cooling' worksheet monthly summer energy balance and monthly ventilation values*

The following sections are being touched on only briefly, as active cooling should not normally be required in the UK. Refer carefully to the technical manual before completing the following two worksheets if active cooling is being used.

4.4 Cooling Units

The 'Cooling units' worksheet:

- determines the latent energy required for dehumidification

- calculates the portion of the cooling demand met by each AC device

- covers a variety of cooling systems

- covers dehumidification (for humid climates not normally applicable to UK).

The cooling systems covered by this worksheet include:

1. simply cooling the supply air (with the supply airflow rates taken from the 'SumVent' worksheet)

2. conventional recirculating air (air from the plant room is drawn into an extra ventilator, cooled down, and blown back into the room)

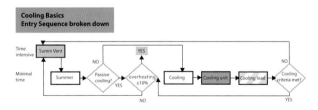

Figure 4.14 *Cooling Basics – cooling units*

COMMON MISTAKES

Assuming that using the supply air for cooling provides a similar cooling capacity to traditional AC

The supply air does not have the capacity to cool the building significantly due to the low airflows. The principle here is similar to the principle for heating through the air. When it comes to cooling, the maximum cooling load that can be delivered by the supply air is approx. $10W/m^2$ for residential buildings.

3. if no air conditioning unit is present or the capacity of points 1 and 2 above is insufficient, surface cooling (thermally activated concrete ceilings) can be used

4. dehumidification units.

If cooling is required in the UK, it is likely that simply cooling the supply air will satisfy the requirements of the building users.

It is important to take into account that the cooling unit will of course impact on cost and energy use and effort ought to be made to avoid active cooling.

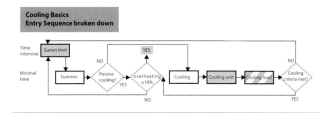

Figure 4.15 *Cooling Basics – cooling load*

4.5 Cooling Load worksheet

The 'Cooling load' worksheet:

- provides a similar function to the 'Heating load' worksheet
- calculates a daily average of the cooling capacity
- calculates a daily temperature fluctuation.

It is worth noting that for the cooling load calculations the PHPP is using daily averages and assumes the building mass can buffer the fluctuations during the day. A separate calculation is included on the 'Cooling load' worksheet to establish if the daily temperature fluctuations are over 3K – if they are, the calculated cooling load may not be sufficient.

If a cooling unit is being used, refer carefully to the technical manual before interpreting the results from this worksheet. Once the cooling criteria have been met (i.e either the cooling demand ≤15kWh/(m2a) or cooling load ≤10kWh/(m2a) if using a mechanical system or the overheating frequency is ≤10% if no mechanical system is being used) this chapter is complete. As discussed previously, although 10% is the limit for overheating it is more acceptable for this figure to be below 5% and ideally around 1%.

Chapter 5

PHPP Primary Energy Basics

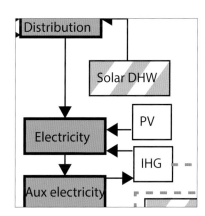

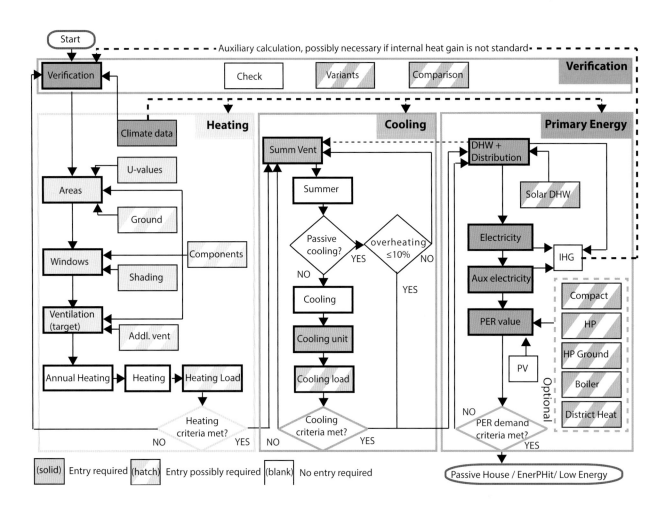

This chapter touches briefly on how to input data that will allow the PHPP to assess how much energy, in total, the building will consume. This value is referred to as either the Specific Primary Energy Demand (PE) or the Specific Primary Energy Renewable Demand (PER). The certification requirements for a Passive House are detailed in Chapter 2.

Primary Energy (PE) and Primary Energy Renewable (PER) we know from Chapter 2 include all of the energy content of the raw material from which energy delivered to the building comes, and thus it also includes the amount of energy from that source which is not delivered to the building but rather is lost in the process of distributing it from source to use, lost in conversion from one form of energy to another, and lost in short, medium, and seasonal storage (notably for PER). In addition PER is based on the specific end use in a specific climate.

It is important to understand that this differs from UK compliance tools such as SAP and SBEM. The Specific Primary Energy Demand in PHPP includes tools to estimate what are referred to as unregulated

emissions in the UK. These are normally excluded from UK compliance tool calculations.

For 'on gas' residential developments, meeting the Primary Energy (PE) requirement is straightforward. However, it can be challenging in 'off gas' situations. Meeting the PE or PER criteria can often be challenging for non-residential buildings. The efficiency of household appliances and building systems is critical to achieving a successful Passive House project.

While PER is new to PHPP9, PHI has given no indication that it will be removing the option to certify Passive House projects using the previous PE value. As such, this chapter refers to both methods of certification.

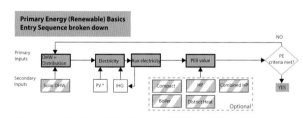

* PV worksheet also links to the Solar DHW and PER worksheets. PHPP9 also provides the opportunity to insert additional renewable energy generation such as offshore wind, refer to the technical manual for further details

Figure 5.1 *(opposite) Primary Energy Basics, flow diagram*

Figure 5.2 *Primary Energy Basics, entry sequence broken down*

This section of the PHPP gets into the more specific M&E specifications for the building. It is not the purpose of this guide to repeat the information in the technical manual and this section of the PHPP does not lend itself to diagrammatic representation. This chapter is therefore fairly brief and will direct users back to the technical manual for full instructions.

5.1 DHW+Distribution

The 'DHW+Distribution' worksheet:

- calculates the heat losses of the distribution systems for the space heating and DHW

- provides a secondary calculation to determine in detail the requirement for DHW for showers and other uses

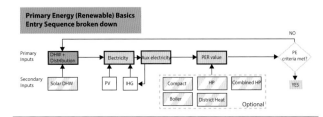

Figure 5.3 *Primary Energy Basics, DHW + Distribution*

- provides a location to input the design flow temperature and the design system heating load

- provides auxiliary tools to:
  - calculate the contribution of hot water heat recovery systems
  - account for patterns of water use in non-residential buildings.
  - calculate the heat loss of multiple storage tanks.

This worksheet has been restructured and improved for PHPP9. It is now possible to input distribution pipes with different properties separately, with five available inputs for pipework within the thermal envelope and a further five for those outside of the thermal envelope.

The worksheet has a new section for inputting data to calculate the heat demand used for showering and it also now has a section for completion if hot water heat recovery is being used.

The final improvement seasoned PHPP users will find is provided through a new tool for calculating tank

Figure 5.4 *(opposite) Heating distribution losses*

storage losses, with this worksheet now combining storage heat loss inputs previously entered on the 'HP' and 'SolarDHW' worksheets.

It is worth noting here that in the term residential hot water (DHW) the 'residential' refers to water used within the building and applies equally to residential and non-residential buildings.

The DHW sections of this worksheet should be straightforward to complete using the guidance notes embedded in the PHPP. The technical manual provides detailed guidance on each section of this worksheet (refer to pp. 181–92).

The results from this worksheet are expanded on in **Figure 5.5**.

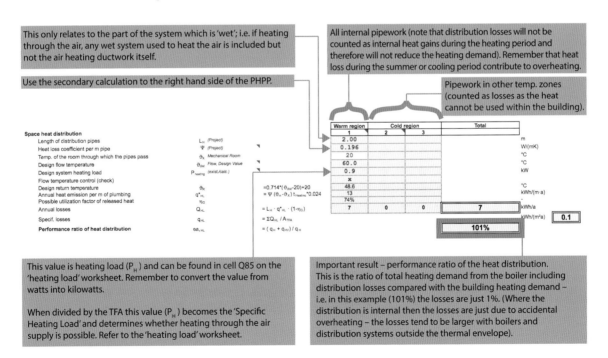

This only relates to the part of the system which is 'wet'; i.e. if heating through the air, any wet system used to heat the air is included but not the air heating ductwork itself.

Use the secondary calculation to the right hand side of the PHPP.

All internal pipework (note that distribution losses will not be counted as internal heat gains during the heating period and therefore will not reduce the heating demand). Remember that heat loss during the summer or cooling period contribute to overheating.

Pipework in other temp. zones (counted as losses as the heat cannot be used within the building).

This value is heating load (P_H) and can be found in cell Q85 on the 'heating load' worksheet. Remember to convert the value from watts into kilowatts.

When divided by the TFA this value (P_H) becomes the 'Specific Heating Load' and determines whether heating through the air supply is possible. Refer to the 'heating load' worksheet.

Important result – performance ratio of the heat distribution. This is the ratio of total heating demand from the boiler including distribution losses compared with the building heating demand – i.e. in this example (101%) the losses are just 1%. (Where the distribution is internal then the losses are just due to accidental overheating – the losses tend to be larger with boilers and distribution systems outside the thermal envelope).

DHW useful heat

47	DHW demand for showers, per person and day (with 60°C)	litre/person/d	16.0
48	DHW demand others, per person and day (with 60°C)	litre/person/d	9.0
49	Performance of shower drain-water heat recovery		0%
50	Effective DHW demand	V_{DHW} litre/person/d	25
51	Average cold water temperature of the supply	ϑ_{cw} °C	11.4
52	DHW demand for washing machines and dishwashers non-electric	kWh/a	0
53	Effective useful heat DHW	Q_{DHW} kWh/a	1374

Tools for (1) non-residential buildings and (2) shower drain heat recovery systems, as previously, the worksheet must be temporarily unprotected to allow these to be expanded.

This is the total heat demand for the DHW system in the home before the losses are accounted for below.

kWh/a	kWh/(m²a)
1374	11.3

55	Auxiliary calculation - DHW demand calculation (for non-res)
83	Auxiliary calculation - shower drain-water heat recovery

DHW distribution

			Inside thermal envelope					Outside thermal envelope					Total values	
			1	2	3	4	5	1	2	3	4	5	Absolute	Specific
145	Temp. of room through which the pipes pass	θ_X °C	20.0	20.0	20.0	20.0	20.0							
146	Design forward flow temperature	θ_{set} °C	60.0	60.0	60.0	60.0	60.0	60.0	60.0	60.0	60.0	60.0		

DHW circulation pipes

149	Length of circulation pipes (forward + return flow)	$L_{Z,B}$ m	1.2											
150	Nominal width of pipe	mm	15											
151	Insulation thickness	mm	25											
152	Insulation reflective coating?	-												
153	Thermal conductivity of insulation	W/(mK)	0.040					0.040	0.040					
154	Heat loss coefficient per m of insulated pipe	W/(mK)	0.164											
155	Insulation quality of mountings, pipe suspensions, etc.	-	3 - Good	1-None	1-None	1-None	1-None	1-None	1-None	1-None	1-None	1-None		
156	Thermal bridge supplement	W/K	0.146											
157	Total heating loss coefficient per m of pipe	Ψ W/(mK)	0.285											
159	Daily circulation period of operation	td_{Circ} h/d	18.0											
160	Design return flow temperature	θ_R °C	55											
161	Circulation period of operation per year	t_{Circ} h/a	6570											
162	Annual heat released per m of pipe	q^*_Z kWh/m/a	70											
163	Annual heat loss from circulation lines	QZ kWh/a	84										84	0.7

DHW individual pipes

167	Exterior pipe diameter	$d_{U,Pipe}$ m	0.010	0.015	0.022									
168	Accumulated length per single pipes	L_U m	15.50	22.20	1.70									
169	Amount of tapping points in building	$n_{tapping point}$	4.00	4.00	4.00									
170	Average pipe length per tapping point	$L_{U, average}$ m	3.9	5.6	0.4									
171	Tap openings per person per day		6	6	6									
172	Utilisation days per year	d	365	365	365									
173	Heat loss per tap opening	$q_{individual}$ Wh/tap opening	0.0090	0.0334	0.0061									
174	Amount of tap openings per year and person	n_{tap} nings per year	2190	2190	2190									
175	Annual heat loss of individual pipes	Q_U kWh/a	59	190	35								284	2.3

178	Total heat losses of DHW distribution	Q_{WL}				kWh/a	368	3.0
180	Performance ratio of DHW distribution pipes	ea_{WL}					127%	

Where more than one column is filled in, the total tapping points in the building should be inserted not just the number on the end of the pipe in question.

Total heat losses from the DHW distribution pipes

This performance ratio is the efficiency of the DHW distribution pipes only, and does not include the efficency of the storage tank, which is calculated in the next section of the worksheet, see figure 5.6. 127% for hot water is the total heating demand of the DHW distribution compared with the actual hot water usage. So this includes distribution losses with the exception that PHPP doesn't include losses that are providing useful winter heating in this figure. An additional 27% of energy consumption for pipe distribution losses is clearly significant. To improve upon this shorter pipe runs would be required. Instant electric water heaters can help to solve this by having the hot water created much closer to its usage point. This can be the best solution for situations such as schools or offices where usage is low and distribution losses potentially large.

Figure 5.5 *DHW + Distribution results*

PHPP9 has a new tool for calculating the heat loss of the storage tank, to view this tool you have to unprotect the worksheet and press the '+' sign next to row 207

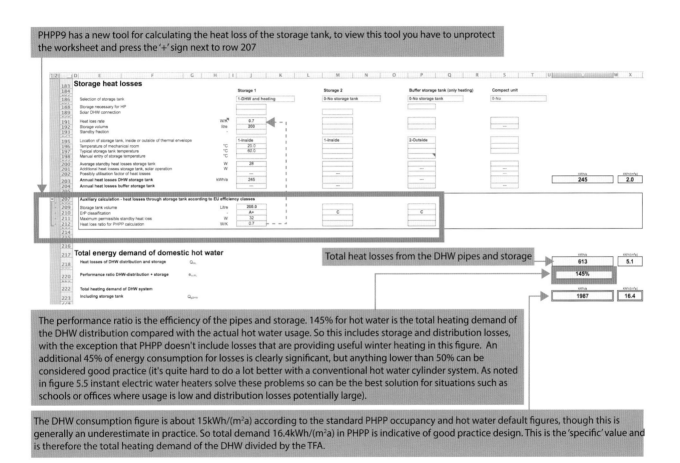

The performance ratio is the efficiency of the pipes and storage. 145% for hot water is the total heating demand of the DHW distribution compared with the actual hot water usage. So this includes storage and distribution losses, with the exception that PHPP doesn't include losses that are providing useful winter heating in this figure. An additional 45% of energy consumption for losses is clearly significant, but anything lower than 50% can be considered good practice (it's quite hard to do a lot better with a conventional hot water cylinder system. As noted in figure 5.5 instant electric water heaters solve these problems so can be the best solution for situations such as schools or offices where usage is low and distribution losses potentially large).

The DHW consumption figure is about 15kWh/(m²a) according to the standard PHPP occupancy and hot water default figures, though this is generally an underestimate in practice. So total demand 16.4kWh/(m²a) in PHPP is indicative of good practice design. This is the 'specific' value and is therefore the total heating demand of the DHW divided by the TFA.

Figure 5.6 *Heat losses results*

5.2 Solar DHW

The 'Solar DHW' worksheet:

- is only to be completed when a solar thermal system is being used

- can normally be used to size a building's solar thermal system (as long as the system is simple in nature)

- calculates the solar thermal system's contribution to DHW

- links to the 'Climate Data' worksheet to calculate an accurate contribution for the solar thermal system

- provides the user with the ability to take shading elements into account that affect the efficiency of the solar thermal system.

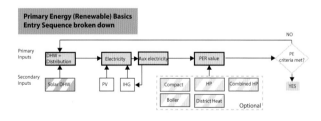

Figure 5.7 *Primary Energy Basics, Solar DHW*

- determines the system PER factors

The technical manual provides guidance (pp. 193–4) on how to link external simulation programs to this worksheet. This may be necessary for more complex systems.

There is also additional guidance on dimensioning the solar thermal. The headline advice is noted below (with the caveat that storage volume required varies with collector type):

1. A small solar thermal system should aim to meet 50–60% of the annual hot water heating demand. This fraction is known as the solar fraction.
2. When facing south this can be achieved with 1m²/person. In apartment buildings this can reduce to 0.5m²/person. It is best to base this on the expected occupancy not the PHPP certification occupancy.
3. The storage tank should have a volume of 70–100l/person. In apartment buildings this can reduce to 50l/person.

This advice is designed to avoid problems of overheating the solar thermal systems in the summer. The full rationale behind this advice can be found in the technical manual (pp. 193–4).

This is the total demand of the DHW (this can be adjusted to include the space heating if the solar thermal panel also contributes to space heating by checking cell M15). The table below this graph in the PHPP breaks these figures down.

As a general rule of thumb in the UK, the most economic small solar thermal system will provide approx. 50% of the DHW heating demand. A 2m² panel has been added to the Case Study house PHPP for illustrative purposes, which is calculated to meet 42% of the DHW demand (the home did not have one included in the design).

This is the contribution of the solar thermal as a percentage of the total hot water demand.

This is the energy reaching the surface of the solar collector.

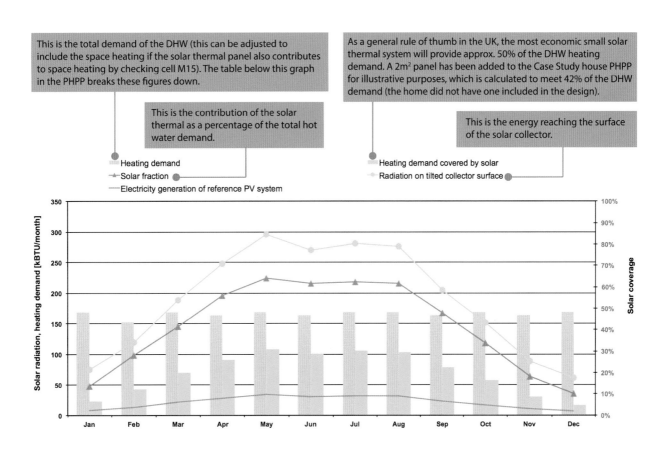

Heating demand
Solar fraction
Electricity generation of reference PV system

Heating demand covered by solar
Radiation on tilted collector surface

Figure 5.8 *Solar DHW graph*

5.3 PV

The 'PV' worksheet:

• calculates yields from the PV systems (up to five different systems can be entered)

• provides the user with the ability to take shading elements into account that affect the efficiency of the PV array.

The technical manual provides good guidance notes (p. 197) on how to extract the relevant information from manufacturers' data sheets and prepare it for inputting into the PHPP.

The provided example in **Figure 5.10** is based on the a small array of 10 panels being added to the Case Study house, as this did not have any PVs. It is worth noting that the PV array contribution does not get subtracted from the Primary Energy (PE) or Primary Energy Renewable (PER) value. This is to prevent a high energy-using building being certified by offsetting energy use against the PV array generation.

A summary of the energy contribution of the PV array is included on the 'Verification' worksheet as a separate entry with the New Passive House Classes incorporating renewable energy generation minimum certification requirements.

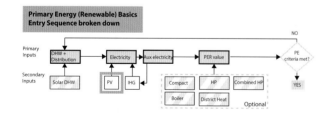

Figure 5.9 *Primary Energy Basics, PV*

Figure 5.10 *(opposite) 'PV' worksheet*

10 PV panels have been added to the Case Study home, for illustrative purposes – as the house did not have PV

	F	G	H	I	J	K	L	M	N	O
9										
10	**Name of system**		System 1	System 2	System 3	System 4	System 5	Reference PV syst.		
11	Location: Selection in 'Areas' worksheet		6-Roof South					6-Roof South		
12	Size of selected area		61.5					61.5	m²	
13	Deviation from North		165					165	°	
14	Angle of inclination from horizontal		50					50	°	
15	Alternative input: Deviation from North								°	
16	Alternative input: Angle of inclination from the horizontal								°	
17										
18	**Information from the module data sheet**									
19	Technology		4-Mono-Si	5-Poly-Si	5-Poly-Si	5-Poly-Si	5-Poly-Si	4-Mono-Si		
20	Nominal current	I_{MPP}	7.84					7.71	A	
21	Nominal voltage	U_{MPP}	30.00					30.50	V	
22	Nominal power	P_n	235	0	0	0	0	235	Wp	
23	Temperature coefficient short-circuit current	α	0.053					0.040	%/K	
24	Temperature coefficient open-circuit voltage	β	-0.035					-0.340	%/K	
25	Module dimensions: Height		1.500					1.658	m	
26	Module dimensions: Width		1.000					0.994	m	
27								1.6	Module area [m²]	
28	**Further specifications**									
29	Number of modules	n_M	10					1.2		
30	Height of module array		5.0					1	m	
31	Height of horizon	h_{Hor}	4.0					0	m	
32	Horizontal distance	a_{Hor}	37.0					1000.0	m	
33	Additional reduction factor shading	r_{other}	97%					90%		
34	Efficiency of the inverter	η_{INV}	95%					95%		
35										
36	**Results**									
37	Area of module field		15.0	0.0	0.0	0.0	0.0	2.0	m²	
38	Free area on the selected building element		44.5					44.5	m²	
39	Allocation to building element		28%					28%		
40	Annual losses due to shading		124					29	kWh	
41									Total	
42	Annual electricity yield after the inverter, absolute		2192					259	2192	kWh/a
43	Related to projected building footprint area		24.6					2.9	25	kWh/m²A_Projected*a
44	Specific PE factor (non-renewable primary energy)		0.42					0.4		kWh_prim_ne/kWh_End
45	Specific CO_2 equivalent emissions of the system		63.7					65.5		g/kWh
46	CO2-equivalent emissions according to 1-CO2 factors GEMIS 4.6 (Germany)		285.0					33.7	285.0	kg/a
47	PE-factor according to 1-PE factors (non-renewable) PHI Certification		0.00	0.00	0.00	0.00	0.00	0.0	0.0	kWh_prim/kWh_End

Assign the PV to one of the building areas; in this case the PV has been placed on the southern roof plane

Insert details from PV data sheet

Insert project specific details. The shading is inserted using the same logic as that set out in chapter 3.

Expand this section to see the specific PE factor and CO_2 equivalent

Energy produced each year

Embodied CO_2 in manufacture divided by useful kWh over a 30-year lifespan

The graph, below the calculations in the PHPP, provides a useful visual representation of the monthly data and the tools below this (expanded using the '+' signs to the left hand side of the worksheet) provide a clear summary of the values on a per month basis.

5.4 Electricity

The 'Electricity' worksheet:

- calculates the electricity demand. Included in the calculation are all services normally provided by electricity, including all auxiliary energy (calculated in a separate worksheet and fed back into this sheet). Excluded from the calculations are services for the DHW and heating, electricity for pumps (which are covered in the 'PER value' worksheet)

- provides the user with the ability to input the energy demand of appliances and set patterns of use

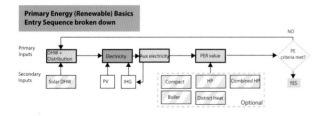

Figure 5.11 *Primary Energy Basics, electricity*

- makes assumptions based on the number of occupants, TFA and room height

- is only to be completed for residential buildings; non-residential buildings are covered by the 'use non-res' and 'electricity non-res' worksheets.

At this stage it is important to check the number of occupants on the 'Verification' worksheet is correct, as this has a significant impact on the electricity calculations. Remember, if the building is non-residential the number of occupants must be inserted manually in the 'Verification' worksheet. If the building is residential and the standard PHPP-calculated number of occupants is significantly different from the actual number of occupants this should be discussed with the certifier. In certain circumstances it is possible to enter the number of occupants manually for residential buildings.

The technical manual works through all of the inputs for each appliance in detail (pp. 200–8). It is important to comply with the Passive House input standards for certification. For example, the energy demand of washing machines should be taken for a 5kg load. These standards are set out in the technical manual or can be seen by hovering over the red tabs in the PHPP.

The Primary Energy or Primary Energy Renewable Factor is the Primary Energy used per unit of Final Energy

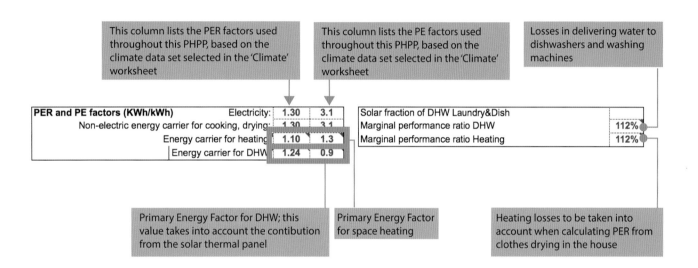

This column lists the PER factors used throughout this PHPP, based on the climate data set selected in the 'Climate' worksheet

This column lists the PE factors used throughout this PHPP, based on the climate data set selected in the 'Climate' worksheet

Losses in delivering water to dishwashers and washing machines

PER and PE factors (KWh/kWh)		
Electricity:	1.30	3.1
Non-electric energy carrier for cooking, drying:	1.30	3.1
Energy carrier for heating	1.10	1.3
Energy carrier for DHW	1.24	0.9

Solar fraction of DHW Laundry&Dish	
Marginal performance ratio DHW	112%
Marginal performance ratio Heating	112%

Primary Energy Factor for DHW; this value takes into account the contibution from the solar thermal panel

Primary Energy Factor for space heating

Heating losses to be taken into account when calculating PER from clothes drying in the house

All values are populated using information designers have entered elswhere.

Figure 5.12 *Primary Energy Factors*

'Electricity' worksheet results section

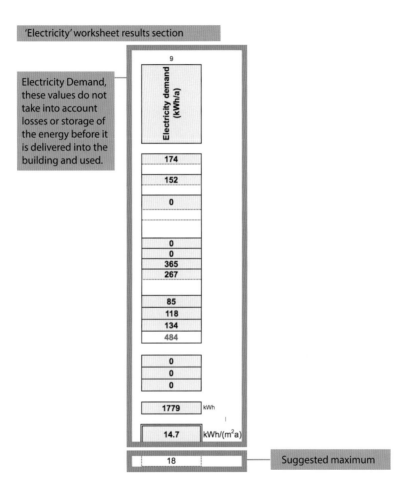

Electricity Demand, these values do not take into account losses or storage of the energy before it is delivered into the building and used.

Suggested maximum

The input cells (D31–33) listed under 'other' can be used to add appliances that have not yet been accounted for and do not fit into the 'Aux electricity' worksheet. An example of this would be for lifts. Refer to the technical manual for further guidance on the inputs.

5.5 Use non-res and Electricity non-res

These two worksheets are only required for non-residential buildings. I have assumed in this guide that by the time the user is working on non-residential buildings in PHPP they are familiar with the software and the technical manual and do not need further instruction here.

These worksheets are fairly straightforward to complete with the guidance supplied by the technical manual. The 'Electricity non-res' worksheet is particularly useful to aid in the estimation of lighting loads based on room geometry and usage patterns, although this can give unrealistically optimistic results, which is worth bearing in mind.

5.6 Aux Electricity worksheet

The term auxiliary electricity refers to all the electricity that is necessary to power and control a building's mechanical systems. For our case study project these are the heating, ventilation, and DHW systems. If solar thermal is included in the design the energy to power and control this system will also be included.

The 'Aux Electricity' worksheet:

- organises the auxiliary electricity into three categories: ventilation, space heating and DHW

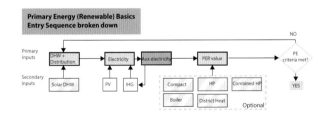

Figure 5.13 *(opposite) Electricity results*

Figure 5.14 *Primary Energy Basics, auxiliary electricity*

• provides standard values but allows for user-defined data to be substituted. Note these values are based on the gross (external) building volume entered on the 'Verification' worksheet

• calculates the heat energy produced by these systems in both the summer and winter.

As with the 'Electricity' worksheet, the technical manual works through all inputs for each of the building's mechanical systems in detail (pp. 215–18). Don't forget to put in a frost heating temperature set point for the ventilation unit.

The key results are presented in the same format as the results in the 'Electricity' worksheet (refer to **Figure 5.13**).

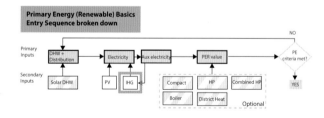

Figure 5.15 *Primary Energy Basics, IHG*

5.7 IHG worksheet

Internal heat gains (IHG) include heat given off by electrical equipment, lighting, cooking, DHW circulation and storage and the occupants themselves. A few processes count as negatives, such as cold water use and evaporation.

It is important to understand that the DHW gains (space heating gains from DHW heat loss) are not included in the winter IHG to prevent it being advantageous to design a poorly insulated distribution system. Of course they do need to be included in the summer IHG, so summer overheating issues can be fully understood. In the current PHPP the summer IHG are based on calculated figures from the IHG sheet, but winter IHG just use a standard figure. Even if the IHG are changed here, the figure for heat load does not change.

Until PHPP9 the IHG for dwellings was fixed at 2.1W/m². However, smaller dwellings often have similar gains (2–3 people, a fridge, freezer, TV etc) but concentrated in a smaller building. Thus we find that the IHG/m² tend to increase as dwellings get smaller.

PHPP9 uses a simple formula to approximate this:

IHG = (2.1 + 50/TFA) W/m² but with a maximum of 4.1W/m² (corresponding to occupant density of one person every 25m² of TFA).

The technical manual recommends that for residential projects the standard IHG are used. These are selected in the 'Verification' worksheet and no further input is then required in respect of IHG contributing to winter heating. However, the inclusion of this worksheet means the user can adjust IHG to make them more building specific.

The other reason to complete this sheet, which is linked to the output of the DHW, electricity and Aux electricity sheets, is that a separate calculated IHG figure is used to determine summer overheating risk.

Another significant change in PHPP9 is that occupancy is no longer based on a linear 35m²/person but instead uses a curve fit that is very similar to that used in the UK SAP.

To test higher occupancies and/or higher IHGs select the user-defined options on the 'Verification' worksheet. It is also possible to un-protect the

'Electricity' worksheet and change the reference quantities to account for higher occupancies. The 'Electricity' worksheet already covers the basic residential appliances and there is space to insert additional building-specific appliances. However, this will not be covered further in this guide, so any variations must be discussed with the certifier.

For the purposes of this guide we will restrict ourselves to observing the effect on using the inputs currently available to us in the PHPP. For certification this sheet was left with the standard values.

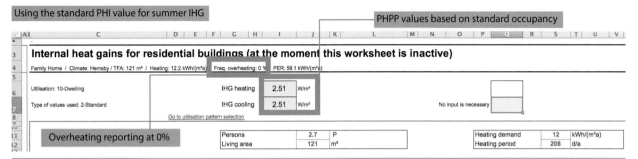

Using the standard PHI value for summer IHG

PHPP values based on standard occupancy

Internal heat gains for residential buildings (at the moment this worksheet is inactive)

Family Home / Climate: Hemsby / TFA: 121 m² / Heating: 12.2 kWh/(m²a) | Freq. overheating: 0 % | PER: 59.1 kWh/(m²a)

Utilisation: 10-Dwelling

Type of values used: 2-Standard

Go to utilisation pattern selection

IHG heating | 2.51 | W/m²
IHG cooling | 2.51 | W/m²

No input is necessary

Overheating reporting at 0%

| Persons | 2.7 | P |
| Living area | 121 | m² |

| Heating demand | 12 | kWh/(m²a) |
| Heating period | 208 | d/a |

For the PHPP to allow the user to insert the IHG figure manually the drop down menu in cell R25 on the 'Verification' page must be changed to PHPP calculation, for residential buildings standard values must be used unless agreed otherwise with the certifier. However, designers may wish to temporarily increase the summer IHG to test the effect on summer comfort. To do this, with the 'Verification' worksheet left on Standard values, the 'IHG' worksheet must be unprotected. Designers have to be **very careful** not to make permanent adjustments to the formula in the formula bar as this could invalidate the building's certification.

Testing higher IHG for summer comfort

IHG value increased by 1.5W/m² (as monitoring in the UK has shown summer IHGs can be as high as 4W/m²) to test effect on overheating. It is important that this adjustment is NOT made on the certification files, as the standard values must be used for certification unless, through agreement with the certifier, alternate values are taken from the 'Electricity' worksheet.

Internal heat gains for residential buildings (at the moment this worksheet is inactive)

Family Home / Climate: Hemsby / TFA: 121 m² / Heating: 12.2 kWh/(m²a) | Freq. overheating: 2 % | PER: 34.1 kWh/(m²a)

Utilisation: 10-Dwelling

Type of values used: 2-Standard

Go to utilisation pattern selection

IHG heating | 2.51 | W/m²
IHG cooling | 4.00 | W/m²

No input is necessary

The heat demand is not affected, as the winter IHG remains the same

Overheating reporting at 2%

| Persons | 2.7 | P |
| Living area | 121 | m² |

| Heating demand | 12 | kWh/(m²a) |
| Heating period | 208 | d/a |

5.8 IHG non-res worksheet

As with the two worksheets covering non-residential electrical use, this worksheet is required only for non-residential buildings. Again, it is assumed that by the time the user is working on non-residential buildings in PHPP they are familiar with the software and the technical manual and do not need further instruction here.

The calculation of the IHG has an important impact on the annual heating demand, and conversely the cooling demand, so careful attention should be given to this section of the PHPP.

5.9 PER Value worksheet

Refer to the introduction to this chapter for the definition of PER.

The 'PER Value' worksheet replaces the previous 'PE value' worksheet and:

- provides for the selection and calculation of the heating source(s)

- calculates the final energy demand for heating, cooling, DHW and household electricity

- calculates the effective PER factor based on the energy source, accounting for the biomass budget and the PER specific value for the building.

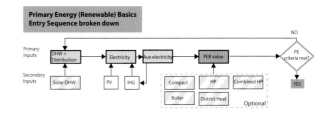

Figure 5.16 *(opposite) IHG worksheet*

Figure 5.17 *Primary Energy Basics, PER value*

- calculates the PE specific value and the CO_2-equivalent emissions depending on the PE factor profile for the building's location.

In the PHPP the user can select primary and secondary heating source. If more than one heat source is selected then the user can state the percentage each source contributes.
Remember that the contribution of solar thermal systems has already been taken into account; solar thermal was entered in the 'Solar DHW' worksheet and is automatically subtracted from the PE/PER Demand. The contribution of PV was entered in the 'PV' worksheet and is automatically transferred into the bottom of this worksheet so that the user can see the planned electrical generation.

Note: this energy is not subtracted from the PE/PER Demand. Buildings have to meet the Passive House certification criteria for energy demand and energy generation independently.

The Case Study house has one heat source, a boiler, (in addition to the solar thermal, added for illustrative purposes, as it did not have any in the design). The boiler accounts for 100% of the total demand as the solar has already been accounted for. The inputs required for the case study house are shown in **Figure 5.18**. And then the 'Boiler' worksheet was completed.

If other heat sources are used, such as electric space heating, electric boilers, heat pumps, compact units, natural gas, fuel oil or wood boilers, district heat or other types, refer to the technical manual for guidance.

It is important that the correct values are taken from data sheets for insertion into the PHPP. For example, SEDBUCK boiler efficiencies have to be converted from gross to net for use in PHPP. Consultants Warm: Low Energy Building Practice have an online conversion tool for this scenario (see www.peterwarm.co.uk/resources/downloads).

One challenge of Passive House design in the UK is the unavailability of small output condensing boilers. This supply problem means larger output boilers than required must be installed, which reduces the efficiency of the systems. The efficiency would be increased if one

Figure 5.18 *(opposite) Primary Energy Renewable, PER inputs*

Select the building's primary and, if used, secondary heat generation systems

Assign a percentage of the heating and DHW covered by each. Do not account for solar thermal heating here, this is covered by the inputs on the 'SolarDHW' worksheet.

Refer to these cells for the next worksheet to be completed. In this example the PHPP indicates the 'Boiler' worksheet should now be completed.

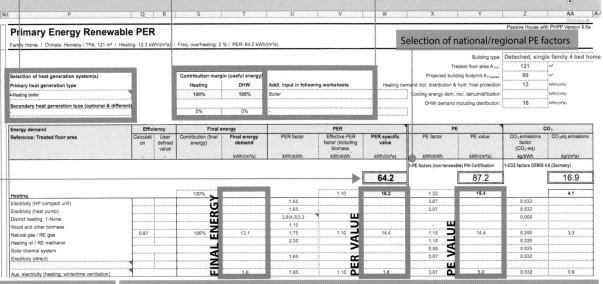

Primary Energy Renewable PER

Family Home / Climate: Hemsby / TFA: 121 m² / Heating: 12.3 kWh/(m²a) / Freq. overheating: 2 % / PER: 64.2 kWh/(m²a)

Passive House with PHPP Version 9.6a

Selection of national/regional PE factors

Building type:	Detached, single family 4 bed home
Treated floor area A$_{TFA}$:	121 m²
Projected building footprint A$_{Projected}$:	89 m²
Heating demand incl. distribution & hydr. frost protection	13 kWh/(m²a)
Cooling energy dem. incl. dehumidification	kWh/(m²a)
DHW demand including distribution:	16 kWh/(m²a)

Selection of heat generation system(s)

Primary heat generation type

4-Heating boiler

Secondary heat generation type (optional & different)

Contribution margin (useful energy)

Heating	DHW	Addl. input in following worksheets
100%	100%	Boiler
0%	0%	-

Energy demand	Efficiency		Final energy			PER			PE		CO₂	
Reference: Treated floor area	Calculation	User defined value	Contribution (final energy)	Final energy demand	PER factor	Effective PER factor (including biomass)	PER specific value	PE factor	PE value	CO₂ emissions factor (CO₂-eq)	CO₂eq emissions
	-	-		kWh/(m²a)	kWh/kWh	kWh/kWh	kWh/(m²a)	kWh/kWh	kWh/(m²a)	kg/kWh	kg/(m²a)
								1-PE factors (non-renewable) PHI Certification		1-CO2 factors GEMIS 4.6 (Germany)	
							64.2		**87.2**		**16.9**
Heating		100%				1.10	16.2	1.32	19.4		4.1
Electricity (HP compact unit)					1.65			3.07		0.532	
Electricity (heat pump)					1.65			3.07		0.532	
District heating: 1-None					2.8|4.5|3.3			-		0.000	
Wood and other biomass					1.10			-		-	
Natural gas / RE gas	0.97	100%		13.1	1.75	1.10	14.4	1.10	14.4	0.250	3.3
Heating oil / RE methanol					2.30			1.10		0.320	
Solar thermal system								0.00		0.025	
Electricity (direct)					1.65			3.07		0.532	
Aux. electricity (heating, wintertime ventilation)				1.6	1.65	1.10	1.8	3.07	5.0	0.532	0.9

FINAL ENERGY   **PER VALUE**   **PE VALUE**

Summary of the Primary Energy Renewable (PER), the Primary Energy (PE) Demands and the CO$_2$ emissions. The first two of which will be displayed on the 'Verification' worksheet, as these are key Certification Criteria.

Rows 20–54 summarise the energy demands by use heating. The worksheet then clearly presents the PER and PE factors of different energy sources for these uses. Designers can easily see that, for the same energy source, the PER factor (unlike the PE factor) varies for different uses. This is the core of the new PER concept, as explained in Chapter 2. And the resulting PER values are then displayed (column W).

Rows 56–63 summarise the renewable energy generation. Again, the energy generation will be displayed on the 'Verification' worksheet, as this is a key Certification Criteria in the new Passive House Classes.

See figure 5.19 for details on the final section (from row 69) of this worksheet.

185

This table provides a summary of the heating, cooling and airtightness Certification Criteria for the new Passive House Classes and states the level the project being modelled is achieving for each. The certification limits for the new Classic, Plus and Premium Classes are the same for these three criteria.

This summary graph provides a visual representation of the Primary Energy Renewable Criteria for each of the new Passive House Classes. And the project being modelled is shown on the graph with an 'X', to indicate which class it has acheived. In this example the Case Study house is a Passive House Classic. This graph shows clearly what would be required for the building to move up to the next Class.

Achievable energy standard through the verification of renewable primary energy (assessment of individual aspects)	Useful energy, performance				Airtightness n₅₀
	Annual heat. dem. Treated floor area kWh/(m²a)	Heating load Treated floor area W/m²	Useful cool. energy Treated floor area kWh/(m²a)	Cooling load Treated floor area W/m²	1/h
Requirement Passive House Premium					
Requirement Passive House Plus	15	10	-	-	0.60
Requirement Passive House Classic					
Requirement PHI Low Energy Building	30	-	-	-	1.00
Current building reaches following class for aspect	12	9	-	-	0.4
	Premium		Premium		Premium

Summary	Final energy	PER specific value	PE value	CO2eq emissions	CO₂eq substitution balance
Though, from the scientific point of view, not entirely correct, different energy carriers will be added together here. This is done to meet the criteria of other energy standards.			1-PE factors (non-renewable) PHI Certification	1-CO2 factors GEMIS 4.6 (Germany)	1-CO2 factors GEMIS 4.6 (Germany)
	MWh/a	MWh/a	MWh/a	kg/a	kg/a
Demand	5.9	7.2	9.13	1800	1800
Generation	-3.0	-2.4	-1.01	306	-1070
Demand, cumulative generation (annual balance)	2.92	4.77	8.12	2106	730
Demand w/o household electricity	4.6	5.5	5.15	1111	1111
Demand w/o household electricity, cum. generation	1.62	3.09	4.14	1417	41

This value omits all unregulated emissions and is the value often quoted in the UK for non Passive House projects. Remember, final energy does not include the energy losses through storage, distribution, conversion and delivery. For figures which are inclusive of this additional energy refer to the figures in the two columns to the right, PER and PE values respectively.

Figure 5.19 *Primary Energy Renewable, PER results*

boiler was shared between multiple homes, but this is not a desirable solution due to billing and control issues.

As this guide is an introduction only, further details are not provided on the optional sheets. The technical manual walks users through the inputs required for these if they are being used. This is also an ideal time to collaborate with the mechanical and electrical consultants, as they will be integral to achieving an optimal energy strategy for the building.

Once this section of the PHPP to completed a user should have a clear idea of whether their building is likely to meet the PER/PE certification criteria (refer to chapter 2 for full details of these). Some redesign is required if the building is missing the target at this stage.

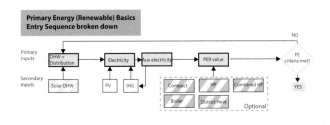

Figure 5.20 *Primary Energy Basics, optional*

Chapter 6

*design*PH SketchUp plugin

by David Edwards

6.1 Overview of *design*PH

Introduction

*design*PH is an extension (or plug-in) for Trimble SketchUp, which provides a 3D interface to the PHPP. It can be used simply as a tool to take-off areas from a 3D computer model and export them to PHPP; in this respect it can save time and effort completing the windows, areas and shading sheets in PHPP. However, it is also capable of calculating a preliminary energy balance (using the annual method for the heating period only) directly from the 3D model, allowing a more iterative design workflow and rapid prototyping to be carried-out.

Fitting *design*PH in to the project workflow

Before deciding to use *design*PH on a project (or before commencing a project on which you expect to use *design*PH), it is important to consider how it will fit into the project workflow.

*design*PH is most valuable at the early design stages when the building envelope is not yet fixed and changes to the form, mass, orientation and fenestration in SketchUp can instantly be understood in terms of their impact on the predicted heating demand. This means that the tool should be ideally suited for in-house use by architects and designers, to make a first assessment of the energy performance at pre-planning stage. However, *design*PH can also work well as an economic solution for independent consultants who do not use or want to invest in expensive CAD software.

Ideally the first contact with *design*PH in a project should be at feasibility stage, well before planning consent has been achieved and the envelope is fixed. The same point applies in general to planning a Passivhaus building and using PHPP, but the 3D nature of *design*PH and the automatic analysis feature (see below) makes it highly suited to this purpose.

How the model will be built-up, organised and adapted as the design develops should also be considered when planning the project workflow. A *design*PH energy model in SketchUp can double as the architectural design and presentation model, but it is important to have some fore-thought for what is required for the energy model in order to keep it well-organised and efficient as the design progresses. If SketchUp+*design*PH is to be used purely as an energy analysis tool alongside a BIM/CAD model, it is important to consider

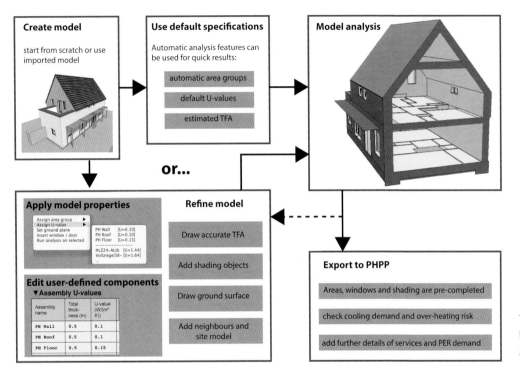

Figure 6.1 *designPH work flow diagram.*

how design changes will be kept in sync between the models; a full import of a 3D BIM model to SketchUp may not be the most effective solution for each design iteration.

Additionally, SketchUp (as of SU2014) now provides a degree of support for IFC attributes, which may present new opportunities for interoperability between *design*PH + PHPP and BIM.

191

Automatic Analysis

One of the great strengths of *design*PH is the automatic analysis; an heuristic algorithm infers the thermal area group of each surface of the model and automatically assigns a default U-value based on that. Each surface is given a coloured rendering according to the PHPP area group (see also section 3.4), allowing the designer to visually confirm which surfaces have been included in the thermal model. The automatic analysis allows the designer to test and compare different building forms without the need to specify the properties of each surface in great detail, allowing greater focus on the 3D modelling aspect (which is the inherent strength of working in SketchUp). To subsequently refine the model, those automatically assigned area groups and default U-values can be modified and for further refinement, custom properties can be assigned to each individual surface.

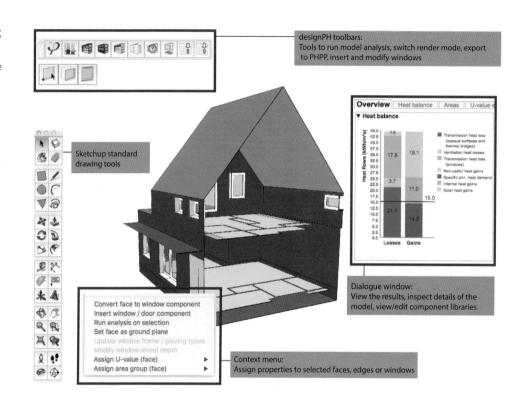

designPH toolbars:
Tools to run model analysis, switch render mode, export to PHPP, insert and modify windows

Sketchup standard drawing tools

Dialogue window:
View the results, inspect details of the model, view/edit component libraries

Convert face to window component
Insert window / door component
Run analysis on selection
Set face as ground plane
Update window frame / glazing types
Modify window reveal depth
Assign U-value (face)   ▶
Assign area group (face)   ▶

Context menu:
Assign properties to selected faces, edges or windows

Figure 6.2 *the designPH user interface*

192

The User Interface

As with other SketchUp plugins, the *design*PH tools are accessed via toolbars and menu items added to the SketchUp interface (see **Figure 6.2**). When the launch button (PHI logo) is clicked, a dialog window also pops up, so it only takes up screen space when it is needed. The dialog window is used for both entering the full details of the building properties and also for retrieving detailed information on the analysis results. The Dashboard, which floats at the top left of the model window, provides a quick overview of the key data; the currently selected climate, the specific space heat demand and the Treated Floor Area from the last analysis result. The Overview sheet (new in *design*PH 1.5) also shows the energy balance and other key data in more detail within the dialog.

6.2 Using *design*PH – Key Concepts

Defining the Energy Model

In general, because the *design*PH model is an energy model, not all details of the architectural design are required unless they have thermal significance. Excluding some elements from the analysis, such as non-thermal internal structures or fittings and purely cosmetic external details, will usually speed up the analysis process and reduce the likelihood of mistakes.

Heat transfer surfaces

As in the PHPP, the heat transfer surface areas that are required for the energy model in *design*PH are the external surface areas of the thermal envelope. For this reason, only a single-skin model comprised of SketchUp faces is required. For a simple model, this should be a closed volume, preferably drawn as a SketchUp Group (although the thermal envelope can be modelled in other ways - see *Different ways of drawing the envelope* later in this chapter). SketchUp is very well suited in this respect, because unlike BIM applications, walls and other building elements need not be drawn in SketchUp as 3D volumes. This does not mean that a building model cannot be drawn and analysed using SketchUp+*design*PH with the walls drawn as solids, but it does mean that there is no inherent need for that additional complexity.

Windows

Unlike some other energy analysis tools which simply tag certain surfaces as transparent, windows in *design*PH are modelled using a realistic 3D component comprising a frame area, glazing area and reveal depth. Windows are initially assigned a default frame and glazing type which allows the installed U-value to be calculated for each separate window, and this will be responsive to changes in the frame to glazing area ratio, perimeter length and coupling to other windows. See the *Windows* section below for further details on inserting windows.

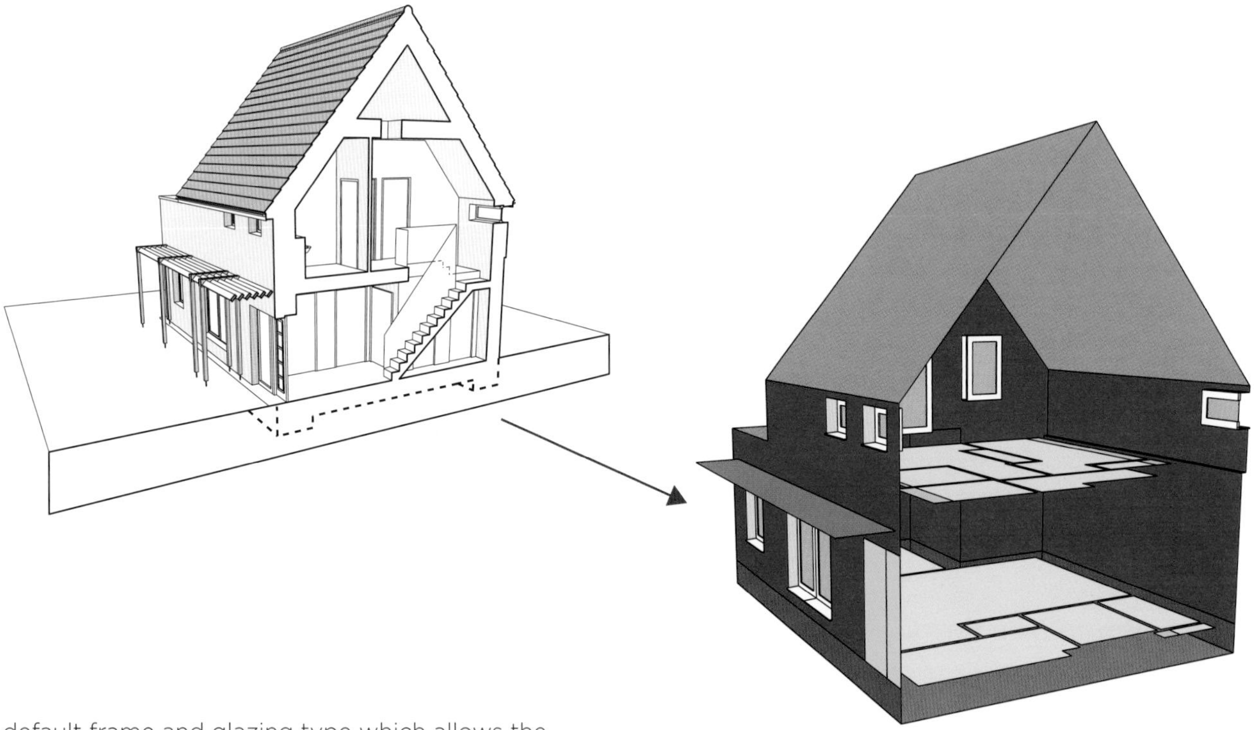

Figure 6.3 *The full architectural model in SketchUp (left) and the energy model (right); only the external skin and shading objects are required for the thermal analysis*

Treated Floor Area

The Treated Floor Area (TFA) is a measure of the usable internal floor area, which is calculated according to a prescribed method – see Chapter 3 for more explanation of this. Currently *design*PH has two possibilities for defining the TFA; the Estimated TFA Calculator and directly drawn TFA surfaces. An overview is given below, see *Defining the Treated Floor Area* later for details on how to use each method.

Estimated TFA Calculator

The 'Estimated TFA Calculator' is essentially a ready-reckoner which starts with the gross floor area from the footprint and applies a number of configurable adjustments to arrive at an estimation for the internal floor area. This feature is intended for use in quick feasibility studies and cannot be used for Building Certification.

Drawn TFA surfaces

Treated Floor Area can also be defined by directly drawing floor areas in the model and assigning them as TFA using the context menu. When this method is used, it is expected to be more accurate, so the value takes priority over any inputs from the estimator.

Applying user-defined properties

Once a basic energy model has been defined, a great deal of further detail can be added if required. The thermal area groups and properties assigned to each surface or window by the automatic analysis can be overridden, either by modifying the global default U-values as a first step, or by directly assigning properties on an element by element basis. Libraries of components for 'assemblies' (wall, roof and floor build-ups), window frames and glazing units are included with *design*PH.

Certified Components

There is an extensive library of components included in *design*PH which have been certified by PHI as being of sufficient thermal quality for Passive House (see also section 3.6). The PHI certified components database can also be searched at http://database.passivehouse.com. Updates to the component libraries in *design*PH are provided in the regular free software updates from www.designph.org, in future these will be accessed directly through the *design*PH software so the latest components will always be available.

User-defined Components

As in the PHPP, user-defined components can also be entered using generic or manufacturer supplied specifications. U-values for assemblies can also be calculated from scratch by using the built-in U-value calculator and assigned to any model surface. Any custom assignments or user-defined components are stored in the SketchUp model so they are retained when the model is saved and re-opened for analysis at a later date.

Climate and Location

More than 500 climate datasets are currently included in *design*PH – these are used for the internal heat balance calculation and also exported to PHPP. The climate data is selected independently of any geolocation settings in SketchUp; the in-built SketchUp sun tool can be used to inform shadow studies, but it does not have any influence on the solar gains nor the heat balance calculation in *design*PH. By default, the Green axis in SketchUp corresponds to the North direction in the model. The north direction can also be modified in SketchUp and this setting will be used by *design*PH when determining the orientation of surfaces and windows.

Running the Analysis: Alternative modes

There are two different ways of running the analysis in *design*PH, depending on whether a part of the model is selected or not.

Run analysis on whole model

If the analysis button is pressed without making any selection in the model, then the whole model is analysed as if it were the thermal envelope. The automatic analysis attempts to assign properties to each surface on the basis that they are all thermal. Any user-assigned properties will take priority. The main disadvantage of using this mode is that where models have a large amount of context (eg for shading), these surfaces would all need to be manually assigned as 'non-thermal'. Conversely, the only real advantage of the whole model mode is that it is simpler to activate (just one click is required), so it is generally more suited to simple models without any context.

Running the analysis
- The quickest way to perform the analysis is usually to run the analysis on a selection
- Organise the thermal envelope using SketchUp Groups; that way they can easily be selected for analysis and won't interact with non-thermal elements (see Tips on Groups)
- Make use of the *design*PH automatic analysis functions for feasibility models; you don't need to directly assign all thermal properties so can focus on the form
- Hide non-thermal elements that are not needed for analysis – this will make it easier to check the thermal model and should speed up the analysis process.
- *design*PH analysis is WYSIWYG; anything that is not seen is not analysed.

Run analysis on selection

If an analysis is made with a part of the model selected, it is assumed that only the selected part includes the thermal model. This means that the context does not need to be manually assigned as 'non-thermal' if it is not included in the selection. The 'Run analysis on selection' command is also available from the context menu (it will be greyed out if no selection is made). A further advantage of this mode of analysis is that it can be used to analyse different buildings or design variants on the same site, all within the same SketchUp model. It could also be used to compare individual units within a block, or analyse the block as a whole, for example to perform a stress test on the most exposed unit.

Analysis rendering and assignment of area groups

The *design*PH analysis automatically assigns a thermal zone (Ambient, Ground or Non-thermal) and by inference a thermal area group (External Wall to Ambient, External Wall to Ground, Roof or Ground Floor/Basement Ceiling) to the surfaces of the thermal envelope. Where the area group has been directly assigned to a surface by user input, that setting takes priority in the analysis. The coloured rendering of the surfaces provides visual feedback on the area group assignment, indicating if they have been categorised successfully. This automatic assignment saves the time of manually categorising each surface, but it is not definitive; in some cases (usually in more complex models) the automatic analysis may not be able to correctly detect the area group for all surfaces, so user intervention may occasionally be required. It is always good practice to

Surfaces are colour-coded by area group

Roof

External Wall – Ambient

Shading

External Door

External Wall – Ground

Floor Slab / Basement Ceiling

User-defined Treated Floor Area

198

Figure 6.4 *designPH model after analysis*

perform a quick visual check of the model to confirm that all surfaces have been coloured as expected and if not, manually assign the required area group and re-run the analysis to update the result. For 'non-standard' area groups such as Party Walls, External Doors, or the group for the user defined temperature reduction factor 'Area Group X', the area group assignment must always be done manually, using the context menu on a selection of one or more surfaces.

6.3 Organising the model and adding details

Organising the model for effective analysis

A well-organised model is always easier to manage and analyse and also makes the task easier when sharing models with other members of a design team. SketchUp provides some useful tools and concepts for organising the model: Layers, Groups and the Outliner. See the following section, '*Different ways of drawing the envelope*' for some examples of their use.

Layers

Layers are a familiar concept from CAD and drawing applications. They are the primary way to control the visibility of drawing elements in a SketchUp model.

Layers in a SketchUp model have no influence on the display hierarchy (there is no layer order) or spatial position (there is no layer stacking or z-offset such as that used to set-up storeys in other CAD software); any object can be assigned to any layer and is therefore either visible or hidden. As a general rule, it is better to keep the number of layers small for the sake of simplicity, so it may be useful to rationalize the layers after importing a CAD model.

Figure 6.5 *SketchUp Layers palette*

Groups

Groups are another familiar organisational concept from other CAD and drawing applications; they are essentially containers for lower-level model entities (faces and edges) that cause those entities to behave as if they were one single object when they are moved, scaled, inherit material properties or their visibility is changed. In SketchUp the normal behaviour is that faces and edges that reside at the same point in space will interact and intersect with each other. Crucially, Groups prevent (or protect) the faces and edges inside them from intersecting with those outside the Group – this is very important when separating thermal and non-thermal elements. Groups can also be nested so that a high-level group may contain many lower-level groups. Groups can be placed in different layers and be given a unique name. In general, to avoid confusion it is safer to keep all the loose faces and edges within groups in Layer0, and put the Group itself into a specified layer to control the visibility.

Figure 6.6 *The Entity Info palette*

199

TIPS

Groups and Layers
- Group related faces and edges together to prevent them from interacting with other entities outside the group.
- Keep Layer0 as the active layer when drawing new geometry.
- Keep all entities that are inside a Group (the loose edges and faces) in Layer0.
- After grouping elements, assign the preferred layer to the group as a whole.
- Control visibilities by hiding the layer of the Group or by directly hiding the Group itself.
- Use the 'Purge' command on the Layers palette menu to remove unused layers.

The Outliner

The Outliner is a palette in the SketchUp user interface which provides a hierarchical tree view of the model, where the branches and nodes of the tree are the grouped elements (Components and Groups) in the model. This is an extremely useful tool as it allows the designer to traverse the structure of the model and find grouped elements without knowing where they are located in space. This means that objects which are hidden from view can be found and selected, without needing to hide any of the other objects that obscure or contain them; this is especially powerful if used in combination with the SketchUp 'X-Ray' view mode. If descriptive names are given to Groups in the model such as blocks, storeys, zones or rooms, or construction elements, this hierarchy of names will be shown up in the Outliner.

TIPS

Outliner
- Naming Groups makes them easier to find in the Outliner
- Group names can be edited directly in the Outliner or the Entity Info palette
- Clicking an element (Group or Component) in the Outliner selects it in the model
- The context menu can also be accessed directly from the Outliner.
- Double-clicking also opens the Group or Component for editing

View modes

SketchUp also provides a number of View modes, some of which are of great help when organising the model. The X-Ray mode is fairly self-explanatory; it renders all faces with a degree of transparency so that elements inside Groups can be seen – this can be particularly handy when combined with the Outliner to find an object that is out of view. The options for 'Hide rest of model' and 'Hide similar components' are useful when editing nested Groups or Components; they either fade-out or hide completely the context (which might otherwise obscure the view) when editing elements inside a Group. It is especially useful if these options are assigned to a shortcut key to toggle quickly between the two modes.

Different ways of drawing the envelope

One of the great attractions of SketchUp is that it is not particularly prescriptive about how models are constructed; it provides some basic tools and concepts, such as Faces, Edges, Groups, Components and Layers which can be combined in many different ways to produce either very simple concept models or rich architectural designs. Likewise, *design*PH aims to fit in with this ethos and allows a degree of flexibility on how the energy model is constructed. Some different ways of drawing the

model are outlined below, with their advantages and disadvantages.

Single skin (grouped or ungrouped)

The simplest form of model comprises a single skin of SketchUp faces to represent the thermal envelope with *design*PH window components inserted into the

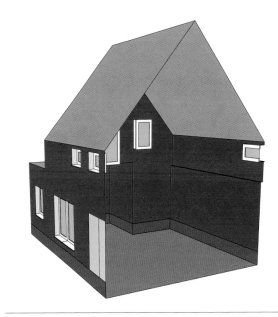

Figure 6.7 *Single skin model*

201

faces. These surfaces could be left as 'free' entities or combined into a single Group. The simplest way to create a single-skin model, whether starting from scratch or working from an imported CAD plan, is usually to draw the floorplate and then extrude upwards using the Push-Pull tool to create a volume. When non-thermal elements are added outside the envelope (for example shading devices, columns, balconies or other adjacent structures) it becomes advantageous to use groups in order to keep the thermal elements and non-thermal elements from interacting. This also means the **Run Analysis on Selection mode** (see p. 197) can be used more easily.

Grouped blocks

A model can be constructed from grouped blocks of surfaces, for example stacked up or arranged as a terrace (these must be SketchUp Groups and not Components). These could be unique blocks or modular units. The shared surfaces between the blocks are automatically detected by *design*PH as internal surfaces and therefore not

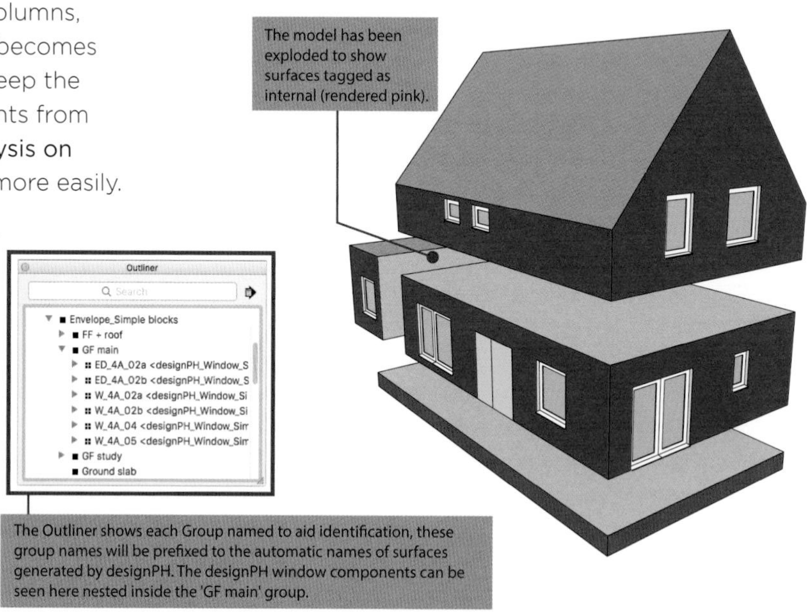

TIP

Don't forget to include the windows when grouping the thermal envelope!

The model has been exploded to show surfaces tagged as internal (rendered pink).

The Outliner shows each Group named to aid identification, these group names will be prefixed to the automatic names of surfaces generated by designPH. The designPH window components can be seen here nested inside the 'GF main' group.

Figure 6.8 *Grouped blocks model (above) with the Outliner (left)*

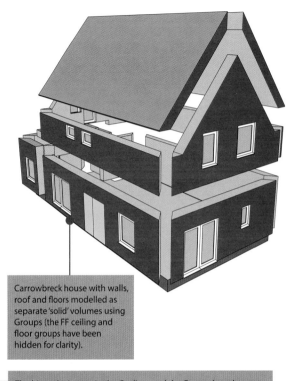

TIP

Any given group name will be prefixed to the automatic names generated by *design*PH (eg walls inside the Group "Top floor" would be named "Top floor_Wall_12345_N" and so on.

part of the thermal envelope. Where adjacent surfaces do not completely overlap they must be appropriately sub-divided so there is no ambiguity about which surfaces are inside and which are exposed to the outside.

Slab model

This is essentially a variant of the grouped blocks scheme, but at a different scale. Blocks can also be used to represent solid construction elements, walls, roof, floors and so on. This scheme could be used for treating the result of 3D model

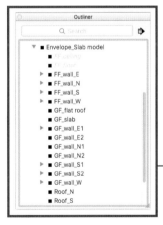

Carrowbreck house with walls, roof and floors modelled as separate 'solid' volumes using Groups (the FF ceiling and floor groups have been hidden for clarity).

The hierarchy is seen in the Outliner and the Groups have been named for easier identification. Note however that *design*PH will automatically name surfaces with the Group name, element type and orientation, so the Groups could just be named 'FF' and so on.

Figure 6.9 *Slab model (above) with the Outliner (left)*

203

imports from some CAD/BIM applications. As with the block model, care should be taken to ensure that surfaces are appropriately sub-divided into thermal and non-thermal parts, since the original CAD/BIM model may not have been built with that distinction in mind.

placed in a separate Layer for TFA. Internal elements such as walls, floors and stairs could also be placed in sub-groups and separate layers in the same manner.

Onion skin model

This scheme is a development of the single skin model, but with nested Groups. The outer Group is a container for the energy model, which can be selected with one click in order to analyse it. Immediately inside this are the surfaces and windows that form the thermal envelope. Within this main Group could be additional Groups for the TFA (eg each floor, zone or even room as a separate Group), these groups could also be

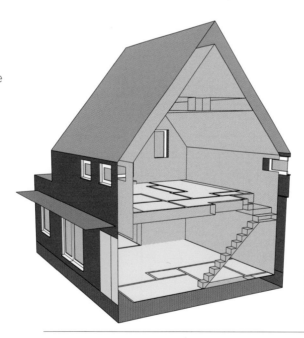
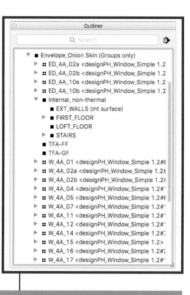

Successive 'layers' of the model are contained in nested groups. Thje first layer is the thermal envelope and the TFA

Figure 6.10 *Onion skin model (left) with the Outliner (right)]*

TIPS

Non-thermal surfaces
- If internal (non-thermal) surfaces are included in the analysis, designPH should detect them as internal and apply a pink rendering – however in a very detailed model it would be difficult to detect a mistake
- In general, it is safer to hide details which are thermally insignificant, such as:
  - internal walls, furniture & fittings
  - external rain water pipes, mouldings, parapets and cornices where these do not have any impact on shading.

Adapting an existing model for analysis

If you need to make an analysis on a model that was already drawn in SketchUp for design development or presentation purposes, or have received a SketchUp model or CAD model by others, in some situations, it can be quicker to draw a new simplified model for analysis purposes. Alternatively, if the model is already relatively simple or well-organised, it may be sufficient to simply add a few dedicated layers for energy analysis, concept design, internal layout and so on, allowing you to hide or show different parts of the model geometry that are required for analysis or design purposes respectively.

COMMON MISTAKES

Defining the thermal envelope
- Each face in the model can only belong to one thermal zone; don't draw faces that cross the boundary of the thermal envelope so that they are both inside and outside, or are in both the ambient or ground zone
- Don't forget to intersect surfaces where adjacent structures overlap the envelope
- Windows must be 'glued' to the parent surface to calculate the areas correctly
- SketchUp Components (except *design*PH windows) cannot be part of the thermal envelope.

See the Members Area at www.designph.org for further examples

205

Single skin model over CAD import

When working on a model that has been imported from BIM software, especially one provided by others, it can often be simpler to place the 3D import in a locked Group or Component, in a separate Layer and draw over it to create a simple single-skin analysis model. This removes the need to spend time understanding the layering and cleaning up the import model to make it usable as an energy model.

Where a design model has already been made in SketchUp by others, without any fore-thought for dual use as an energy model, in some cases it may be simpler to take the same approach as for a BIM import and not spend time re-organising the model and splitting surfaces into thermal and non-thermal parts. That said, simply analysing a design model without correctly splitting the surfaces into thermal and non-thermal will usually yield a result, but the fabric heat loss may be over-estimated due to increased surface area where non-thermal elements have been treated as thermal. This margin of error would only be acceptable at the very early stages.

While small discrepancies in the opaque surfaces of the thermal envelope will not prevent a successful analysis, particular attention should be paid to

TIPS

Drawing the envelope – keep the model simple
- Clean-up and simplify the model where possible (reduce the number of surfaces)
- A CAD import may contain over-triangulated faces – you can either try to simplify these yourself or search for a tool; many third-party plugins exist for this kind of task.
- Keeping the model simple in SketchUp means less surfaces that will be exported to PHPP, so it will be easier to manage the PHPP and compare changes.
- Purge unused Layers & Components after importing and simplifying a complex CAD model, using the 'Purge' commands found on the Components and Layers palettes.
- In general, the simplest models are achieved by drawing directly in SketchUp rather than using a BIM/CAD import.

windows, since they *must* be defined using the *design*PH window component in order to correctly apply the properties from the component libraries.

Windows

Windows must be modelled using the window component provided with *design*PH – this is so that *design*PH can correctly calculate the window, glazing and frame areas in detail and link the windows to the thermal properties from the built-in library of frame and glazing types. These properties, along with the precise window geometry, are essential so *design*PH can calculate the installed U-value for each individual window, based on the frame and glazing areas and the lengths of the thermal bridges. This does mean that the shape of windows in the energy model is restricted to rectangular shapes, but this restriction is commensurate with the inputs in the current PHPP version. See the online resources at *www.designph.org* for further tips and suggestions. Additionally, *design*PH windows must be correctly 'glued' to their parent wall (or roof) surface so they cut an opening. This is so that *design*PH can calculate the opaque and transparent surface areas correctly. Two alternative ways of inserting windows are provided by *design*PH; the 'Insert Window' tool and the 'Convert Face to Window' tool.

The Insert Window tool

This tool invokes the SketchUp 'place component' command, with the *design*PH window component pre-selected. Simply move the cursor to the desired

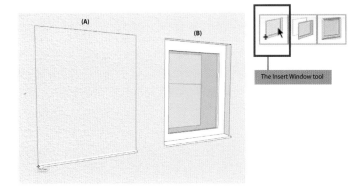

Figure 6.11 *The Insert Window tool*

position on a face in the model and click to specify the insertion point (bottom left corner). When the cursor is moved over the faces in the model, the outline of the window will be shown (Fig. 6.11 A) and it will 'snap' to different directions as the orientation of the faces changes. This is the 'glue-to' behavior of SketchUp components; when the window is placed it will remain attached to the face and will automatically cut an opening in the surface (Fig. 6.11 B).

The Convert Face to Window tool

This tool allows the dimensions of the opening to be specified before the window is placed. It is usually more efficient for placing several windows at a time. Firstly draw an outline on a face using the rectangle or line tool (it must be within the same group as the parent face so that the edges intersect). Select the tool and hover over each face to be converted, it will become highlighted (Fig. 6.12 A), click to place

the window. The edges of the window outline are deleted and replaced with the window component (Fig. 6.12 B).

The Window Installation factor tool

This tool is used to specify which frame edges are coupled to adjacent windows and which edges are installed in the adjoining wall or roof structure. The installation factor determines whether or not the

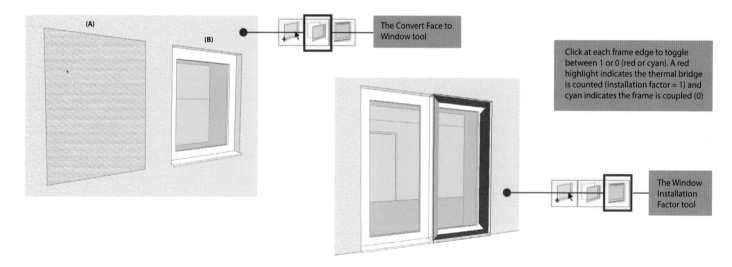

(A)

(B)

The Convert Face to Window tool

Click at each frame edge to toggle between 1 or 0 (red or cyan). A red highlight indicates the thermal bridge is counted (installation factor = 1) and cyan indicates the frame is coupled (0)

The Window Installation Factor tool

Figure 6.12 *The Convert Face to Window tool*

Figure 6.13 *The Window Installation Factor tool*

thermal bridge coefficient for that frame edge is taken account of in the calculation of the installed window U-value (used in the *design*PH energy balance calculation). This input is also used to pre-complete the matrix of 1's and 0's on the PHPP Windows sheet (see **Figure** 3.36).

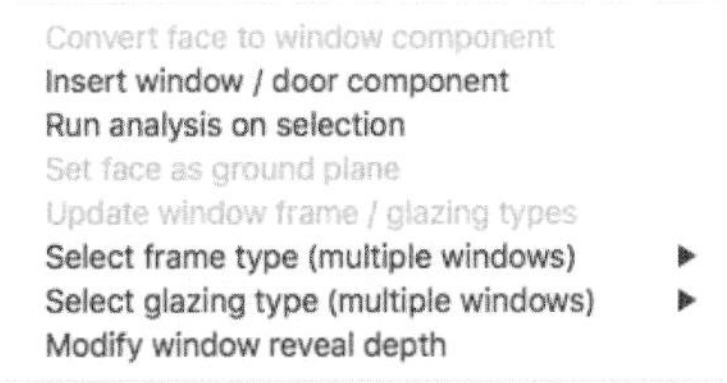

Editing window properties

The *design*PH window components are SketchUp 'Dynamic Components'. The Dynamic Components Extension (which is shipped as a standard part of the SketchUp package) must be enabled by the user for windows to work correctly in *design*PH, but a warning will be displayed by *design*PH if Dynamic Components has been disabled.

It is no longer necessary to configure *design*PH window properties using the native 'Dynamic Components Options' dialog (in fact this is not recommended) - all of the window properties can now (from *design*PH 1.1.60) be modified either directly in the model (modifying the dimensions using the Scale Tool) or via commands which are added to the context menu when a window is selected. In particular it is recommended <u>not</u> to edit multiple windows using the Dynamic Components Options dialog as this can lead to problems; multiple selected

Figure 6.14 *Context menu options for multiple windows*

windows can safely be edited using the *design*PH context menu commands.

Dimensions

The window dimensions can be modified directly in the model using the SketchUp scale tool; either by typing a scale factor or directly entering a dimension with the appropriate units in the input box. The dimensions of a single window can also be modified using the Dynamic Components Options dialog (take care not to select multiple windows). In the preliminary design, the structural opening size of windows should be used as the dimension. When manufacturers window sizes are known, the overall frame dimensions can be used, refer to **Figure** 3.33 on p. 115.

Choosing Frame types and Glazing types

Frame and glazing types can be chosen from the built-in libraries (user-defined or certified components). These can be selected for one or several windows via the context menu.

209

COMMON MISTAKES/TIPS

Reversed faces and windows

Faces in SketchUp have an orientation, if they are reversed they will report the wrong orientation for the opaque surface and can result in an inserted window becoming reversed!

- The designPH 'by Area Groups' render mode (default mode) now renders the reverse side of faces with a texture, so reversed faces can easily be spotted after running analysis
- Face orientation can be corrected by choosing "Reverse Faces" or "Orient Faces" from the context menu
- Fix a reversed window using "Flip along" -> "Components blue" from the context menu.

Reveal depth

Window reveals do not need to be modelled separately - the recess is included in the *design*PH window component and this is taken into consideration when analysing shading. The reveal depth of one or several windows can be edited through the context menu.

Defining the Treated Floor Area

The TFA estimator

The estimated TFA calculator is intended for getting quick first results; when used in conjunction with the automatic assignment of area groups and default U-values this means a full energy balance can be calculated with minimal direct input of properties. The calculator starts with the number of stories multiplied by gross floor area, taken from the slab area detected through the analysis. A number of adjustments are then applied to arrive at the estimated TFA; each of these can be turned on or

COMMON MISTAKES

The TFA estimator

If the slab area is not detected correctly (in which case you may need to manually assign the area group) or you have lifted the model off the ground, then the TFA estimator will have no basis value to work from and an error message will be displayed. It may be easier to simply draw the TFA directly in these situations.

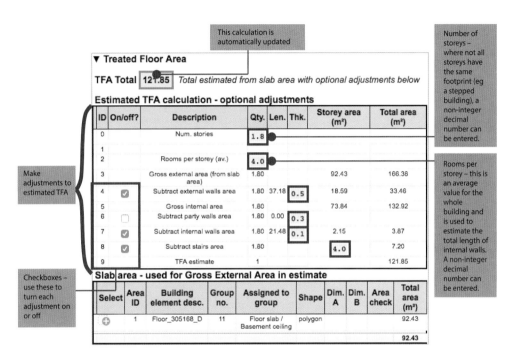

Figure 6.15 *The Treated Floor Area estimator*

Drawn or User-defined TFA

When the room layout is known, the areas can be drawn directly in SketchUp to obtain a more precise figure. It is important to get this accurate, since variance in the TFA has a significant effect on the specific space heat demand. Once the surfaces are drawn, they should be tagged as TFA using the context menu. The percentages refer to the weighting factors applied for different usages of the space (see **section 3.4.3** and the technical manual for further details); 50% for low ceilings between 1–2m, 60% for service/circulation spaces and 30% where both reductions apply. Multiple surfaces can have the same factor assigned in one action. After first drawing or updating the TFA surfaces, the analysis

off with the adjacent checkboxes and each one has a configurable value that can be edited in the yellow input boxes. Each of the adjustments is multiplied by the number of stories and subtracted from the total.

TIPS

Drawing and analysing the Treated Floor Area

- You can draw the TFA surfaces outside of the building envelope in order to find and edit them more easily. However, you must ensure that they are included in the selection when running analysis on a selection
- Including the TFA as a nested Group inside the thermal envelope Group (note that Groups just define a hierarchical, not a spatial relationship) means that it does not get forgotten when running the analysis on a selection (see Onion Skin model).
- In older versions of *design*PH, it was possible for TFA faces to have a shading effect if it was drawn outside of the thermal envelope and stacked up according to the floor levels – so if you are still using an old version, ensure you draw the TFA at ground level (or better, keep the software up-to-date!)

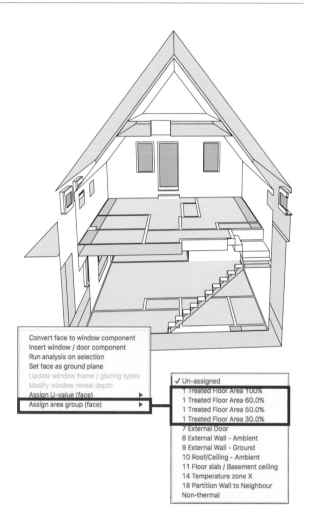

Convert face to window component
Insert window / door component
Run analysis on selection
Set face as ground plane
Update window frame / glazing types
Modify window reveal depth
Assign U-value (face) ▶
Assign area group (face) ▶

✓ Un-assigned
1 Treated Floor Area 100%
1 Treated Floor Area 60.0%
1 Treated Floor Area 50.0%
1 Treated Floor Area 30.0%
7 External Door
8 External Wall - Ambient
9 External Wall - Ground
10 Roof/Ceiling - Ambient
11 Floor slab / Basement ceiling
14 Temperature zone X
18 Partition Wall to Neighbour
Non-thermal

Figure 6.16 *(opposite) Drawing and assigning the TFA*

must be run to update the result, the Dashboard and Overview sheet will also indicate whether the estimator or user-defined method is active.

Shading analysis

Entering the shading details in the PHPP can be one of the more arduous parts of completing the spreadsheet manually (see also **section 3.8**), since it requires the shading effect on each window to be considered separately and up to six separate dimensions are entered to describe the shading situation for each window. However, *design*PH is able to automatically detect these dimensions from the 3D model and export that data to PHPP. The *design*PH heat balance calculation also makes use of the same algorithm as in PHPP to calculate the shading reduction factors and hence the effect on solar gain (during the heating period only).

Shading detection method

The concept of the current (*design*PH v1.0 – v1.5) shading detection is based on (and constrained by) the manual input method of the PHPP; development of a far more sophisticated algorithm is in progress for *design*PH 2.0 but this book will focus on the currently available tools. A simplified ray-trace method is used to scan the model, where a sweep is made in the horizontal and vertical planes perpendicular to each window. This detects the most prominent shading edges for the lateral reveals, overhang and horizon shading objects. Therefore if what is drawn in the model can be easily interpreted in terms of the dimensions that would be entered in the PHPP (horizon, lateral reveal, overhang) then it is usually detected correctly; if it is more complex then *design*PH may not interpret it exactly as the designer might have intended. For this reason users may find it helpful to model shading objects in a simplified way, with these three input types in mind. The shading analysis is performed individually for each window, giving a high degree of differentiation, albeit with a simple methodology. Visual feedback about the shading detection process is given by *design*PH; dotted rays are shown drawn from the reference edge of the window to the shading edge and shading surfaces are rendered blue-violet (NB not all surfaces that contribute to shading become coloured; only the one that contains the most prominent edge is used and if a surface already has a rendering due to its thermal area group, that takes priority).

Horizon and Overhang shading

Horizon and overhang shading edges are detected by scanning in the vertical plane perpendicular to the centre of each window. The largest gap between objects is assumed to be the sky and this determines the position of the two shading edges. See also figure 3.39 for horizon shading inputs in PHPP and figure 3.41 for overhang. More details on the method used can be found on Passipedia.

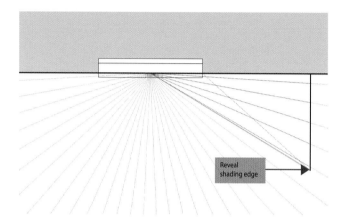

Figure 6.18 *Lateral Reveal (vertical) shading detection*

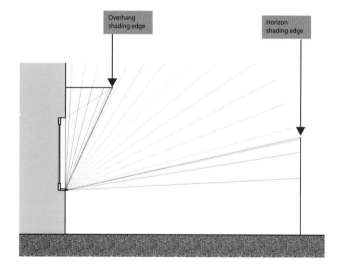

Figure 6.17 *Horizon and Overhang shading detection*

Lateral reveal (vertical) shading

Primarily this is the shading caused by the vertical surfaces of the lateral reveals to the window opening. However, shading by any vertical obstruction to the side of the windows is counted in this category. To avoid over-counting reveal shading from distant objects, lateral reveal shading is only counted by *design*PH if it is caused by a surface that is part of the thermal envelope (self-shading) or explicitly

TIP

Drawing shading objects
Always simplify the shading objects in the model to get the most predictable results (remember it is an energy model which is never a perfect representation of reality!); draw the shading objects as you would input them into PHPP, if necessary hide some of the 'architectural' context model and draw a proxy shading object.

marked by the user as a non-thermal surface. Although *design*PH detects separate dimensions for the distance to the most prominent shading edge at the left and right side, the results are averaged to produce the single pair of input dimensions required by PHPP. See also figure 3.40 for lateral reveal shading inputs in PHPP.

6.4 Interpreting the results and auditing the model

Analysis process
During the analysis process, *design*PH also gives a number of helpful warning messages to assist finding surfaces that could not be assigned automatically, or require some special attention. In most such cases, the message will give a choice between applying a specified action to selected model elements, or to select those elements and inspect them without completing the analysis. The highlight-select feature (see p. 218) can be particularly useful for locating selected elements in these cases.

One particular warning message you may see is regarding the automatic assignment of surfaces to the Ground zone; by default, surfaces below the zero-plane in SketchUp (the plane defined by the red and green axes) are automatically assigned to the Ground zone. However, if a surface continues both above and below the zero-plane, *design*PH cannot automatically assign a thermal zone – in this case you must either manually split the surface with an edge along the zero-plane, or manually assign the required area group.

Energy balance graph

The energy balance bar chart (a new feature in *design*PH 1.5), already a familiar concept to PHPP users (see also **fig. 3.56**) is also presented in *design*PH as part of the 'Overview' tab, providing a quick way of checking the overall performance. The Overview sheet also contains a summary of the key results for the building geometry (including the form factor – see section 1.2) and reports a summary of some model integrity checks which can assist with troubleshooting.

The Heat Balance sheet

The Heat Balance tab in *design*PH shows a breakdown of the energy balance – this is similar to the Annual

NOTE

It is important to note that *design*PH cannot completely verify if you have reached Passivhaus standard - but it will help you achieve a design that is capable of achieving the standard. The *design*PH heat balance calculation is not as detailed as PHPP and you should always check the overheating risk and any cooling demand in PHPP.

The energy demand calculation within *design*PH uses the annual method (seasonal method according to EN ISO 13790– see also section 3.11) to calculate a specific space heat demand for the heating season only. For cooling climates you can still use *design*PH to enter the building geometry then perform the full analysis after exporting to PHPP. Further information on the *design*PH calculation methodology can be found at designph.org and on Passipedia.

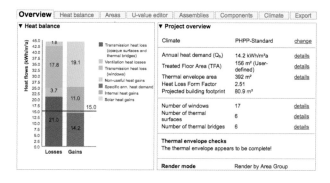

Figure 6.19 *Energy balance graph and project overview. (Example only – results shown are from a model of the Kranichstein Passivhaus).*

Heat Demand sheet in PHPP. Here you can get a more detailed summary of the heat losses and gains in the project. The figures in the highlighted green boxes are those that are displayed in the bar chart.

The Areas sheet

To inspect the results at an even more fine-grained level, you can use the Areas tab; this lists all of the areas, windows and edges (thermal bridges) that have been

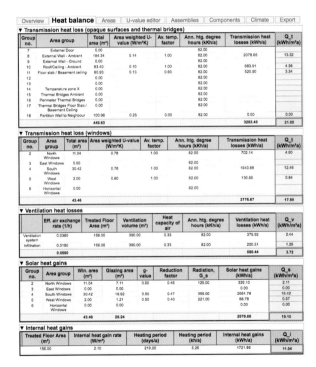

Figure 6.20 *The Heat Balance calculations sheet*

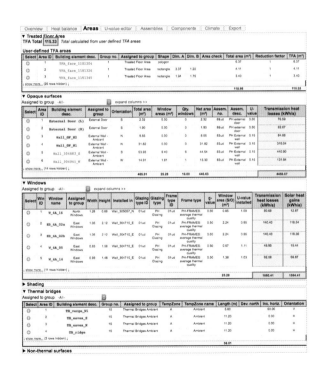

Figure 6.21 *The Areas sheet*

taken into account for the energy model. Each sub-table presents the energy balance results and properties of each individual surface or window in the project.

The Highlight-Select feature

This feature (new in *design*PH 1.5) provides invaluable assistance when trying to cross-reference between rows in the results tables with the elements (surfaces and windows) in the model. It can be useful when looking more deeply into the results to optimize the design, and also for QA purposes when doing a Building Certification. Hovering over the rows in the results table highlights the corresponding elements in the model and conversely, selecting the elements in the model highlights the table rows. The name of each element can also be edited (overriding the automatically generated name) directly in the table, which makes it easier to cross-reference the elements after exporting to PHPP.

Heat loss by element render mode

In this render mode (new in *design*PH 1.5), a colour value is assigned to each face of the thermal envelope according to its

specific heat loss (kWh/m²a). This provides a quick visual method to assess the thermal quality of the model and more easily spot weak points in the thermal envelope. It is analogous to viewing the model through an infrared camera, although it is only showing the average heat flows for each separate surface as modelled by the U-values and will therefore only reveal as much detail as has been modelled.

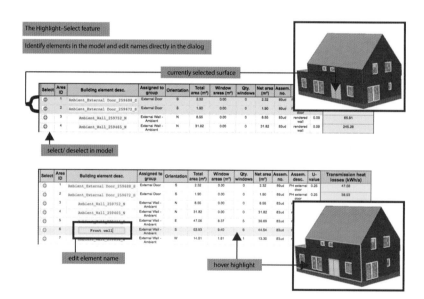

Figure 6.22 *The highlight-select feature*

Assigned component render mode

In this render mode (new in *design*PH 1.5), a colour code is assigned to each face according to the construction or component type. This provides a quick visual method to assess the range of component specifications and construction build-ups that have been used in the project and therefore provides a useful tool to rationalise them. This is a worthwhile exercise, since a greater variety of component types means more potential combinations in the junction details that need to be considered and therefore more thermal bridges to try to design-out. Therefore in most cases this could have design time and construction cost implications. See chapter 7 for more information on thermal bridges and why these should be avoided.

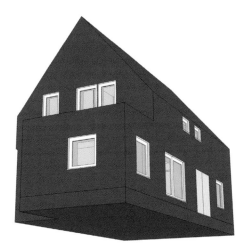

Figure 6.23 *Heat loss render mode; orange shows greatest heat loss and blue-purple shows the least heat loss – the door has been modelled as an opaque component to emphasise the differences in thermal quality*

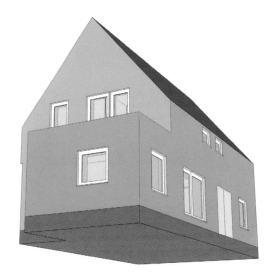

Figure 6.24 *Component render mode; each construction type is rendered with a different colour*

6.5 Exporting to PHPP

Once the model has been completed and a first analysis made, it can be exported to the PHPP. The *design*PH analysis *must* be run, before the export can be made. This provides the opportunity for a plausibility check; since *design*PH automatically

renders the faces of the thermal envelope that have been included in the analysis, a quick visual check of the model can be made before export to ensure that no areas have been missed.

Import/Export process

The export is begun by clicking one of the export buttons on the *design*PH toolbar. The export to PHPP8 (or PHPP-IP8) immediately brings up a save dialog where you select the location to save the PPP export file. The export to PHPP9 (or PHPP-IP9) button brings the 'Export' sheet of the main dialog into focus – here you can find the 'Selective Export' options – clicking one of these buttons will bring up the save dialog, but will save different sets of data to the PPP export file, depending on the profile chosen. Usually, the

PHPP sheet name	What is exported
Areas	Surfaces: thermal area group, dimensions and area, orientation, assembly (U-value) TFA: composite area with reduction factors applied Thermal bridges: thermal area group, length and Psi-value
Windows	Rough opening dimensions, frame installation factors, frame type, glazing type
Shading	Horizon, lateral reveal and overhang shading object dimensions
Ventilation	Some defaults to allow complete calculation (n_50=0.6, default MVHR unit, indicative duct losses)
Components	User-defined components and calculated U-values

What is exported Key data that is exported to pre-complete the PHPP

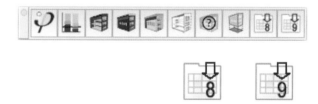

Figure 6.25 *The export buttons on the designPH toolbar*

'Standard export' should be used for the first export. To import to PHPP9, the PHPP_Tools Excel workbook must be used, this is found in the "Additional Tools" folder of the CD. Additionally the destination PHPP must also be opened.

Selective Export

Another new feature that was introduced in *design*PH 1.5 is 'Selective Export'; which gives greater control over what is exported to PHPP when doing a subsequent export after making changes to the

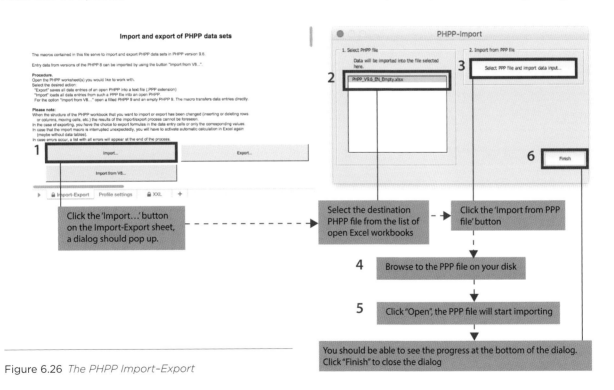

Figure 6.26 *The PHPP Import-Export*

221

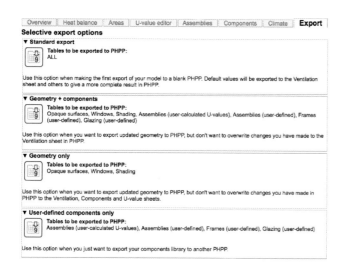

Figure 6.27 *Selective export options*

model. In the standard export mode, all the data in the table above will be exported to the PHPP, overwriting any existing content. If you manually enter details in the PHPP after making an export, but then want to import details from a design change in the model (for example if you have entered details of the MVHR unit and blower-door test result in the Ventilation sheet), you can prevent this from being overwritten by using the appropriate export profile.

Large models: Extending the PHPP

The PHPP has a pre-determined number of rows available for entering Areas, Windows and Thermal Bridges. If your model has more than 100 surfaces, 152 windows or 100 thermal bridges defined, then you will need to extend the PHPP by adding rows. It is important to use the 'XXL' tool provided with PHPP9

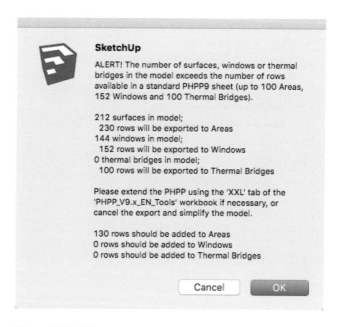

Figure 6.28 *XXL export messages in designPH*

to do this and not to manually insert rows in the spreadsheet as you could risk breaking the formulae. When you click the export button in *design*PH, you will see a pop-up message advising you that the model is larger than a standard PHPP.

The first part of the message will report the size of the model and how many rows will be exported; *design*PH will always export the standard (minimum) number of rows, overwriting any existing content in the PHPP. When the size of the model exceeds a standard PHPP, *design*PH will add up to 20 'padding' rows to the export to accommodate changes to the size of the model in subsequent exports.

ALERT! The number of surfaces, windows or thermal bridges in the model exceeds the number of rows available in a standard PHPP9 sheet (up to 100 Areas, 152 Windows and 100 Thermal Bridges).

212 surfaces in model;
230 rows will be exported to Areas
144 windows in model;
152 rows will be exported to Windows
0 thermal bridges in model;
100 rows will be exported to Thermal Bridges

Please extend the PHPP using the 'XXL' tab of the 'PHPP_V9.x_EN_Tools' workbook if necessary, or cancel the export and simplify the model.

130 rows should be added to Areas
0 rows should be added to Windows
0 rows should be added to Thermal Bridges

The second part of the message will report how many rows should be added to the standard PHPP using the XXL tool. If you are still using PHPP8, you cannot extend the PHPP, but you can use the larger PHPP_XXL sheet (500 rows) which is also provided on the CD.

6.6 Further information and learning resources

This chapter aims to give an overview of the concepts of *design*PH sufficient to decide how it might fit into your project workflow and to provide some tips for getting the best out of the software. However this book does not aim to provide a comprehensive tutorial, for further information you should refer to the user manual, now available online at designph.org (customer account required to login) as a Wiki-style resource. Also available for registered users at designph.org are extensive user forums and an FAQ section.

Chapter 7

PHPP Heating Demand Details

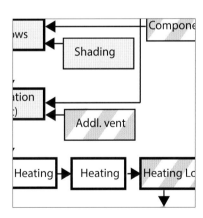

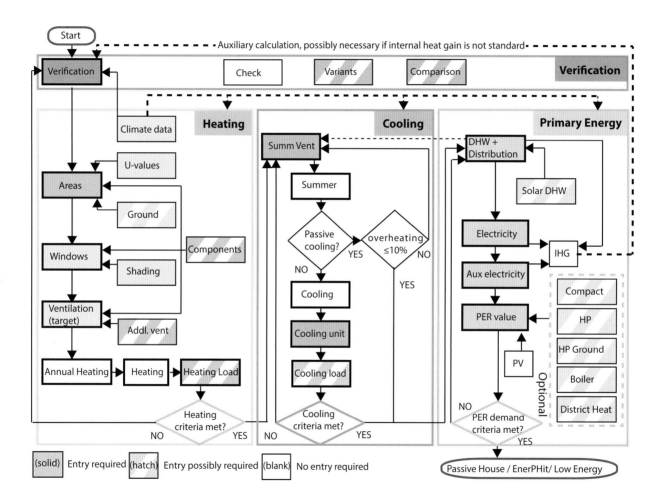

This chapter looks in more detail at some of the PHPP worksheets introduced in Chapter 3 and will enable readers to add an additional level of details as their design advances. The chapter will focus on thermal bridging, both in general and specifically around windows and will also look briefly at two other areas:

- Ventilation

- Individual room analysis – for meeting the heat load requirements.

As with the other chapters, this chapter focuses on residential buildings. It is assumed users are familiar with the PHPP and technical manual by the time they are modelling non-residential buildings.

NB. On many or most retrofits, it is highly likely that some modelling will be required as there may be existing structural elements that cannot be removed and may need modelling, not just for heat loss estimates, but equally for surface temperature calculations to assess potential risk of condensation and discomfort.

Figure 7.1 *(opposite) Heating Demand Details – flow chart*

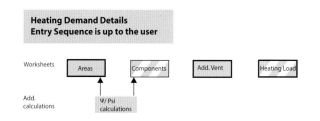

Figure 7.2 *Heating Demand Details – sequence breakdown*

7.1 General Thermal Bridging (Areas Worksheet)

This section of the 'Areas' worksheet:

- allows users to account for the thermal performance of junctions

- provides users with a simple tool for the conversion of heat loss coefficients that reference interior dimensions to exterior dimensions, as required for Passive House projects.

It is important to understand that the calculation of thermal bridges should not be a particularly laborious part of the PHPP. If the principles of thermal bridge free construction are followed, no modelling may be

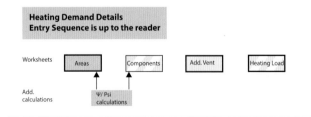

Figure 7.3 *Primary Heating Demand Details, thermal bridging generally*

required at all. However, in reality this is difficult to achieve and designers should expect to have to model at least a handful of details.

As discussed in Chapter 3, external dimensions are used in the PHPP, so losses resulting from geometrical thermal bridges are generally already accounted for within the transmission losses. This is if thermal bridge free detailing is used. Thermal bridge free detailing is described on the PHI resource Passipedia as:

'A building envelope is considered to be free of thermal bridges if the transmission losses under consideration of all thermal bridges are not greater than the result calculated using the external surfaces and regular U-values of the standard building elements alone. Regularly occurring thermal bridges in standard building components must already be taken into account in the regular U-values.'*

On the Passive House Institute website (https://database.passivehouse.com/en/components/) there are many examples of construction systems for which

* https://passipedia.org/basics/building_physics_-_basics/what_defines_thermal_bridge_free_design

all connection details that are normally required have been certified as "thermal bridge free". The technical manual (pp. 84–5) also provides specific advice on how to account for soil vent pipes (SVPs) that vent to air through the roof. Passipedia has more guidance on thermal bridge free detailing, which can be particularly useful when dealing with difficult junctions.

Now, we must establish whether the building has any thermal bridges that do not meet the thermal bridge free criteria and therefore require calculation.

What is a thermal bridge?

A thermal bridge is a portion of the building envelope with substantially faster (and greater) heat transmission than adjacent areas. It effects energy demand and comfort in both winter and summer. Also, it affects the thermal quality of adjacent areas because instead of heat moving perpendicular to the plane of the assembly, it moves laterally – sideways – through the assembly. Therefore, a thermal bridge allows heat to "sidestep" even robustly-insulated areas of an assembly adjacent to the thermal bridge.

Thermal bridges can occur at any junction where two or more elements come together or where

w/(mK)

w/(mK) – is Watts for each meter of length of the thermal bridge per degree Kelvin difference between the indoor and outdoor air temperature.

there is a change in the building fabric. The main effects associated with thermal bridges in buildings are increased heat loss and a reduction in internal surface temperature, increasing the risk of condensation and mould growth and reducing the comfort of the building occupants.

There are two categories of thermal bridges: (1) repeating thermal bridges and (2) non-repeating thermal bridges. Repeating thermal bridges are accounted for in the U-value calculations. An example of a repeating thermal bridge would be timber studwork in an insulated wall. Non-repeating thermal bridges will be covered here. An example of a non-repeating thermal bridge would be the junction where a wall and roof meet.

A thermal bridge is measured by the heat flow through the bridge, which is represented by its linear

229

Calculating Thermal Bridges – Psi values

Three variations on a typical parapet detail from the Mayville Community Centre

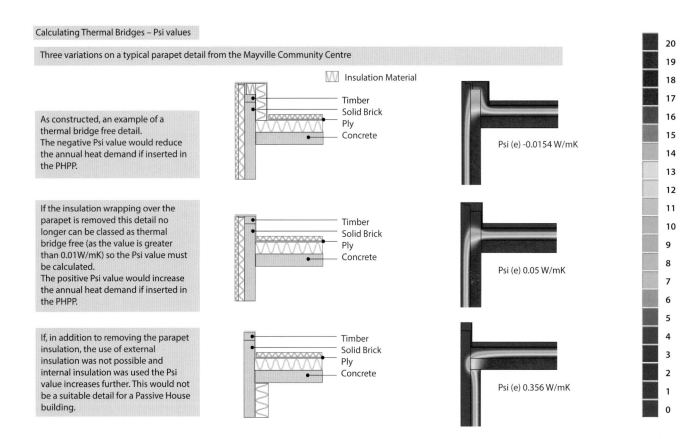

As constructed, an example of a thermal bridge free detail.
The negative Psi value would reduce the annual heat demand if inserted in the PHPP.

If the insulation wrapping over the parapet is removed this detail no longer can be classed as thermal bridge free (as the value is greater than 0.01W/mK) so the Psi value must be calculated.
The positive Psi value would increase the annual heat demand if inserted in the PHPP.

If, in addition to removing the parapet insulation, the use of external insulation was not possible and internal insulation was used the Psi value increases further. This would not be a suitable detail for a Passive House building.

Insulation Material

Timber
Solid Brick
Ply
Concrete

Psi (e) -0.0154 W/mK

Timber
Solid Brick
Ply
Concrete

Psi (e) 0.05 W/mK

Timber
Solid Brick
Ply
Concrete

Psi (e) 0.356 W/mK

20
19
18
17
16
15
14
13
12
11
10
9
8
7
6
5
4
3
2
1
0

Figure 7.4 *Thermal Bridge (Psi) Values*

thermal transmittance coefficient, or Ψ-value (psi value – pronounced 'si') in W/(mK). The Ψ-value represents the extra heat flow through the linear thermal bridge over and above the adjoining thermal element(s).

Which thermal bridges require calculation?

Junctions only have to be calculated if the Ψ-value is greater than 0.01W/(mK).

It is useful to note that the supplementary heat loss can be a negative value, resulting in less heat transmission. As long as all junctions with Ψ-values greater than 0.01W/(mK) are calculated, it is up to the user whether to calculate the remaining thermal bridges.

If further Ψ-values are calculated designers have two methods for accounting for them:
(1) include only positive Ψ-values or
(2) include both positive and negative Ψ-values.

It is very important that designers do not include only the negative values as this will not be acceptable for certification. In our Case Study house the thermal bridges were all calculated, however for certification only the junctions with Ψ-values greater than 0.01W/(mK) were included in the PHPP. If, in addition, all of

the negative Ψ-values had been included there would have been a reduction in the overall heat demand. The decision not to include the negative values was due to the additional cost of having the Ψ-values checked by the certifiers. With the heat demand around 12kWh/(m²a) including these negative values in the PHPP files was not necessary, if the heat demand had been over the certification limit of 15kWh/(m²a) these values could have been accounted for.

It is difficult to estimate Psi values without modelling them. However, with experience of working on Passive House projects, users should become familiar with the type of detailing required to obtain a thermal bridge free detail and thus be able to establish which details require calculations.

How to calculate a thermal bridge

2D modelling is recommended in the technical manual as being sufficient for the calculation of ambient (to air) thermal bridges. Calculations of thermal bridges to the ground are slightly more complicated.

Thermal bridges to the ground can either occur in the middle of the floor slab, load-bearing interior walls that penetrate the insulation layer, or around the perimeter

231

Calculating Thermal Bridges – A Light Introduction

The BRE guide 'BR497 – Conventions for calculating linear thermal transmittance and temperature factors' is a useful reference document. However, remember that UK conventions require the calculation of internal Psi values while PHPP requires external Psi values.
Refer also to BS EN ISO 10211 and DIN 10211-1.

First decide which junctions require calculation and remember any repeating thermal bridges will have been accounted for in the U-value sheet; do not double account for these here. If two junctions are less than the thickness of the building element apart they should be included in the same model, otherwise they should be treated separately. When refining the mesh size, it is more important to concentrate the grid elements around the structural elements that are likely to cause significant heat flow.

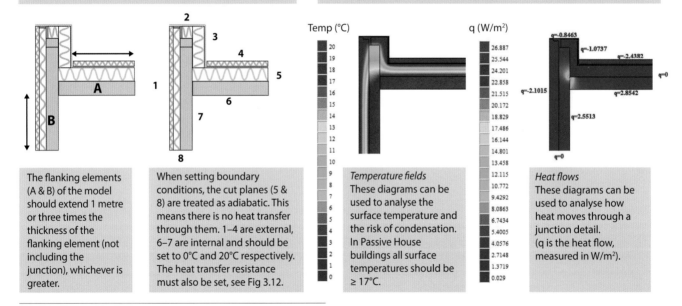

The flanking elements (A & B) of the model should extend 1 metre or three times the thickness of the flanking element (not including the junction), whichever is greater.

When setting boundary conditions, the cut planes (5 & 8) are treated as adiabatic. This means there is no heat transfer through them. 1–4 are external, 6–7 are internal and should be set to 0°C and 20°C respectively. The heat transfer resistance must also be set, see Fig 3.12.

Temperature fields
These diagrams can be used to analyse the surface temperature and the risk of condensation. In Passive House buildings all surface temperatures should be ≥ 17°C.

Heat flows
These diagrams can be used to analyse how heat moves through a junction detail.
(q is the heat flow, measured in W/m².)

Figure 7.5 *General rules for calculation of thermal bridges*

Add a description here (try to keep these clear and ideally match file names of Ψ-value calc. files)

Refer to the group list at the top of the worksheet (rows 23–25 refer to thermal bridges)

This plot does not have a SVP venting through the roof

Thermal bridges are measured in lengths, in metres

Insert the results of Ψ-value calcs. remember to use external values

Thermal bridge inputs

No.	Thermal bridge - denomination	Group No.	Assigned to group	Quantity	x (	Length [m]	-	Subtraction length [m]	)=	Length l [m]	User determined psi value [W/(mK)]	User determined $f_{Rsi=0.25}$ (optional)
1	SVP	15	Thermal bridges Ambient	0	x (	4.00	-		) =	0.00	0.192	
2	Gas pipe	15	Thermal bridges Ambient	1	x (	1.00	-		) =	1.00	0.140	
3	(500)Ren Foundation Perimeter	16	Perimeter thermal bridges				-		) =	0.00	-0.010	
4	(500)Tim Foundation Perimeter	16	Perimeter thermal bridges		x (		-		) =	0.00	-0.010	
5	(504)Tim-Tim Ext. Corner	15	Thermal bridges Ambient		x (		-		) =	0.00	-0.051	
6	(504)Tim-Ren Ext. Corner	15	Thermal bridges Ambient		x (		-		) =	0.00	-0.062	
7	(504)Ren-Ren Ext. Corner	15	Thermal bridges Ambient		x (		-		) =	0.00	-0.060	
8	(506)Ridge	15	Thermal bridges Ambient		x (		-		) =	0.00	-0.070	
9	(508)Parapet	15	Thermal bridges Ambient		x (		-		) =	0.00	-0.040	
10	(509)Tim Verge	15	Thermal bridges Ambient		x (		-		) =	0.00	0.040	

Inputs left blank for negative Ψ-values, as these were not being validated for certification

Note: In the case of a point thermal bridge the length to be entered is 1

New to PHPP9, this section allows Ψ-values to be selected from certified building systems

New tool (row 247) for calculating Ψ-values for rain water pipes and SVPs that penetrate the thermal envelope/vent to air

To thermal bridge list

or	Selection building system	Ψ-Value [W/(mK)]	f_{Rsi}-Requirement met?
or		0.192	
or		0.140	
or		-0.010	
or		-0.010	
or		-0.051	
or		-0.062	
or		-0.060	
or		-0.070	
or		-0.040	
or		0.040	

Links to certified systems in the 'Components' worksheet

Auxiliary calculation rain water pipes		
Nominal width:	100	mm
Insul. thickness:	50	mm
Thermal conductivity	0.040	W/(mK)
Interior pipe diameter:	0.100	m
Exterior pipe diameter:	0.200	m
α-Surface	6.80	W/(m²K)
Ψ-value	0.285	
Reduction factor	0.68	
Ψ–value	0.192	W/(mK)
To enter as group 15 thermal bridge		

Figure 7.6 *Areas worksheet*

of the floor slab. For the first scenario, the thermal bridge can be calculated with 2D software ignoring the presence of the surrounding ground. These Ψ–values can be entered in the 'Areas' worksheet along with all the other non-repeating thermal bridges.

For the second scenario, the software should consider both the building elements and the adjacent ground. 3D software may give more in-depth understanding of the heat flows involved, but may require specialist consultancy. Calculations can be state-steady (to save on costs), only establishing the heat flow in reference to the temperature difference between the interior and ambient air (2D software is sufficient). In this case, heat flows can be added to the entries in the 'Areas' worksheet. In addition, calculations can be dynamic. To establish harmonic thermal bridge heat loss coefficients, refer to the technical manual (p. 93). If calculated, harmonic thermal bridge heat loss coefficients are inserted into the 'Ground' worksheet. More detail can be found on this topic on Passipedia.

The technical manual (p. 83) recommends 2D software, THERM, HEAT2 and the newer Flixo and HT Flux are all commonly used by designers. THERM and HT Flux are free while HEAT2 and Flixo require a subscription. Basic training is helpful for new users. I would recommend doing this in-house as it provides a deeper understanding of the building fabric.

The technical manual refers to DIN 10211–1 for the calculation of thermal bridges. BS EN ISO 10211 is the UK standard. When referring to UK-based standards that may reference internal dimensions, remember to use external dimensions for PHPP. The key point is that the thermal bridge has to be calculated with respect to the same dimensions as the heat loss areas – eg a timber rain screen is discounted from areas dimensions in PHPP so the rain screen is also discounted from thermal bridge calculations.

These standards provide the specifications of the geometrical model, boundary conditions and accuracy criteria. There are also a number of short courses covering the topic around the UK.

7.2 Window Thermal Bridging (Components Worksheet)

The performance of the windows is highly dependent on how they are installed. It is very important to design good robust window details that are practical to install on site. Any thermal bridging within the window has already been accounted for in the values inputted into the 'Components' worksheet. Here we are only interested in the junctions where the window meets the building.

The technical manual (p. 106) gives some example Ψ-values. These can be used if they match the construction detail being used. If these do not cover

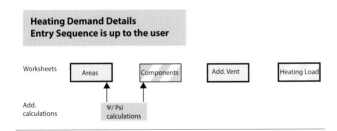

Figure 7.7 *Primary Heating Demand Details, thermal bridging around windows*

the designed construction detail then the Ψ-value should be calculated.

When the 'Components' worksheet was covered in Chapter 3, an installation value of 0.04W/(mK) was inserted. This was a conservative value and well-designed details at this stage should be able to reduce this initial value, thus reducing heat transfer through these junctions. This change can have a significant impact on the overall heat demand for the building. In our Case Study house if all the junctions are reduced from 0.04W/(mK) to 0.02W/(mK), the overall heat demand reduces by 1kWh/(m²a).

It is important to remember that conversely poor window detailing, either at design stage or on site, can increase the heat demand by a couple of kWh/(m2a) and make the difference between the building achieving Passive House Certification or not.

The example in **Figure 7.8** is illustrating a solid timber frame window, supplied by the Green Building Store. Solid frames are becoming more common in UK Passive House projects; if the frame can be detailed so it is completely covered with insulation it is not necessary to also have an insulated frame.

235

The U-value of a solid frame on its own is significantly over the recommendations; however with careful details the installed U-value of the window shown in **Figure 7.8** is 0.86W/(m²K), which only slightly exceeds the Passive House recommendation for an installed vertical window of 0.85W/(m²K) based on the climate data for the Case Study home.

Such products can be used in the UK (due to our milder winters) through agreement with the certifier, providing significant cost savings. This compromise makes the installation detailing extremely important. It is recommended that discussions with the certifier are started early if components are being used that would not ordinarily meet the PHI recommendations.

Figure 7.8 *Window thermal bridges*

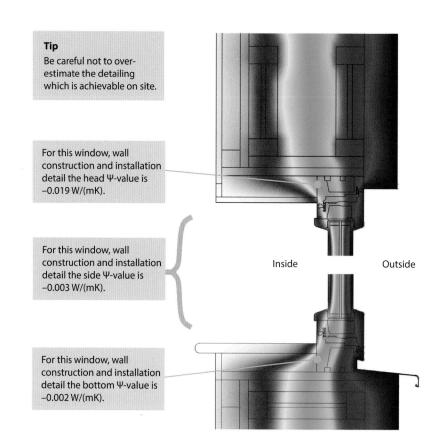

Tip
Be careful not to over-estimate the detailing which is achievable on site.

For this window, wall construction and installation detail the head Ψ-value is –0.019 W/(mK).

For this window, wall construction and installation detail the side Ψ-value is –0.003 W/(mK).

For this window, wall construction and installation detail the bottom Ψ-value is –0.002 W/(mK).

Inside   Outside

Note: most window Psi values will be positive numbers, the main reason these are negative is due to the fact the window frame itself is not insulated and the fact the frame is very well lapped with insulation.

7.3 Ventilation (Additional Vent Worksheet)

The 'Additional Vent' worksheet:

- provides for projects with multiple heat recovery ventilation units
- is an extension of the 'Ventilation' worksheet, i.e. when using this worksheet the 'Ventilation' worksheet is still required
- does not need to be completed for single-family homes.

This worksheet has been included in this guide even though it is normally not required for single-family homes; it is required for semi-detached houses and terraces as well as non-residential buildings. It is also one of the worksheets first introduced in PHPP8 and benefits from a brief explanation.

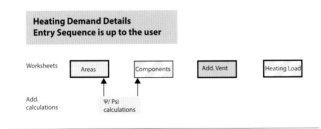

Figure 7.9 *Primary Heating Demand Details, additional vent*

It should be noted that, as with the 'Ventilation' worksheet, this worksheet provides only a rough assessment of the size of ventilation units required for the building. A specialist should always be consulted regarding the final specifications.

When designing a non-residential Passive House it is common to design a ventilation system that turns off when the building is unoccupied. Unlike dwellings, which are in use 24 hours a day, buildings such as a

COMMON MISTAKES

Increasing the airflow to compensate for high VOC materials

It is important that a holistic approach is taken to the design of low energy, healthy buildings and this includes the specification of furniture, fittings and soft furnishings. Increasing the airflow to compensate for preventable pollution is the wrong approach. Where the designer is not engaged to specify furniture, etc, it is good practice to add recommendations regarding low VOC furniture to the user manual.

1 It is easiest to start with the 'Ventilation unit selection' in the middle of this worksheet – from row 88

Without going into too much detail, this section of the worksheet facilitates the input of the following data:
The quantity of each ventilation unit – '1' unless there are identical ventilation setups e.g. in flatted developments, where flats are identical.
The type of unit - this drop down menu links back to the 'Components' worksheet, refer to Chapter 3.
The pressure loss of the duct design has to be entered, this is calculated on a per-project basis, if at an early stage in the design the services consultant will be able to provide some preliminary data to use here.
The location of the unit, inside or out and finally the efficiency of a subsoil heat exchanger, if used.

2 Then move onto entering the air flows 'design of air quantities' towards the top of this worksheet - from row 53

The number of rooms this row relates to. If more than one, these must be identical.

This assigns the design air qualities in this row to a ventilation unit. See notes above.

The supply and extract volume flow rates must meet the acceptable indoor air qualities, 20-30m³/(h person) refer to manual P129-130.

The values shown below are for dwellings and should be adjusted to suit occupation patterns in non-domestic projects

Room no.	Amount a	Room name	Allocation to ventilation unit (No.)	Area A m²	Clear height h m	Room vol. A x h m³	Volume flow per room			Air chng. rt. per room n 1/h	Utilisation times	
							V_{SUP} m³/h	V_{ETA} m³/h	V_{TRANS} m³/h		h/d h	d/week d
1	1	Dwelling unit	1	156	2.70	421	152	152		0.36	24	7

Enter the number of days during the heating period that the ventilation system will be turned off e.g school holidays.

The PHPP will assume the ventilation unit is operating at the maximum volume flow rates unless a reduction factor is entered. Up to 3 different rates can be entered and the percentage of time they are each in use.

Duration of holidays d	Reduction factor 1	Operation red. 1	Reduction factor 2	Operation red. 2	Reduction factor 3	Operation red. 3	Annual average value:			
							V_{SUP} m³/h	V_{ETA} m³/h	V_{TRANS} m³/h	Change rate 1/h
	77%	100%					117	117		0.28

Must total 100%

Figure 7.10 *'Additional vent' worksheet 1*

school or office may only be in use for eight hours a day. By turning off the ventilation system during unoccupied hours, a lot of energy can be saved. It is important to design the ventilation system to come on a few hours before the intended occupation period when using this intermittent operation strategy in order to allow any emissions that have accumulated overnight to be removed.

Some inputs in this worksheet are similar to those discussed in Chapter 3. It can be easy to make mistakes in this worksheet and end up with inaccurate results, so take time to carefully fill in the entries, referring to the technical manual for further details.

3 Now move onto 'data entries for duct sections between the ventilation unit and the thermal envelope', towards the bottom of this worksheet -from row 109

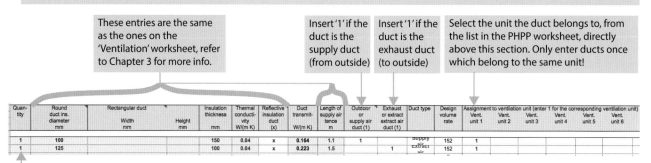

These entries are the same as the ones on the 'Ventilation' worksheet, refer to Chapter 3 for more info.

Insert '1' if the duct is the supply duct (from outside)

Insert '1' if the duct is the exhaust duct (to outside)

Select the unit the duct belongs to, from the list in the PHPP worksheet, directly above this section. Only enter ducts once which belong to the same unit!

Quan-tity	Round duct ins. diameter mm	Rectangular duct		Insulation thickness mm	Thermal conducti-vity W/(m K)	Reflective insulation duct (x)	Duct transmit-tance W/(m K)	Length of supply air duct (1) m	Outdoor or supply air duct (1)	Exhaust or extract or extract air duct (1)	Duct type	Design volume rate	Assignment to ventilation unit (enter 1 for the corresponding ventilation unit)					
		Width mm	Height mm										Vent. unit 1	Vent. unit 2	Vent. unit 3	Vent. unit 4	Vent. unit 5	Vent. unit 6
1	100			150	0.04	x	0.164	1.1	1		Supply air	152	1					
1	125			100	0.04	x	0.223	1.5		1	Extract air	152	1					

Quantity of ducts should be set at 1, however if users run out of space and need to enter multiple ducts in a single row refer to the additional guidance in the technical manual. Users should take care when doing this.

4 Finally, refer the the results section at the very top of the worksheet which summarises what has been entered - from row 8

Results of ventilation design and unit selection:

Venti-lation Unit no.	Description of the unit	Design				yr. Air ch.rt. 1/h
		V_{SUP} m³/h	V_{ETA} m³/h	V_{SUP} m³/h	V_{ETA} m³/h	
1	Unit 1	152	152	117	117	---
2						---
3						---
4						---
5						---
6						---
7						---
8						---
9						---
10						---

Takes into account the reduction and utilisation factors

	Effective heat recovery efficiency	Spec. input power	Heat recov. efficiency SHX
	82%	0.40	31%

Performance of each unit

Result for overall vent. syst.	152	152	117	117	0.30

82%	0.40	31%

Performance of total system

Figure 7.11 *'Additional vent' worksheet 2*

7.4 Ventilation (Final Protocol Worksheets)

This worksheet can be a useful tool at early design stages to establish air flow rates based on expected occupancy, so is being touched on briefly here. The purpose of this worksheet is to give the commissioning engineer the target airflow rates and provide a place to record all the balanced, commissioned airflows. This worksheet will form part of the submission to achieve certification of a building. If the MVHR system has not been properly commissioned the building will not perform optimally. This worksheet comes with its own manual in pdf format, so further details are not given here.

7.5 Individual Room Analysis (Heating Load Worksheet)

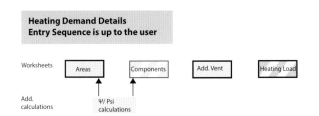

Figure 7.12 *Primary Heating Demand Details, individual room analysis*

This tool is relevant only for air heating, which as discussed in earlier sections of this guide is not normally used in the UK.

If air heating is being used then this tool is a useful check to make sure an individual room does not have an abnormally high heating load compared to the rest of the building. If this is the case, supplementary heating may be necessary. This check could be relevant if, for example, a room has a particularly high percentage of exterior walls or a very large percentage of glazing.

Remember, as discussed in Chapter 3, the 'Heating load' worksheet is concerned with the specific scenarios that result in the highest heat load throughout the year. Refer back to Chapter 3 for more details regarding how this is determined.

This chapter has introduced some new themes to the reader and, when used in conjunction with the technical manual, readers should feel confident about adding more detail to their PHPP models.

Heating load – risk assessment

Risk determination of group heating for a critical room

Figure 7.13 *'Heating load' worksheet, individual room analysis*

Ground Floor Master Bedroom	(1 = Yes / 0 = No)

Building satisfies Passive House criteria **1**

The air quantity should comply with current standards.

Room floor area	16	m²
Planned ambient air quantity for the room	27	m³/h
Planned ambient air quantities for the remaining rooms	51	m³/h

Supply air per m² living area
1.69 m³/h/m²

Add specific details about the room; note windows automatically subtract from the wall area. This is the same as the logic used on the 'Areas' worksheet. Refer to Chapter 3 for more details.

Building assembly	Temperature zone	m²		W/(m²K)		always 1 (except "X")		K		Room trans. loss W
Above ground Exterior wall	A	10.0	*	0.12	*	1.00	*	19.0	=	22
Below ground Exterior wall	B	8.0	*	0.13	*	1.00	*	7.9	=	8
Roof/Ceiling	D		*	0.08	*	1.00	*	19.0	=	
Below ground Floor slab	B	16.0	*	0.11	*	1.00	*	7.9	=	14
	A		*		*	1.00	*	19.0	=	
	A		*		*	1.00	*	19.0	=	
	X		*		*	1.00	*	19.0	=	
Windows	A	8.0	*	0.77	*	1.00	*	19.0	=	117
Exterior door	A		*		*	1.00	*	19.0	=	
Exterior thermal bridges (length/m)	A	6.0	*	−0.01	*	1.00	*	19.0	=	−1
Perimeter thermal bridges (length/m)	A	4.0	*	−0.05	*	1.00	*	19.0	=	−3
Floor slab thermal bridges (length/m)	A	4.0	*	0.04	*	1.00	*	19.0	=	3
House/DU partition wall	I		*		*	1.00	*	3.0	=	

= 160

Answer each of these questions either 1 = Yes or 0 = No.

	Enter: 1 = Yes 0 = No	$P_{T/Room}$ W	$P_{Supply\ Air}$ W	Ratio	Risk summand
Transmission heat losses		160	285	0.56	−0.44
Concentrated leakages	0				0.00
Insulation towards other rooms: R > 1.5 m²K/W	1	(2 = no thermal contact except door)			0.50
Room is on the ground floor.	1				0.50
Open staircase	1				0.50
TOTAL of the risk summands					1.06
Interior doors predominantly closed	0			Risk factor	1.00

Total room risk	**17.7%**

Analysis is given here.

Assessment and advice	**Normally no problem**

Chapter 8

PHPP Variants and Comparisons

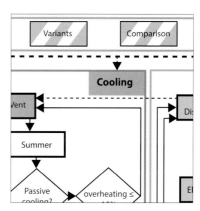

8.1 Introduction to new advanced PHPP features

PHPP9 introduced a number of new features, including four new worksheets in the main PHPP workbook. This chapter will look briefly at three of these new worksheets – 'Variants', 'PHeco' and 'Comparison'. The fourth 'Check' worksheet is already covered in Chapter 3.

The three worksheets covered in this chapter are considered advanced features in PHPP and it is recommended that designers are familiar with the standard PHPP features and data entries before working with these. As such, the standard blank PHPP file does not have these worksheets visible and activated. PHI has created a suite of new blank PHPP workbooks with these worksheets activated, i.e. there is a Variants PHPP and a PHeco PHPP (the 'Comparisons' worksheet is activated in both of these options). Designers can import their standard PHPP file into either of these activated versions very easily. It is also possible, although not recommended, to activate the new worksheets in an existing PHPP. If this route is taken, designers should pay close attention to the additional guidance in the technical manual to make sure these advanced features are fully activated. This option is not as simple, and requires more set-up work by the designer, as such where possible designers should start with the Variants PHPP or PHeco PHPP as appropriate.

In addition to these new worksheets, PHPP9 saw the introduction of new tools for retrofit projects. This chapter will take a look at the new output file 'EnerPHit Retrofit Plan' (ERP) and briefly cover the criteria for pre-certification of step-by-step retrofits.

8.2 Variants

8.2.1 Variants Worksheet

The 'Variants' worksheet:
- is a new tool in PHPP9
- allows input of buliding design variants or refurbishment steps
- results of each variant are calculated and displayed in parallel
- can be used to evaluate difference fabric efficiency options in a single building
- can be used to evaluate several buildings which differ only in some aspects, for example individual homes in a terrace (if not being assessed as a block)
- can be used in conjunction with the 'Comparison' worksheet to understand the costs implications of various options.

By expanding these sections users can view the impact of their design variations on either preset results or specific results they set up

Up to 99 variants can be calculated. Designers must give each variant a title in row 8. If more than five variants are being assessed refer to the technical manual for additional set-up guidance. Note: too many variants will use up computer processor capacity, slowing down your computer

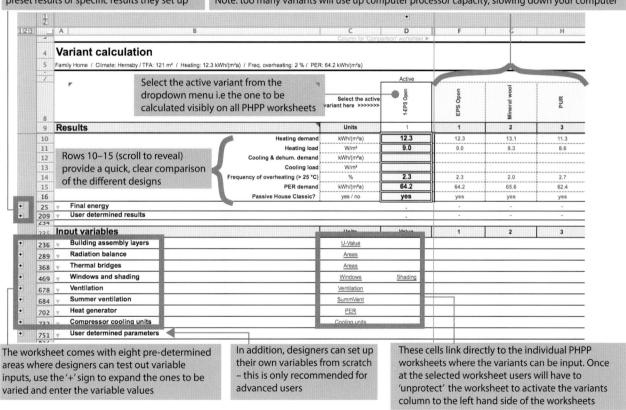

Select the active variant from the dropdown menu i.e the one to be calculated visibly on all PHPP worksheets

Rows 10–15 (scroll to reveal) provide a quick, clear comparison of the different designs

Variant calculation

Family Home / Climate: Hemsby / TFA: 121 m² / Heating: 12.3 kWh/(m²a) / Freq. overheating: 2 % / PER: 64.2 kWh/(m²a)

Select the active variant here >>>>>>>

Results	Units	1-EPS Open (1)	EPS Open (1)	Mineral wool (2)	PUR (3)
Heating demand	kWh/(m²a)	12.3	12.3	13.1	11.3
Heating load	W/m²	9.0	9.0	9.3	8.6
Cooling & dehum. demand	kWh/(m²a)				
Cooling load	W/m²				
Frequency of overheating (> 25 °C)	%	2.3	2.3	2.0	2.7
PER demand	kWh/(m²a)	64.2	64.2	65.6	62.4
Passive House Classic?	yes / no	yes	yes	yes	yes
Final energy		-	-	-	-
User determined results		-	-	-	-

Input variables

	Units	Value	1	2	3
Building assembly layers	U-Value				
Radiation balance	Areas				
Thermal bridges	Areas				
Windows and shading	Windows	Shading			
Ventilation	Ventilation				
Summer ventilation	SummVent				
Heat generator	PER				
Compressor cooling units	Cooling units				
User determined parameters					

The worksheet comes with eight pre-determined areas where designers can test out variable inputs, use the '+' sign to expand the ones to be varied and enter the variable values

In addition, designers can set up their own variables from scratch – this is only recommended for advanced users

These cells link directly to the individual PHPP worksheets where the variants can be input. Once at the selected worksheet users will have to 'unprotect' the worksheet to activate the variants column to the left hand side of the worksheets

Figure 8.1 *Variants Worksheet*

245

When working with the 'variants' worksheet it is recommended to use the 'Variant PHPP'. It is simple to import existing PHPP files into the 'Variant PHPP'; when this is done all calculations should run automatically. If using the standard PHPP9 worksheet, to run a calculation follow the steps on p. 42 of the technical manual. In this case it is very important to make sure that the correct cells are selected for the calculation.

Variant calculation

Family Home / Climate: Hemsby / TFA: 121 m² / Heating: 12.3 kWh/(m²a) / Freq. overheating: 2 % / PER: 64.2 kWh/(m²a)

Select the active variant here >>>>>>>

Results	Units	Active 1-EPS Open	EPS Open	Mineral wool	PUR
		1	1	2	3
Heating demand	kWh/(m²a)	12.3	12.3	13.1	11.3
Heating load	W/m²	9.0	9.0	9.3	8.6
Cooling & dehum. demand	kWh/(m²a)				
Cooling load	W/m²				
Frequency of overheating (> 25 °C)	%	2.3	2.3	2.0	2.7
PER demand	kWh/(m²a)	64.2	64.2	65.6	62.4
Passive House Classic?	yes / no	yes	yes	yes	yes
Final energy		-	-	-	-
User determined results		-	-	-	-

Input variables	Units	Value	1	2	3
Building assembly layers	U-Value				
a External Wall Insulation	W/(mK)	0.031	0.031	0.04	0.021
	mm	220	220	220	220
b	W/(mK)	0			
	mm	0			

To input the variables, first expand the section to be varied. In this example the type of insulation in the walls is being varied, so the 'Building Assembly Layers' is expanded. And the three different insulations being assessed are input, as shown here. Note the thickness is to be input in mm; in this example the thickness was left consistent and only the type of insulation varies.

Note: pp. 45–6 of the technical manual walks through the inputs required for all of the eight categories as well as providing details for how to set up a new User Determined category.

Figure 8.2 *Variants Worksheet running the calculation*

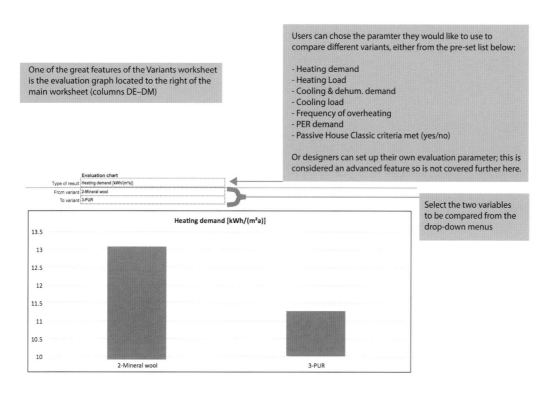

Users can chose the paramter they would like to use to compare different variants, either from the pre-set list below:

- Heating demand
- Heating Load
- Cooling & dehum. demand
- Cooling load
- Frequency of overheating
- PER demand
- Passive House Classic criteria met (yes/no)

Or designers can set up their own evaluation parameter; this is considered an advanced feature so is not covered further here.

One of the great features of the Variants worksheet is the evaluation graph located to the right of the main worksheet (columns DE–DM)

Select the two variables to be compared from the drop-down menus

Figure 8.3 *Variants Evaluation Chart*

Designers often need to look at multiple design solutions in parallel to be able to develop a solution that meets the varying demands of project budgets, programmes and sustainability aspirations. This previously lead to

Passive House designers running multiple PHPP files for a single project looking at, for example, different building systems or window performances. This new worksheet streamlines this process.

Another way to use this worksheet is in retrofit projects where designers may wish to compare the performance of the original and renovated building, and possibly look at the buildings performance at intermediate stages in a step-by-step retrofit. All of this data is now easily assessable, comparable and presentable in a single worksheet.

To efficiently use the capabilities of this worksheet it is recommended that users are first comfortable and familiar with using the main PHPP workbook. Then, before getting started on the 'Variants' capabilities of the PHPP, read pp. 39–47 of the technical manual. These pages provide essential information on setting up the 'Variants' worksheet.

When using this worksheet results are continuously calculated in parallel, with the results of each variant or group of variants displayed. Users select the variant(s) they want to be actively calculated in all of the PHPP worksheets in the 'Variants' worksheet.

8.2.2 PHeco

We will now take a very brief look at the new PHeco calculation sheet; this sheet is used to assess the profitability of various different energy efficiency

measures both for new-build projects and for renovations. Usefully, this worksheet can be directly linked with the 'Variants' worksheet so that the calculation results in the PHPP are available on a column-by-column basis for different EnerPHit steps (variants).

The 'PHeco' worksheet:
*   is a new tool in PHPP9 and comes with a separate guidance document as it is not covered in the technical manual
*   is designed as an economical assessment tool to be used for EnerPHit (retrofit) projects
*   requires designers to provide detailed costings for retrofit measures in a separate spreadsheet
*   links through to the 'Variants' worksheet.

This worksheet provides a detailed view on operational and investment costs of different EnerPHit steps. Before starting to use this worksheet, designers must have set out these EnerPHit steps in the 'Variants' worksheet.

The energy efficiency market is subject to high price variability, so it was not possible for PHI to set cost ranges for difference building efficiency or retrofit measures. Instead, to be able to use this worksheet, designers must calculate the costs for each retrofit measure in detail in an external spreadsheet. It is

This graph looks at two main factors: the cost of the energy required to operate the building (for a period of 30 years) and the capital investment cost of the renovation steps (all present value costs)

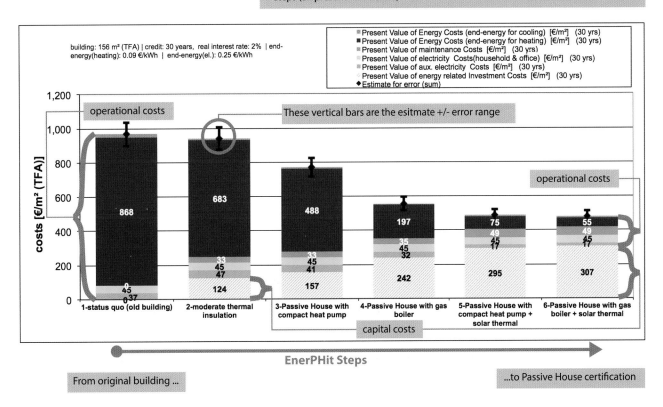

Figure 8.4 *Final Energy and Capital Investment Cost Graph*

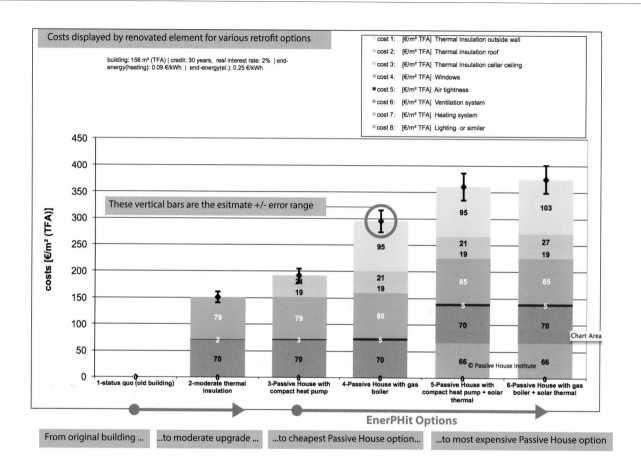

Figure 8.5 *EnerPHit Measure Cost Chart*

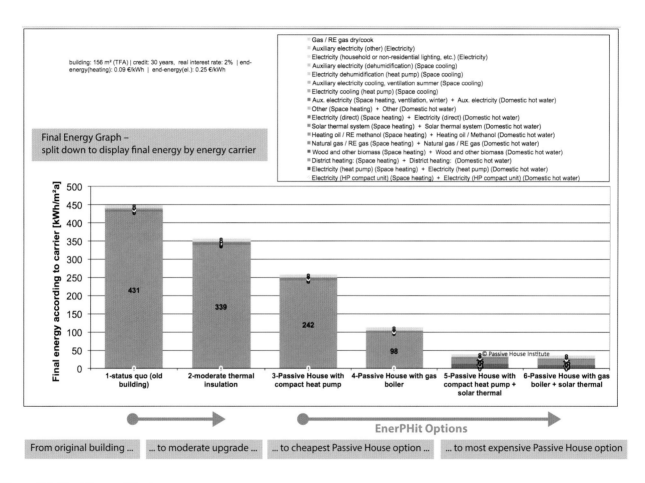

Figure 8.6 *Final Energy Chart*

important that all costs are calculated in €/m² treated floor area. This is especially important for assessing combinations of retrofit measures, otherwise no comparison is possible.

This book this worksheet is classed as an advanced PHPP feature and it is not the purpose of this guide to cover advanced features in detail. Therefore further guidance is not provided on the specific inputs required for this worksheet. Instead, we will look briefly now at the output graphs that are produced by the worksheet, so readers can get a feel for the capabilities of this worksheet. Some notes are also provided at the end of this section directing readers to further guidance.

Further reading on passipedia:

http://passipedia.org/basics/affordability/economic_feasibility_of_passive_house_design (or, **http://goo.gl/gkgSWb**)

https://passipedia.org/planning/refurbishment_with_passive_house_components/economic_analysis_for_the_retrofit_of_a_detached_single_family_house_to_the_enerphit_standard (or, **http://goo.gl/oCoiQ6**)

8.3 Comparisons

The 'Comparisons' worksheet:
- is a new tool in PHPP9
- can only be used once the 'Variants' worksheet has been activated
- compares the energy demand and the cost-effectiveness of two design variants from the 'Variants' worksheet.

This worksheet is limited to considering energy demand for heating, cooling, dehumidification, ventilation and relevant auxiliary electricity. It does not consider energy for DHW, household electricity, lighting etc. The aim of the worksheet is to be able to provide a detailed comparison between two variants (set out in the 'Variants' worksheet), specifically looking at the energy and cost implications. As such the worksheet can only be used once the variants to be assessed have been entered into the 'Variants' worksheet.

To efficiently use the capabilities of this worksheet it is recommended that users are first comfortable

Figure 8.7 *(opposite) Comparison Worksheet*

By expanding these sections users can view the impact of their design variations in further detail

Select the comparison to be analysed below from the drop-down menu; this menu is linked to the inputs here ▬ ▬ ▬ ▬ ▬ ▬ ▬ ➤

Designers can select any two variants from the 'Variants' worksheet to be compared here. Designers must input cost accurate data.

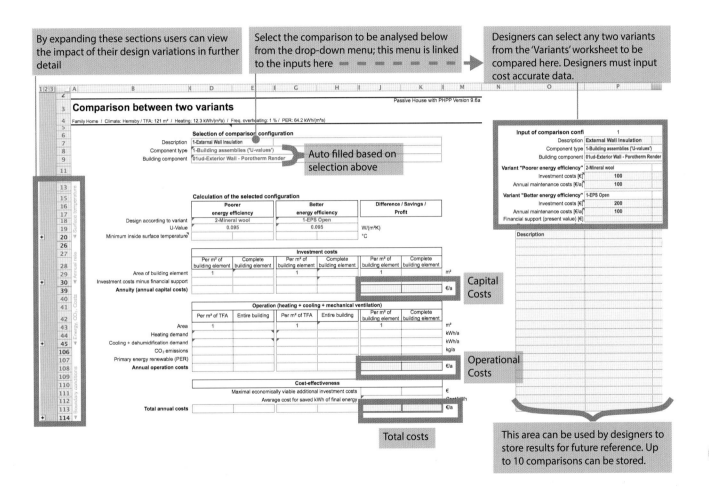

Comparison between two variants

Passive House with PHPP Version 9.6a

Family Home / Climate: Hemsby / TFA: 121 m² / Heating: 12.3 kWh/(m²a) / Freq. overheating: 1 % / PER: 64.2 kWh/(m²a)

Selection of comparison configuration

Description	1-External Wall Insulation
Component type	1-Building assemblies ('U-values')
Building component	01ud-Exterior Wall - Porotherm Render

Auto filled based on selection above

Input of comparison confi   1

Description	External Wall Insulation
Component type	1-Building assemblies ('U-values')
Building component	01ud-Exterior Wall - Porotherm Render

Variant "Poorer energy efficiency" 2-Mineral wool
Investment costs [€] 100
Annual maintenance costs [€/a] 100

Variant "Better energy efficiency" 1-EPS Open
Investment costs [€] 200
Annual maintenance costs [€/a] 100
Financial support (present value) [€]

Calculation of the selected configuration

	Poorer energy efficiency	Better energy efficiency	Difference / Savings / Profit	
Design according to variant	2-Mineral wool	1-EPS Open		
U-Value	0.095	0.095		W/(m²K)
Minimum inside surface temperature				°C

Investment costs

	Per m² of building element	Complete building element	Per m² of building element	Complete building element	Per m² of building element	Complete building element	
Area of building element	1		1		1		m²
Investment costs minus financial support							
Annuity (annual capital costs)							€/a

Capital Costs

Operation (heating + cooling + mechanical ventilation)

	Per m² of TFA	Entire building	Per m² of TFA	Entire building	Per m² of building element	Complete building element	
Area	1		1		1		m²
Heating demand							kWh/a
Cooling + dehumidification demand							kWh/a
CO₂ emissions							kg/a
Primary energy renewable (PER)							
Annual operation costs							€/a

Operational Costs

Cost-effectiveness

Maximal economically viable additional investment costs			€
Average cost for saved kWh of final energy			Cent/kWh
Total annual costs			€/a

Total costs

Description

This area can be used by designers to store results for future reference. Up to 10 comparisons can be stored.

253

and familiar with using the main PHPP workbook. Then, before getting started on the 'Comparison' capabilities of the PHPP, read pp. 48–51 of the technical manual. These pages provide essential information on using the 'Comparison' worksheet. The worksheet assesses two variants in terms of the final energy demand for the whole building when each of the variants is used. If we use the same example as on the 'Variants' worksheet, this worksheet would be looking at how the final energy demand (CO_2 emissions and renewable primary energy (PER)) of the whole building changes when the wall insulation is changed. The worksheet displays the difference between the two calculations, so designers can see how much energy (operational costs) is saved when the higher performing variant is used, along with the impact on the capital investment.

To understand the impact on the capital investment, the second part of the calculation looks at the cost-effectiveness of the different variants. This cost-effectiveness calculation is based on a dynamic annuity method that is integrated into the worksheet. The final energy demand savings determined previously are multiplied with the corresponding costs for the energy sources used. This results in the annual energy cost savings. The annual capital costs for the additional investment in the higher performing variant are deducted from these savings, resulting in the annual total saving over the poorer performing variant. Usefully, the investment cost per saved kilowatt hour is also given on the worksheet.

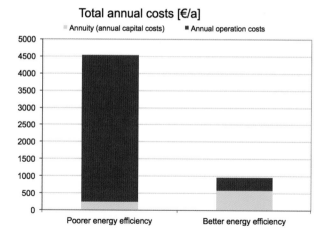

Figure 8.8 *Total Annual Cost Graph*

8.4 EnerPHit Retrofit Plan

Refer back to Chapter 2 for a reminder of the EnerPHit certification criteria and remember the component criteria vary by climatic zone. This section is now going to look at the new output-file for step-by-step retrofits, which was introduced with PHPP9 – the EnerPHit Retrofit Plan (ERP).

The EnerPHit Retrofit Plan:
- is linked to the main PHPP (this should be a 'Variants' enabled PHPP, see figure 8.2)
- enables the user to present component qualities and efficiency results of single retrofit steps
- includes a scheduler to help designers plan their retrofit
- provides worksheets for designers to record detailed descriptions of the proposed work and paste drawings directly into the ERP
- has the ability to set up links to more detailed drawings
- provides a worksheet to record detailed costing information
- facilitates the process of pre-certification during the first retrofit step
- records the whole retrofit process in a single workbook and can generate a PDF file of this

for the building owner, so that they can keep the document and refer to it at each step of the refurbishment
- creates diagrams summarising costs, energy use and CO2 emissions
- comes with its own pdf manual.

Many building owners may aspire to upgrading their buildings to the EnerPHit or full Passive House Standard but are only able to upgrade sections or elements of the building one at a time, as repairs are required. By upgrading the individual components when a replacement/upgrade would be required anyway creates a low-cost route to an EnerPHit/Passive House. However, to make sure that each retrofit step supports the next, a plan is required ahead of time. It is easy to imagine how, for example, the application of external wall insulation could either make future window replacement easier or harder to achieve depending on how well thought through the detailed design was. By planning everything out ahead of time, building owners can be sure that once the final steps are completed, potentially many years into the future, the result will be an EnerPHit/Passive House Standard building as they originally envisaged without wasteful abortive work.

Figure 8.9 *Step-by-step Retrofit Plan*

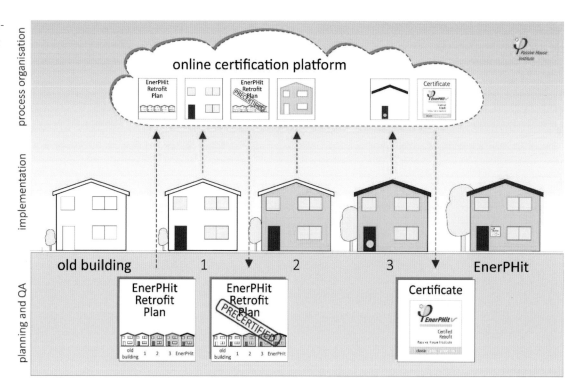

Entering the data into the ERP is fairly straightforward, with the PDF manual providing additional guidance where necessary. As such, further notes are not being added here.

The summary graphics provided in this worksheet will be particularly useful in describing the retrofit steps and the impact of these steps to building owners and users.

Figure 8.10 *Summary graph*

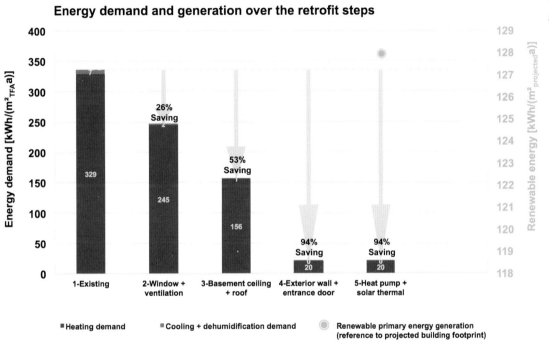

Energy demand and generation over the retrofit steps

- ■ Heating demand
- ■ Cooling + dehumidification demand
- ◉ Renewable primary energy generation (reference to projected building footprint)

The criteria for pre-certification of step-by-step retrofits is fairly straightforward but does require that the EnerPHit Retrofit Plan (ERP) is completed first. The ERP provides a methodology for this type of overall plan. For additional quality assurance, the PHI offers a pre-certification as an EnerPHit (or a Passive House) project. This requires an ERP to be submitted, where the first retrofit step has already been implemented with minimum energy savings of at least 20%. The pre-certification provides assurance to the owners and planners that following the implementation of all retrofit steps, the desired Standard will be achieved.

Recommended further reading:
Any designer who is planning a step-by-step retrofit, aiming for EnerPHit certification, should read these excellent articles before getting started:

http://bit.ly/2euMsh8

http://europhit.eu/certification-retrofit-plans

Appendix

Mandatory Envelope Performance – Passive House – All regions	
Draft-free	$\leq 0.6h^{-1}$@50Pa
External building envelope should be thermal bridge free	$\Psi \geq 0.0058$ Btu/hr.ft. F must be inserted into the PHPP
For component quality recommendations see component requirements for certification according to component standard, below	

Mandatory Envelope Performance - EnerPHit and EnerPHit+i – All regions	
Draft-free	$\leq 1.0h^{-1}$@50Pa §
External building envelope should be thermal bridge free	$\Psi \geq 0.0058$ Btu/hr.ft. F must be inserted into the PHPP
For component quality recommendations see component requirements for certification according to component standard, below	

§ This is a limiting value in recognition of the greater difficulties associated with existing buildings, however the target remains ≤ 0.6h⁻¹@50Pa

Mandatory requirements for certification according to the component standard – EnerPHit/ EnerPHit+i - Cool temperate regions only*
(recommendations for Passive House and EnerPHit/ EnerPHit+i according to heating demand)

Exterior building elements U-value external insulation	$f_t \cdot R \leq 37.86$ Btu/h.ft^2.$^\circ$F †	*Note: In exceptional circumstances where it is not possible to meet all of these criteria in renovation projects the PHI has provided a set of absolute minimum thermal comfort requirements. These can be downloaded from http://www.passiv.de/downloads/03_enerphit_ criteria_en.pdf*
Exterior building elements U-value internal insulation	$f_t \cdot U \leq 16.22$ Btu/h.ft^2.$^\circ$F †	
Window installed U-value (U$_{W,installed}$)	≤ 0.15 Btu/h.ft^2.$^\circ$F‡ (vertical)	
	≤ 0.18 Btu/h.ft^2.$^\circ$F‡ (sloping rooflights)	
	≤ 0.20 Btu/h.ft^2.$^\circ$F‡ (flat rooflights)	
Door installed U-value (f$_t \cdot$ U$_{D,installed}$)	≤ 0.15 Btu/h.ft^2.$^\circ$F§	

* For all other regions refer to Table 2 'EnerPHit criteria for the building component method' on page 8 of the 'Criteria for the Passive House, EnerPHit and PHI Low Energy Building Standard' document, which can be seen at - http://www.passiv.de/downloads/03_building_criteria_en.pdf)

† With temperature factor f$_t$: in contact with the outdoor air f$_t$ = 1 in contact with the ground 'ground reduction factor' from the PHPP 'Ground' Sheet

‡ This is based on a design temperature for the coldest day in winter for Central European climates which is 14°F. Once climate data has been selected in the PHPP, these values will be adjusted for the location.

§ Door f$_t \cdot$ U$_{D,installed}$ with temperature factor f$_t$: in contact with the outdoor air f$_t$ = 1or in contact with the unheated basement: f$_t$ ="ground reduction factor" from the PHPP "Ground" Sheet

Recommended Services Performance (Mandatory for component standard)		Recommended Thermal and Acoustic Performance	
MVHR system efficiency	$\geq 75\%^\dagger$	Overheating frequency	>77°F≤10%of yr (target >77°F≤5% of yr)
MVHR unit electrical efficiency	≤ 0.765 W/cfm	Maximum sound from MVHR unit	35 dB(A)
		Maximum transfer sound in occupied rooms	25dB(A)

† MVHR unit efficiency must be calculated according to Passive House standards not manufacturer's rating, if Manufacturer's rating is used 12 percentage points must be deducted

Table 9.1 *This table provides a summary, in the IP system, of the key component limits for cool temperate regions (e.g. UK), the SI system table 2.2 can be seen on page 43 of this book and full details can be found in the technical manual. The official Passive House Institute climate regions can be seen in figure 2.3, on page 46*

Basic conversions from SI to IP (values given to 3dp)

Energy and Energy Intensity

Energy Conversion	1 kWh = 3.412 kBTU
Energy Intensity Conversion	$1 \text{ kWh/m}^2 = 0.317 \text{ kBTU/ft.}^2$

Power and Power Intensity

Power Conversion	1W= 3.412 BTU/hr
Power Intensity Conversion	$1\text{W/m}^2 = 0.317 \text{ BTU/hr.ft}^2$

Temperature

$1°C = 33.8°F$

SI U-values to IP R-values - Thermal Transfer

This conversion is from SI thermal transmittance (U) to IP Resistance (R)
$1\text{W/m}^2\text{K} = 5.678 \text{ Btu/h.ft}^2.°F$

Conductivity

$1\text{W/(mK)} = 0.578 \text{Btu/hr.ft.}°F$

Thermal Capacity

$1\text{W/K} = 1.896 \text{ BTU/hr.}°F$

Some Key Certification Criteria Conversions

Values for Passivhaus Buildings

Specific Space Heat Demand	$15 \text{ kWh/(m}^2\text{a)} = 4.75 \text{ kBTU/(ft.}^2\text{a)}$
Heating Load	$10 \text{ W/m}^2 = 3.17 \text{ BTU/(hr.ft}^2)$
Primary Energy	$120 \text{ kWh/(m2a)} = 38.04 \text{ kBTU/(ft.}^2\text{a)*}$

*this value varies by location, refer to PHPP file

Primary Energy Renewable	- Classic	$60 \text{kWh/(m2a)} = 19 \text{ kBTU/(ft.}^2\text{a)}$
	- Plus	$45 \text{kWh/(m2a)} = 14 \text{ kBTU/(ft.}^2\text{a)}$
	- Premium	$30 \text{kWh/(m2a)} = 10 \text{ kBTU/(ft.}^2\text{a)}$
Renewable Energy Generation	- Plus	$60 \text{kWh/(m2a)} = 19 \text{ kBTU/(ft.}^2\text{a)}$
	- Premium	$120 \text{kWh/(m2a)} = 38 \text{ kBTU/(ft.}^2\text{a)}$

> Note: all values are m^2 or $ft.^2$ of the TFA except for Renewable Energy Generation which is m^2 or $ft.^2$ of the Projected Building Footprint

Values for EnerPHit Buildings

Specific Space Heat Demand	$25 \text{ kWh/(m}^2\text{a)} = 7.92 \text{ kBTU/(ft.}^2\text{a)}$

Values for Low Energy Buildings

Specific Space Heat Demand	$30 \text{ kWh/(m}^2\text{a)} = 9.51 \text{ kBTU/(ft.}^2\text{a)}$
Primary Energy Renewable	$75 \text{kWh/(m2a)} = 24 \text{ kBTU/(ft.}^2\text{a)}$

Overheating and humidity thresholds - all Passivhaus levels

Frequency of overheating calculated at temperatures >25°C equivalent to 77°F

Frequency of excessive humidity calculated at humidity >12g/Kg equivalent to 0.012lb/lb

Table 9.2 *This table gives some basic conversions from SI to IP. Designers should refer to and use the 'Conversions' worksheet within the (IP) imperial PHPP for a full list of conversions. This worksheet makes it easy for designers to move between the two systems of measurement. This table also provides some key Certification Criteria Conversions. Again, when working with the IP-PHPP, all of the criteria will be displayed using the Imperial system.*

Glossary

Definitions in this glossary are specific to the context of this guide.

Active cooling   Mechanical cooling systems, not normally required in residential buildings in the UK.

A/V ratio   Ratio of the external building envelope to the internal volume

EnerPHit   It is often difficult to achieve the Passive House Standard in older buildings for a variety of reasons. Buildings that have been retrofitted with Passive House components and, to a great extent, with exterior wall insulation can achieve the slightly lesser EnerPHit certification as evidence of both building quality and fulfilment of specific energy values.

EnerPHit+i   The EnerPHit+i designation is similar to the EnerPHit standard but is applied if more than 25% of the opaque exterior wall surface has interior insulation.

Evaluation Criteria   These are the criteria set by the PHI for the certification of Passive House projects.

g-value   How much solar heat gain is admitted through the glass

Heat transfer resistance   Measured in m^2K/W

Lambda 90/90   This is the European standard for the calculation of thermal conductivity. Before European product standards, UK manufacturers for the most part based their claims on typical or mean values. The 90/90 values are subject to strict analysis to provide a value which, among other things, is representative of 90% of production within a 90% confidence level.

n50   This measurement is the total air changes per hour at 50 Pascals (@50Pa). It must be an average of the pressurisation and depressurisation tests using the Vn50.

Overheating   In the context of this guide overheating refers to temperatures >25°C.

q50   This measurement is the m³ of air passing through each m² of the building fabric per hour at 50 Pascals (@50Pa). It is measured in (m³/h/m²@50Pa). This is often quoted as the most favourable result – either pressurisation or depressurisation. For Passive House projects the air test result must be an average of pressurisation and depressurisation, whereas UK regulations allow the best result to be picked.

NB: Both figures are of similar magnitude to each other and are related by the ratio of the building's surface area and volume. See equation, right.

$$Q_{50} = n_{50} \frac{V}{S}$$

Rain screen cladding   In the context of this guide, a cladding material is considered to be a rain screen if there is an opening exceeding 1,500mm² per m length for vertical layers and per m2 for horizontal layers.

Retrofit   Refurbishment of an existing building; usually consisting of significant fabric and performance upgrades

Specific Cooling Load   The Specific Cooling Load is the maximum energy required to maintain a comfortable internal temperature, on the hottest day of the year. As that day can vary depending on the solar declination, two calculations are completed in the PHPP and the worst-case scenario is then displayed. It is measured in watts (W) per metre squared (m²) of floor area. Note that the use of the word 'Specific' refers to the fact that the target is 'a per m² target'. 'Cooling Load' without the word 'Specific' is technically referring to the total figure.

Specific Heat Load   The Specific Heat Load is the maximum heat required on the coldest day of the year. As that day may be cloudy or sunny, there are two calculations completed in PHPP and the worst-case scenario is then displayed. It is measured in watts (W) per metre squared (m²) of floor area. Note that the use of the word 'Specific' refers to the fact that the target is 'a per m² target'. 'Heat Load' without the word 'Specific' is technically referring to the total figure.

Specific Primary Energy Demand   Primary Energy includes not only the energy content of the raw material but also the losses from distribution, conversion and delivery to the end-user. For electricity usage, Primary Energy includes the fuel needed to generate electricity, and this leads to a much higher Primary Energy Factor for electricity compared with gas, for example. Specific Primary Energy Demand is the sum of all the Primary Energy demands for heating, domestic hot water (DHW), auxiliary and household electricity divided by the floor area. It is measured in kilowatt-hours per metre squared of floor area per year $(kWh/(m^2a))$. Note that the use of the word 'Specific' refers to the fact that the target is 'a per m^2 target'. 'Primary Energy Demand' without the word 'Specific' is technically referring to the total figure.

Specific Space Heating Demand   The Specific Space Heating Demand is the total energy required to heat the building for a year. It is measured in kilowatt-hours (kWh) per metre squared (m^2) of floor area per year (a). Note that the use of the word 'Specific' refers to the fact that the target is 'a per m^2 target'. 'Space Heating Demand' without the word 'Specific' is technically referring to the total figure.

Specific Total Cooling Demand   The Specific Total Cooling Demand is the energy required to meet the cooling demand excluding the energy used for dehumidification and cooling system losses. It is measured in kilowatt-hours (kWh) per metre squared (m^2) of floor area per year (a). Note that the use of the word 'Specific' refers to the fact that the target is 'a per m^2 target'. 'Total Cooling Demand' without the word 'Specific' is technically referring to the total figure.

TFA   The internal treated floor area is specific to building type – either residential or non-residential; refer to Figures 3.19 and 3.24.

Thermal bridge   A localised weak area in the envelope of a building where heat flow is increased compared to adjacent areas

Thermal conductivity   The property of a material to conduct heat. It is measured in watts per metre kelvin (W/(mK)). The lower the thermal conductivity value the better the thermal insulation qualities of a material.

Thermal mass   This is the effective thermal storage capacity and is measured in $Wh/(m^2K)$.

U-value   A U-value is a measure of heat loss through a building element.

Uw   U-value of the window (glass and frame combined)

Uw,installed   U-value of the installed window

Vn50   This is the internal volume according to the EN13829 standard, which states the following: '3.2 internal volume – deliberately heated, cooled or mechanically ventilated space within a building or part of a building subject to the measurement, generally not including the attic space, basement space and attached structures.'

With the following additional exceptions: do not include the air volumes within partition walls, suspended ceilings and floor cassettes, behind plasterboard and in inaccessible closed-off areas under stairs (apart from these areas, the stairwell is included). Attics can be included if accessible and fully within the thermal envelope. Generally, door and window reveals are also excluded; it may be possible to include these but it is better if you can make the grade without these extra few m^3.

List of Abbreviations and Acronyms

Air Changes an Hour [ACH]
Building Research Establishment [BRE]
Certified European Passive House [CEPH]
Domestic Hot Water (DHW)
EnerPHit Retrofit Plan [ERP]
Indoor Air Quality [IAQ]
Internal Heat Gains [IHG]
International Passive House Association [iPHA]
Mechanical Ventilation with Heat Recovery [MVHR]
Passive House Institute [PHI]
Passive House Planning Package [PHPP]
Post Occupancy Evaluation [POE]
Retrofit for the Future (RftF)
Simplified Building Energy Model [SBEM]
Standardised Assessment Procedure [SAP]
Volatile Organic Compound [VOC]

List of Standard Acronyms

BS British Standards are the standards produced by BSI Group, which is incorporated under a Royal Charter and is formally designated as the National Standards Body (NSB) for the UK.

DIN Deutsches Institut für Normung, the German institute for standardisation

EN European standards maintained by CEN (European Committee for Standardization), CENELEC (European Committee for Electrotechnical Standardization) and ETSI (European Telecommunications Standards Institute)

ISO The International Organisation for Standardisation, known as ISO, is an international standard-setting body composed of representatives from various national standards organisations.

Further Reading

iPHA website – www.passivehouse-international.org
iPHA is the global hub for Passive House knowledge. The iPHA website provides, among other things, information of iPHA Affiliate organisations, a full directory of printed material relevant to Passive House and an events calendar. It also provides useful links to, for example, the Passive House database and certified products/tradespeople. The website also runs a useful forum for members.

Passipedia – www.passipedia.org   A Wikipedia-style website containing a vast array of Passive House information from basic principles to technical scientific papers.

Passivhaus Trust – www.passivhaustrust.org.uk
The Passivhaus Trust is an independent, non-profit organisation that provides leadership in the UK for the adoption of the Passivhaus standard and methodology.

An Introduction to Passive House, **Justin Bere (RIBA Publishing 2013)**   contains essays and international case studies that reveal the technical and creative secrets of Passive House design.

It serves as an introductory text to the subject, covering the key topics and issues; dispels the widespread myths and misconceptions; and will ultimately inspire architects, developers and clients alike, with case studies of aesthetically breath-taking projects from around the world.

Passive House Handbook, Adam Dadeby and Janet Cotterell (Green Books 2012)   A practical guide to constructing and retrofitting buildings to the Passive House standards. A second edition is expected in 2018.

The Passivhaus Designer's Manual: A technical guide to low and zero energy buildings, **Christina J. Hopfe and Robert S. McLeod (Routledge 2015)**   Comprehensive technical guide for those wishing to design and build Passivhaus and Zero Energy Buildings.

Residential Retrofit: 20 Case Studies, **Marion Baeli (RIBA Publishing 2013)**   presents a series of innovative and best practice case studies of residential low-energy retrofit projects, and illustrates what has been achieved in practice in the UK.

Low Carbon Productions in the US have published a suite of Passive House books available for free download   http://www.lowcarbonproductions.com. Here are two of the books available:

The most recent title is *New England Forges Ahead*, produced by Tad Everhart and Mary James (2017) and includes 50 case studies from seven New England states.

Net Zero Energy Buildings, Passive House + Renewables, North American Passive House Network (NAPHN) (Low Carbon Productions) Free to download - http://naphnetwork.org. This book showcases Passive House projects across North America.

265

International Conference technical papers:

Conference Proceedings 14th International Passive House Conference 2010 (28–29 May 2010 Dresden) ISBN: 978-3-00-031174-1

Conference Proceedings 15th International Passive House Conference 2011 (27–28 May 2011 Innsbruck) ISBN: 978-3-00-034396-4

Conference Proceedings 16th International Passive House Conference 2012 (4–5 May 2012 Hannover) ISBN: 978-3-00-037720-4

Conference Proceedings 17th International Passive House Conference 2013 (19-20 April 2013 Frankfurt) ISBN: 978-3-00-041345-2

Conference Proceedings 18th International Passive House Conference 2014 (25-26 April 2014 Aachen) ISBN: 978-3-00-045215-4

Conference Proceedings 19th International Passive House Conference (17–18 April 2015 Leipzig) ISBN: 978-3-00-048604-3

Conference Proceedings 20th International Passive House Conference (22–23 April 2016 Darmstadt) ISBN: 978-3-00-052227-7

These can be ordered from the Passive House Institute, Rheinstrasse 44/46, D-64283 Darmstadt.

These are a valuable record of all of the technical presentations given at the International Conferences. Each presentation is summarised in a six-page extended abstract.

Index

Picture Credits

Fig 0.1: National Institute of Building Sciences and the Whole Building Design Guide 'cost-influence' graph; **Fig 1.1:** ©Jefferson Smith; **Fig 1.2:** ©Jefferson Smith; **Fig 1.3:** © Hamson Barron Smith; adapted by S. Lewis; **Fig 1.4:** © Hamson Barron Smith; adapted by S. Lewis; **Fig 1.5:** © Hamson Barron Smith; adapted by S. Lewis; **Fig 1.6:** © Hamson Barron Smith; adapted by S. Lewis; **Fig 1.7:** © Hamson Barron Smith; adapted by S. Lewis; **Fig 1.8:** © Hamson Barron Smith; adapted by S. Lewis; **Fig 1.9:** © Hamson Barron Smith; adapted by S. Lewis; **Fig 1.10:** © Hamson Barron Smith; adapted by S. Lewis; **Fig 1.11:** © Hamson Barron Smith; adapted by S. Lewis; **Fig 1.13:** © Hamson Barron Smith; adapted by S. Lewis; **Fig 1.14:** © Jefferson Smith; **Fig 2.1:** Brief Instructions Worksheet, PHPP ver9; **Fig 2.2:** Data from various PHI sources; **Fig 2.3:** © PHI; **fig 2.4 :** © PHI; **Fig 2.5:** Verification Worksheet, PHPP ver9; **Fig 2.6:** Verification Worksheet, PHPP ver9; **Fig 2.7:** Verification Worksheet, PHPP ver9; **Fig 2.8:** Verification Worksheet, PHPP ver9; **Fig 2.9:** Verification Worksheet, PHPP ver9; **Fig 2.10 :** Verification Worksheet, PHPP ver9; **Fig 2.11:** Verification Worksheet, PHPP ver9; **Fig 2.12:** Verification Worksheet, PHPP ver9; **Fig 2.13:** Verification Worksheet, PHPP ver9; **Fig 2.14:** Verification Worksheet, PHPP ver9; **Fig 2.15:** Adapted from PHPP manual ver 9; **Fig 3.1:** Adapted from PHPP manual ver 9; **Fig 3.4:** Verification Worksheet, PHPP ver9; **Fig 3.06:** Verification Worksheet, PHPP ver9; **Fig 3.8:** BRE; reproduced with their kind permission; **Fig 3.9:** Climate Data Worksheet, PHPP ver9; **Fig 3.11:** U-value Worksheet, PHPP ver9; **Fig 3.13:** Extracts from U-value Worksheet, PHPP ver9; **Fig 3.18:** ©PHI/ S.Lewis; **Fig 3.19:** © Hamson Barron Smith; adapted by S. Lewis; **Fig 3.20:** ©Tim Crocker; **Fig 3.21:** ©Tim Crocker; **Fig 3.22:** © Hamson Barron Smith; adapted by S. Lewis; **Fig 3.23:** © PHI/ S.Lewis; **Fig 3.24:** Areas Worksheet, PHPP ver9; **Fig 3.26:** Contains public sector information licensed under the Open Government Licence v2.0.; **Fig 3.27:** Table adapted from PHPP Manul ver9; **Fig 3.28:** Ground Worksheet, PHPP ver9; **Fig 3.29:** Ground Worksheet, PHPP ver9; **Fig 3.31:** Components Worksheet, PHPP ver9; **Fig 3.34:** Windows Worksheet, PHPP ver9 ; **Fig 3.35:** Windows Worksheet, PHPP ver9 ; **Fig 3.41:** Shading Worksheet, PHPP ver9; **Fig 3.43:** Ventilation Worksheet, PHPP ver9; **Fig 3.44:** Ventilation Worksheet, PHPP ver9; **Fig 3.47:** Check Worksheet, PHPP ver9; **Fig 3.49:** Verification Worksheet, PHPP ver9; **Fig 3.50:** Heating Worksheet, PHPP ver9; **Fig 3.51:** Heating and Annual Heating Worksheets, PHPP ver9 ; **Fig 4.1:** Adapted from PHPP manual ver 9; **Fig 4.5:** SummVent Worksheet, PHPP ver9; **Fig 4.6:** SummVent Worksheet, PHPP ver9; **Fig 4.9:** SummVent Worksheet, PHPP ver9; **Fig 4.11:** Summer Worksheet, PHPP ver9; **Fig 4.13:** Cooling Worksheet, PHPP ver9; **Fig 5.1:** Adapted from PHPP manual ver 9; **Fig 5.4:** DHW + Distribution Worksheet, PHPP ver9; **Fig 5.5:** DHW + Distribution Worksheet, PHPP ver9; **figure 5.6:** DHW + Distribution Worksheet, PHPP ver9; **Fig 5.8:** Solar DHW Worksheet, PHPP ver9; **Fig 5.10:** PV Worksheet, PHPP ver9; **Fig 5.12:** Electricity Worksheet, PHPP ver9; **Fig 5.13:** Electricity Worksheet, PHPP ver9; **Fig 5.16:** IHG Worksheet, PHPP ver9; **Fig 5.18:** PER Worksheet, PHPP ver9; **Fig 5.19:** PER Worksheet, PHPP ver9; **Fig 6.01:** © PHI, adapted by S. Lewis; **Fig 6.02:** © PHI; **Fig 6.03 (b):** © PHI; **Fig 6.04:** © PHI; **Fig 6.05 (a) & (b):** © PHI / SketchUp; **Fig 6.06:** © PHI / SketchUp; **Fig 6.07:** © PHI; **Fig 6.08 (a) & (b):** © PHI / SketchUp; **Fig 6.09 (a) & (b):** © PHI / SketchUp; **Fig 6.10 (a) & (b):** © PHI / SketchUp; **Fig 6.11:** © PHI; **Fig 6.12:** © PHI; **Fig 6.13:** © PHI; **Fig 6.14:** © PHI; **Fig 6.15:** © PHI; **Fig 6.16:** © PHI; **Fig 6.17:** © PHI; **Fig 6.18:** © PHI; **Fig 6.19:** © PHI; **Fig 6.20:** © PHI; **Fig 6.21:** © PHI; **Fig 6.22:** © PHI; **Fig 6.23:** © PHI; **Fig 6.24:** © PHI; **Fig 6.25:** © PHI; **Fig 6.26:** © PHI; **Fig 6.27:** © PHI; **Fig 6.28:** © PHI; **Fig 7.01:** Adapted from PHPP manual ver 9 ; **Fig 7.06:** Areas Worksheet, PHPP ver9; **Fig 7.10:** AdditionalVent Worksheet, PHPP ver9; **Fig 7.11:** AdditionalVent Worksheet, PHPP ver9; **Fig 7.13:** Heating Load Worksheet, PHPP ver9; **Fig 8.1:** Variants Worksheet, PHPP ver9; **Fig 8.2:** Variants Worksheet, PHPP ver9; **Fig 8.3:** Variants Worksheet, PHPP ver9; **Fig 8.4:** PHeco Worksheet, PHPP ver9; **Fig 8.5:** PHeco Worksheet, PHPP ver9; **Fig 8.6:** PHeco Worksheet, PHPP ver9; **Fig 8.7:** Comparison Worksheet, PHPP ver9; **Fig 8.8:** Comparison Worksheet, PHPP ver9; **Fig 8.9:** © PHI; **Fig 8.10:** ERP Workbook, PHPP ver9.